D1030350

THE PROPHETS

AND THE

WORD OF GOD

THE PROPHETS
AND THE
WORD OF GOD

by Carroll Stuhlmueller, C.P.

With a foreword by
Bernard Cooke, S.J.

FIDES PUBLISHERS, INC.

NOTRE DAME, INDIANA

Library of Congress Catalog Card Number: 64-16501

Scriptural quotations, except in those cases where the author has made his own translation, are from the Confraternity of Christian Doctrine translation.

For

MY BELOVED PARENTS

God's First Word to Me

FOREWORD

Renewed and educated interest in Sacred Scripture has become one of the most noticeable characteristics of Christianity in our own day. Not just in Catholic circles, but among other Christians also, the scholarly research of biblical experts is being translated into high-level popularization that is having its impact on the religious beliefs and practices of people. A great deal remains, however, to be done in this regard, and so it is with joy that one welcomes a book like that of Father Stuhlmueller on the prophets.

There is much that any age can learn from the great prophetic oracles of the O.T., but the message of the prophets seems particularly pertinent in our own day. With the world in full ferment, with new nations and cultures contesting the position of eminence recently occupied by Western civilization, with men searching for values and faiths that can give meaning to their existence, the task of Christian witness assumes unprecedented importance. More than one great religious leader today has pointed to the need for the prophetic voice in our present world; yet any true Christian prophecy must learn from and be the continuance of the inspired prophecy of Old Testament times.

In many people's minds the word "prophecy" signifies predictions about the future. Such, however, was not the principal function of the great Israelitic prophets; and if one restricts prophecy to this special aspect he will miss the most important dimension of the prophetic office. Above all else, the prophet stands in the midst of his own contemporaries and reveals to them the deeper meaning of the life situation in which they find themselves. The prophet recalls the past, points to the future, but does so in order to indicate the way in which man should seize the opportunity of the present moment. Past and future throw light upon the demands of the present moment of decision.

One might state much the same thing in remarking that the prophetic word is a call to action, a call to change. No man, no age, lives out with full fidelity the demands placed upon human persons by the love of God. Invited to familiar intimacy with the divine, men always look for some way to avoid the forgetfulness of self that true love requires. All the charismatic prophets of Israel called for a changed heart in man; Christ who came after them and fulfilled their historical role called for exactly the same thing—and the message carried to us today by Scripture's inspired record of prophet and Christ remains just that: we must turn away from inadequacy and self-centeredness, and open our personalities and lives to the transforming power of love.

Israel's prophets speak, then, with a voice that is never old, never irrelevant. Prophecy in Israel is not a matter of interesting historical fact; it is an enduring challenge to the men of every epoch and culture. Once the prophets of Israel have spoken, there is a pattern of human responsibility, a demand of human behavior, that cannot be ignored by anyone who accepts the God of Israel.

Every age, our own included, must come to the prophetic books of the Bible to listen and learn. For most people, however, the writings of the prophets will remain a closed book, too difficult for their understanding, unless there be someone to assist them. This is the great value of books like this present one: in language and ideas that are more familiar to our own day, scholars like Father Sthulmueller can explain the historical situation and thought world of the Old Testament prophets, and so make it possible for interested people to approach the prophetic writings themselves.

There is another valuable aspect of this present book that should be drawn to the attention of the reader, so that he will not miss the contribution that it can make to his own contact with God's word. In tracing as it does the course of the development of prophetic thought in Israel, this book is treating of a large segment of that process which is referred to as "salvation-history," this century-long process in which God acted in the history of Israel to shape that people which would be fulfilled by the coming of Christ and the Church. It is this entire process, not just an isolated event or passage of Scripture, that is meant to inform us of God's intent for mankind, meant to tell us of the human free response that must accept the divine vocation if man is to reach his destiny.

It is the meaning of this "salvation-history" that the prophets clarified. It was, above all, their own period's significance in terms of this process to which they bore witness. It is from the prophets' interpretation of human life that Christians in our day are meant to see the relationship of their own lives and deeds to the action of God in their midst.

BERNARD COOKE, S.J.
Chairman, Department of Theology
Marquette University

ACKNOWLEDGMENTS

These chapters were prepared over a long period of time, and many kind persons have made important contributions to them. Some, like Sister M. Judith Therese, C.S.C., have patiently checked the style. Others, like Sister Ann Patrick, S.L., helped in transcribing lectures into manuscripts. The material, however, would never have fitted together into a book were it not for the constant encouragement and helpful suggestions of Mr. Theodore J. Berg. He and Mr. Eugene S. Geissler of Fides Publishers transformed this work into a joy.

Permission to reprint material in this book is gratefully acknowledged from the following publishers and periodicals: Chapter 1, *The Passionist* (December, 1962); Chapter 2, *The Bible Today* (February, 1963); Chapter 4, *Cross and Crown* (June, 1960); Chapter 5, *Marian Studies* (Volume XII, 1961); Chapter 6, *Catholic Biblical Quarterly* (October, 1959); Chapter 7, *The Postexilic Minor Prophets* (The Paulist Press, 1961); Chapter 8, *Sponsa Regis* (December, 1960); Chapter 9, *Ave Maria* (March 25, 1961); Chapter 10, *Catholic Biblical Quarterly* (July, 1958); Chapter 11, *Jubilee* (January, 1963).

CONTENTS

INTRODUCTION

"Salvation is from the Jews" (John 4:22). These words of Our Lord to the Samaritan woman of Sichar rightly deserve a place at the beginning of every work of biblical theology. God revealed Himself to the world through Jewish minds and hearts. If we ignore this Jewish origin of salvation, we lay ourselves open to the charge: "You worship what you do not know."

First of all, it was through a Jewish maiden, the holiest and loveliest woman ever to live, that the Son of God became man in the fulness of time. As mother of the Savior she gave Him her Jewish language, physical features and ways of thought. No son was ever so much his mother's son as Christ who had no human father. But there are other reasons why "salvation is from the Jews." Saintly Jewish men and women had been "heralds of [this] good news" of salvation, for they had been summoned by God with the command: "In the desert [of sin] prepare the way of the Lord! Make straight in the wasteland a highway for our God! Every valley [of human weakness] shall be filled in, every mountain [of stubborn pride] shall be made low" (Is

13

40:3-4, 9). This highway along which God gradually approached the human race lay through Jewish lands and history. Jewish writers related the story of this divine advent. Just as Our Lord's physical features and interior characteristics of soul were cast in the mold of His Semitic ancestry, so also His approach through the ages was through the transforming medium of Jewish history and geography, minds and hearts.

To grasp the full significance of such a statement we must make a comparison with Christian preaching today. The truths of our faith have been revealed by God and are reaffirmed in every century by the Holy Spirit living in the Church. Nevertheless, the gospel message is somehow modified in various ways by the different priests and teachers who transmit it to the people: by their nationality, family background, education, talents, sanctity, and even their lack of sanctity.

The same is true of God's revelation through the ages of the Old Testament. This divine message of salvation came through the Jews, and we are obliged to adapt ourselves to their Semitic mentality. If we fail to do this, we would be like a nearsighted person who, without his glasses, can only surmise about the vague and indistinct things at a distance. We run the risk of seeing in Scripture only the mirages of wishful thinking. We will worship what we do not know. Since God's message comes to us through the genius of Jewish writers, there is no other way to look into the mind of God except through their eyes or from their point of view. Each sacred writer, in the words of Pope Pius XII, was "the living and reasonable instrument of the Holy Spirit ... [and God so used] his faculties and powers, that from the book composed by him all may easily infer 'the special character of each one and, as it were, his personal traits.' Let the interpreter, then, with all care and without neglecting any light derived from recent research, endeavor to determine the peculiar character and circumstances of the sacred writer [as well as] the age in which he lived. . . . There is no one indeed but knows that the supreme rule of interpretation is to discover and define what the writer intended to express." Biblical exegesis, therefore, demands an appreciation of Jewish psychology, outlook, civilization, culture, aspirations and literary rules.

To listen intelligently and profitably to the preaching of the prophets, we must first of all know them as human beings. We must feel that we can sit down and converse with them, call them by their name and inquire about their parents, their family and their work. We must be aware of their political sympathies with the north or with the south, as well as their origin on a farm or in the city. Otherwise, we are not only liable to make social blunders but we are also in danger of misunderstanding what they say. This failure to grasp what the prophets mean would deprive us of the full force of the word of God.

Part one of this book provides some of the literary, political and religious background of the prophetic movement. The second series of chapters helps us to know the prophets as human beings just like ourselves. Only thus will their message become the *living* word of God, relevant to our lives this moment and important for our salvation in Christ Jesus. The third part takes up explicitly the messianic preparation of the prophets. A final section shows that the word of God is never to be considered so many letters rolled out flat in a book but rather a vibrant reality vitalized by the hopes and the needs of a living society. To hear the word of God spoken by the prophets we must have the courage to be alive ourselves, questioning, seeking, investigating as they

did. Only by being absorbed now in the mystery of the Word
Incarnate in Christ Jesus and in the Church can we ever appreciate what the prophets meant by the living word of God.

It is hoped that this book will enable an ever growing
number of readers to open their Bible and to hear God's
word spoken by the prophets. No other qualification is asked
of them than a desire to strengthen their life with God's
thoughts and decisions. Technical footnotes and involved
arguments have been edited out of the book. Scholars who
want such strong fare as that already have at their elbow the
learned periodicals in which some of the chapters of this
book originally appeared.

"And Philip, running up, heard him reading the prophet
Isaia, and he said, 'Dost thou understand what thou art reading?' But he said, 'Why, how can I, unless someone shows
me?'" (Acts 8:30-31).

PART I

Wisdom . . .
   penetrates and pervades all things
   by reason of her purity,
And passing into holy souls from age to age,
   she produces friends of God and prophets.
She reaches from end to end mightily
   and governs all things well (Wis 7:24, 27; 8:1).

CHAPTER 1   THE PROPHETS
AND THE WORD
OF GOD

WHENEVER the prophet spoke, his voice flared "like fire" and struck "like a hammer shattering rock" (Jer 23:29). He whipped "a whirling storm that burst upon the heads of the wicked" (Jer 23:19). His words came "from the mouth of the Lord," for the prophet "has stood in the council of the Lord . . . has heeded his word, so as to announce it" (Jer 23:16, 18).

God's word, heard through the voice of the prophets, not only shattered rocks of stubborness and prejudice, but it also pulled down mountains of pride and turned the rugged terrain of persecution into the broad valley of peace. God's word laid out a highway whereon all mankind could move quickly towards the revelation of "the glory of the Lord" (cf. Is 40:3-5).

Biblical religion, established by the vigorous power of

God's word, surrounded its worshippers with peace and security. Never, however, did the true prophets confuse peace with sleep! Though thanking God for the "comfort" and the "delight" of His word, the psalmist still prayed:

> . . .that I might be firm.
> . . .let me not stray.
> . . .I cling to your decrees.
> . . .I was prompt and did not hesitate (Ps 118).

For many Israelites of Jeremia's day, as for many Jews and Christians today, God's word erects a wall of false security around hunchbacked, insular religion. A lazy, sentimental people think to rest safely within the wall of God's promise, and they say to one another, "Peace shall be yours! No evil shall overtake you!" (Jer 23:17). Jeremia thunders back, "There is no peace!" (Jer 6:14).

The hammer of God's word had shattered their mind, and they had stopped thinking. The prophet crying out the word of God prepared a superhighway, so straight and so well paved, that even believers raced down it, lulled by the monotony of the way, many of them dozing off and crashing! Because of a superstitious trust in the security of the Word of God, the chosen people of Old Testament times provoked Jeremia's scornful indictment:

> They grow powerful and rich,
>   fat and sleek,
> They go their wicked way (5:27-28).

Nothing so quickly deforms and destroys the message of the prophets than to accept it passively, with a yawn. Regretfully, God confessed to Isaia, that His word can "make the heart of this people sluggish, to dull their ears and close their eyes" (Is 6:10).

Many persons today accept the phrase, "The prophets, God's voice," with a shrug of the shoulders. "Oh, yes!" comes the drone of their reply, "What God speaks, the prophet repeats. The Bible, consequently, is the word of God."

Is the word of God, we ask, just an eternal truth, whispered into the prophet's ear and then solemnly mouthed with human sound? How can such a word crash down like a hammer shattering and pulverizing? How can it lift valleys and pull down mountains and heriocally change men's lives? God's word, in fact, does more than change men's lives; it even asks the sacrifice of life. God's word comes forth "a sharp two-edged sword" (Apoc 1:16), cutting deeply, through the demands which it makes, and if it encounters resistance, then, as God declared through the prophet Osee, "I slew them by the word of my mouth" (Os 6:5).

There must, however, be more to God's word than idea and sound. The apostle St. John declared that God's word was such that it could not only be heard, it could also be "seen with our eyes" and "felt with our hands" (1 John 1:1).

God called His word "spring rain that waters the earth" (Os 6:3), "a mist covering the earth" (Sir 24:3), a river running over like the Euphrates with understanding and like the Nile sparkling with knowledge (Sir 24:24-25). The word has the "miraculous" power of water. No sooner does water touch the dry earth of semi-tropical Palestine than a lush carpet of green spreads across the land. No sooner does the word fall upon a heart of good will than the fruit of faith and charity appear.

Behind all this symbolism of hammer and sword, spring rain, mist and river their abides a reality. We must investigate the extraordinary reality behind the phrase, "The prophet speaks the Word of God."

THE WORD OF GOD IN ANCIENT
NEAR EASTERN LITERATURE

The answer to questions about the word of God must come from the land which bred and reared the Israelite prophets. This homeland, however, is vaster than the six thousand square miles of Palestine. The prophet Ezechiel, alive with cosmopolitan ideas, could apply to himself and to his fellow prophets what he addressed to the inhabitants of Jerusalem: "By origin and birth you are of the land of Chanaan; your father was an Amorrite and your mother a Hethite" (Ez 16:1-3). In an ancient Israelite creed, the worshipper made this honest confession: "My father was a wandering Aramean who went down to Egypt with a small household . . ." (Deut 26:5). These references to Chanaan, Amorrite, Hethite, Aramean and Egyptian indicate that the prophetic style, like the people themselves, had deep roots in the ancient Near East.

The Full Strength of the Word

From studying the early literature of Egypt and Mesopotamia, we can conclude that the inhabitants of these countries did not consider "the word" a product exclusively of the intellect. The ancient Near Easterners, and here we classify the Israelites, never distinguished between intellect and will; nor, for that matter, did their thinking separate body and soul. The Hebrew language possessed various words ordinarily translated intellect and will, body and soul; but never did these words denote our highly abstract notions. The modern word "body," for instance, presumes a philosophical mentality which can reason about man's material element which is distinct from the soul, its source of life, but which is not to be identified with a corpse, lying soul-less in a coffin. The Israelites never rose to such abstract speculation.

The Hebrew word *basar,* ordinarily translated *body,* changes its meaning like the colors of a chameleon. Its precise signification varies with the hues and tints of local circumstances. In general, *basar* indicates a man who seems "all flesh!" We today describe such a person as sickly or sensuous or unreliable. In the Bible *basar* does not so much represent a part or a characteristic of a person but the *person himself* physically weak (Is 31-3) or afflicted with sickness (Lev 13:2-43). *Basar* is the person morally depraved (Gen 6:2; 2 Paral 32:8). What is excellently translated "your lustful neighbors" in the Confraternity edition of the Old Testament reads in the Hebrew "your neighbors of great flesh *(basar)*" (Ez 16:26). *Basar* can even mean anybody and everybody, corresponding to our phrase "a seething mass of people" (Gen 6:12; Is 40:5), yet the word can reach even still further beyond our concept so as to include animals (Gen 6:17; Num 18:25). Finally, *basar* denotes a dead man (Gen 40:19), for then the full weakness of human existence appears.

Attention can be directed to other Hebrew words like spirit (ru'ah), soul (nepes), man ('enos), and body (gewiyya). In each case, however, the word does not designate a quality separated from the person possessing it, but the person himself, absorbed by one or other dominant trait.

According to this ancient "psychology," each man acted as a totality, a single, living unit. All of his faculties moved at once, in concert unity. It is true that our faculties do act in this same way, thoroughly dependent upon one another, constantly influencing one another, but whereas we neatly distinguish a cold objective concept of the intellect from the warm, subjective impulse of the will, the Hebrews understood the reaction as "totality thinking." An impulse of love vibrated in their understanding of the act of knowing; a steady control of knowledge directed the élan of the will. Man, with vigorous spirit (ru'ah), reacted against man with weak flesh (basar); man, rich in wisdom, opposed man, impoverished with foolishness. It was always man struggling with man in the arena of reality. This arena could be confined to the reality of *one* man, so that the person gradually evolved into that quality or disposition most dominant in him. As he became flesh or spirit, the full reality of this person lived within that weakness or strength.

Johannes Pedersen, Thorlief Boman and Claude Tresmontant among many others have investigated the ancient Near Eastern psychology. Their investigations release the full strength—perhaps, it would be more accurate to say, the full blast—of the divine word. The word like the idea, vibrated with the speaker's varied tones of character. The very concept of *word* in the ancient Near East possessed resonances of far wider extent that it has in ancient Greece. *Dabar,* the Hebrew expression for "word," possessed a background and usage much different from its Greek equivalent *logos.*

Dabar, in its deepst etymological meaning, signified: "to push" or "to drive forward" according to Edmond Jacob and Thorlief Boman; "to go away with" in Gensenius' Hebrew lexicon. The etymology of *logos* or *lego,* on the contrary, expressed the idea: to collect, to order, to arrange.

In the earliest biblical traditions *dabar,* used as a noun, frequently designates an action or series of events. Abimelech asked Abraham: "What had you in mind in doing *this thing?"* (this *dabar*—Gen 20:10; cf. Gen 22:1; 24:66; 3 Kgs 11:41). Because its meaning differs so much from our modern notion of "word," it will often be difficult to recognize the Hebrew *dabar* in the English translations of the

Bible. Good translators, as St. Jerome advised them, "render sense for sense and not word for word" (*Letter* LXII, 5). This advice is especially imperative when the word is *dabar!*

In very early Greek tradition *logos* had little or nothing to do with the function of speaking. Homer, for instance, ordinarily uses another word, *muthos.* The deepest level of meaning in the term *logos* did not denote action, not even the articulation of a thought, but concerned itself with the well-ordered, reasonable content. When the Greeks later accepted *logos* as the term for *word,* they seized upon the deepest or the most speculative one possible. The Hebrews, on the other hand, chose a term on the surface of life, involved in daily activity. Speaking, therefore, implied more than a communication of well-ordered thoughts; it achieved an active influence of one living person upon another.

When a prophet announced, "Hear the word of God," he was more than a teacher arranging his thoughts in logical sequence, so as to elucidate a doctrine or truth; he was a herald of divine presence. God was *there* in those words, irresistibly "pushing" or "driving forward" the action which his words uttered. The simultaneous "thrust" of speaking-acting is told by Deutero-Isaia:

Things of the past I foretold long ago,
they went forth from my mouth, I let you hear of them;
then suddenly I took action and they came to be (Is 48:3).
In this single verse Deutero-Isaia baffles our modern mind by the ease with which he swivels from past to future to present. Knowledge is communicated in the "long ago," yet, no sooner does it go forth from the mouth of God, then suddenly, by surprise, the action has been done.

God's Word in the Liturgy

God's word *is* God Himself acting upon the listener. God does not act in blind, uncontrollable movements but in a carefully determined way. There is a consistency about God; He is trustworthy. Knowledge is imparted by His actions, but the knowledge itself acts upon man. When the Jerusalem priests mock the words of Isaia as gibberish, and with drunken revelry roar out the refrain: "rule on rule, here a little, there a little" (Is 28:10), Isaia shouts that God's word will fall upon them in the measured steps of dread and terror:

> Rule on rule, rule on rule,
>   here a little, there a little!
> So that when they walk, they stumble backward,
>   broken, ensnared and captured (Is 28:13).

Each faint sound of the shortest syllable will act with fierce revenge.

The Israelites shared the ancient Near Eastern idea of the *word* as an active, dynamic presence of the one speaking. If the one speaking is God, then the word touched the earth with the omnipotent, creative presence of God. Both in Egypt and in Mesopotamia worshippers celebrated the mighty power of the word of their God.

There exists, for instance, the *Hymn to Sin*, the Moon god, a bilingual text belonging to the reign of Assurbanipal (668-632 B.C.), but composed in the archaic languages of thee Sumerians and the Akkadians of the third millenium. The hymn proclaims the vitality of the god's sovereign word. The opening word of each line identifies the divine word with the deity:

> You! your word settles down on the earth and green vegetation
>   is produced.
> You! your word makes stout the sheepfold and the stall;
>   it makes living creatures widespread....
> You! your word who can comprehend it, who can equal it?

Many other quotations could be advanced from the ancient Near East, witnessing to a belief that the word contained within its syllables the presence of the gods. Egyptian documents, in fact, proclaim the *creative* power of the sacred word. One of these announces that the Memphite god Ptah was the original creator-god. The extant text dates only to the eighth century, but linguistic evidence traces it back over another two thousand years. The god Ptah is "heart" conceiving what is to be made; he is "tongue" speaking and thereby creating. Still another Egyptian text of the nineteenth dynasty expresses an idea very similar to Deuteronomy 8:3, "Not by bread alone does man live, but by every word which comes forth from the mouth of the Lord." The Egyptian document thus addresses the god Ptah, "you in whose mouth is the creative word." Commenting on this document Hellmut Brenner notes that the creative power of the word is not exhausted by the first work of creation but extends energetically into each present moment.

With the ancients, the creative acts of the gods must continue into the contemporary life of the worshipper. Otherwise, the world would crack apart and collapse into chaos. The wondrous, divine act of stretching a firmament (or sky) into the heavens to hold back the roaring of its depths or, as we find in Egyptian texts, lifting the earth like mud out of the fertile waters of the Nile, must continue in a cyclic rhythm of life—birth, puberty, marriage and death.

The earth, the rain, the stars, the sun, these and all the other "wondrous" elements of the universe became gods, offspring of the creator-god and themselves continuing the divine work of creation year by year according to the seasons. Each spring the moment of creation burst freshly upon the earth; during the dry season of July-August when vegetation withered and died, the people mourned the death of the gods. In Egypt the cycles vary from those in Mesopotamia, but in both places the people's reaction was basically the same. Death would have been final, if the divine word of creation could not be spoken again. The rainy season in Mesopotamia, or in Egypt the inundation of the Nile, was assured by the power of the sacred liturgical word.

In this conception of time, life does not continue on this earth in a straight line so that a point once passed cannot be retrieved. Time proceeds in the divine-human rhythm of ever recurring acts. The word which created the world is spoken repeatedly, re-enacted liturgically at the sanctuaries of the gods. In Egypt, the great shrines of Memphis, Thebes and Hermonthis were named "the divine emerging primeval island." Each could claim to be the spot where the primeval mud emerged from the waters of the Nile to begin life. Through faith that the liturgical rites and sacred words re-enacted and *thereby* renewed the first act of creation, the worshiper recognized a power divine within the sacred, liturgical word.

This discussion has crisscrossed the ancient Near East from Mesopotamia across the west into Syria and down into Egypt; it has led us into the mysterious chambers of the ancient sanctuaries. We have become involved in the recital and the re-enactment of the sacred myths. What these myths were and how they reflected the experiential, psychosomatic character of ancient man are questions which we cannot pursue here. We have investigated the intellectual and religious habits of the ancient Near East, so that we will understand the biblical faith in the word of God. This word must not be fossilized into a mere concept or idea, but rather be clothed with all the qualities of the one speaking. The word *is* the active presence of the speaker.

BEARER OF FAITH IN A PERSONAL GOD

Left to themselves the Israelite would have been no different from their Amorrite, Aramean and Chanaanite neighbors. The blood of these people flowed in the veins and nourished the minds of Abraham, Moses, Samuel, David and the other great leaders of Israel. History evidences the close ties between Israel and her neighbors. In language and architecture, in social practices and civil laws, even in the rubrics of divine worship, Israel copied freely. When the children of Abraham, however, seem to melt into the multitude of ancient Near Eastern peoples, they emerge from the crowd, separate and unique. This religious difference is made clear from the archeological discoveries of Palestine. History reveals the Israelites, copying from their neighbors' architecture and agriculture, even from their language and ritual, and yet history also points out the uniqueness of Israelite morality and concept of the deity. Why is it that Israel is culturally very much the same, yet religiously very different? History raises this question, but only Theology can answer it by claiming the intervention of God. For us at this moment the problem narrows down to this: like her neighbors Israel proclaims the power of the divine word, but unlike her neighbors Israel recognized within this word the personal love and kindly interest of her God.

> For *love* of your fathers he *chose* their descendants and *personally* led *you* out of Egypt by his great power. . . . This is why you must now know, and fix in your heart, the *Lord is God* in the heavens above and on earth below, and that there is no other (Deut 4:37-39).

Clearly this similarity of Israel to her neighbors was hazardous. The Hebrews were constantly in danger of absorbing not only the cultural habits of pagan peoples but also their religious beliefs and practices. In that eventuality the surrounding nations would have peacefully destroyed Israel's identity as a separate nation. Israel's greatness did not depend on what she was but rather on who God was. The word of God in Israel was different from the divine word in Mesopotamia or in Egypt because of Him who spoke.

God's Word to Abraham

When the cultic patterns of the ancient Near East were in danger of suppressing the word of a *personal, loving* God, rolling it out flat and indistinguishable from the word of any other god, then it was that the prophets arose and spoke. Their voice was God's, calling the nation back to the faith of Abraham. God had entered sacred history by speaking a word, and through that word He pointed that history in the direction of world salvation. When Israel began to swerve into the way of other nations, the prophets once again spoke the word of faith. To understand the prophetic message, therefore, we must know clearly the faith established in Abraham's soul by the word of God. When the word of God first came to Abraham, it called to him:

> Leave your country, your kinfolk and your father's house,
>   for the land which I will show you;
> I will make a great nation of you.
>   I will bless you and make your name great,
>   so that you shall be a blessing. . . .
> In you shall all the nations of the earth be blessed (Gen 12:1-3).

The divine word transmitted a message about land, posterity and blessing, but it was weighted with a mysterious element, which remained unspoken, and which turned out to be far more important than what the words actually said. God did not explain at first the situation of the land and to the very end Abraham remained a *ger*, an immigrant without citizenship. Abraham had to *wait* upon God trustfully and would eventually be canonized not as a man of great possession, but rather as a man of heroic faith. "Abraham believed God, who accredited the act to him as justice (Gen 15:6). Faith, which comes from hearing the word of God (cf. Rom 10:17), relies upon something not explicitly presented in the word. It is "the evidence of things that are not seen" (Heb 11:1).

God's word to Abraham held a mysterious power, sweeping the soul of the patriarch towards God and transforming him into "the friend of God" (James 2:23). The dynamic power within the word was, of course, none other than God Himself, speaking the word and thereby revealing the secret of His divine life. The word pulsed with the personal love and the tender concern of Almighty God.

The word emerged from God's deepest life. It was not something created outside of Him, like the universe, but a secret thought, a mystery, at the very heart of His being. So deep in God lies this mystery that it can be called God Himself.

Abraham's response to God's word was faith, an unconditional, total surrender of *himself* to God. As with God, so with Abraham, the interchange involved nothing primarily material, but rather something deeply personal—his very self.

The word of Scripture presents many examples of Abraham's new life of personal faith. For instance, he will listen in on divine soliloquies; he will hear God reasoning within Himself: "Can I keep from Abraham what I am about to do?" (Gen 18:17). "The friend of God"—*El Khalil* according to the Arabic form even today—will not be surprised at any demand from God. Love reacts that way.

Abraham quickly submits when he understands that God wants the sacrifice of the child of promise, Isaac. The bibli-

cal words manifest the poignant rending of someone closer
to him than his own life: "Take, I pray you, your son, your
only one, the one whom you love, Isaac" (Gen 22:2).
Cornelius a Lapide commented: "Quot hic verba, tot sunt
stimuli, tot tentationes." Each word not only tempted Abraham but coming from God it also contained the power of
God's presence so that God and Abraham were more closely
pledged to one another.

God will reward the heroic faith of Abraham. When
Moses later asked the name of the one speaking to him
from the burning bush, the first answer declared: "I am the
God of your father, the God of Abraham" (Ex 3:6). This
reply reflects as delicate a charity as though a man today
would suppress his own name and for his son's sake call
himself simply "the father of Jimmy Smith."

God was the father of Abraham, because by His word He
had begotten new life within the Patriarch. Life, it surely
was, for God's word had vitalized that area of Abraham's
person where Abraham thought, loved, judged, put to death
and brought back to life.

God's Word to Moses

The faith of Abraham became the life-blood of his many
descendants. This life would be transmitted as it was originally bestowed, through the *word* spoken by God to Moses
and through Moses to all the people.

God, it is true, performed great wonders as He brought
His people out of Egypt: the plagues, the miracle of the
Red Sea, the manna and the water. God acted stupendously
in the sight of all. "Yet with most of them," wrote St. Paul,
"God was not well pleased" (1 Cor 10:5). Unless God
spoke His word within the soul and unless the Israelite re-

sponded with faith as did Abraham, the murmur of unbelief
would continue.

God's redemptive acts would continue to save and redeem through the sacred word recited at the sanctuary. The
day of Moses endured in the word which was vibrant with
life.

> Hear, O Israel, the statutes and decrees which I proclaim
> in your hearing *this day. . . .* The Lord, *our* God, made a cov-
> enant *with us* at Horeb [= Sinai]; not with our fathers did
> he make this covenant, but with *us, all of us who are alive here*
> *this day* (Deut 5:1-2).

Each generation responded with faith, yet even this answer
of faith was breathed into them by the utterance of God's
word. *"Hear, O Israel!"* Each listened, as God repeated
what He once spoke to Moses:

> I have witnessed the affliction of my people Israel in Egypt
> and I have heard their cry of complaint. . . . Therefore, I have
> come down to rescue them (Ex 3:7-8).

This life, begotten by the word within the soul of the
people, was the same as Abraham's, a personal bond, attach-
ing God and His people to one another. No word, of course,
contained so fully the life of God as the sacred name,
Yahweh. What this name really means is still controverted
by scholars. Some question whether God in revealing this
name added any new idea to the heritage of biblical faith.
The name, according to these scholars, succinctly expressed
what had been the faith given to Abraham. It pledged God's
continuous presence, and by responding with faith to this
presence Israel came to know God better and better. In this
case, the sacred name Yahweh confesses: *He who is always*
there with you.

This "new" name, as the late Albert Gelin beautifully

declared, becomes a prayer when spoken by man and a promise when uttered by God. By it man asks of God: "Come, be with me"; and by it God replies to man, "I am with you." For man to hear this word, he must believe. As he hears it with faith, his life becomes a waiting upon God. During each moment of man's life, God reveals Himself by love and care, and as man experiences this "word" of protection, he comes to know the mystery of God. It is a knowledge which is life, for it extends God's personal concern to every segment of man's being.

The Mosaic tradition provides a second example of the creative power of the word of God. This instance is drawn from one of the earliest law codes of Israel, Exodus 21-23. German scholars have given it the name *Bundesbuch, Book of the Covenant.*

Most of the laws are expressed conditionally: i.e., if such and such happens, then this is what shall be done. These laws are called casuistic or case laws, because they represent a decision handed down by a judge on a particular case or problem. Almost all ancient legal codes consisted of these casuistic laws. Hammurabi's code listed nearly three hundred such cases. These enactments were not properly laws; like decisions of the United States Supreme Court, they established a norm or precedent for the future. Each new case would be judged not only according to this traditional "norm" but also on its own merits.

As we watch the Israelites share the jurisprudence of their neighbors, we must admit that the children of Abraham seem to fade into the common horizon of the ancient Near East. In many ways, moreover, the Hebrews were definitely inferior to others, because the biblical laws are poorly arranged, in sharp contrast to the orderly and comprehensive legislation of Hammurabi. Just when the distinct genius of Israel seems absorbed by the higher culture of other countries, the Israelites step forward to stand alone. Their juridical system is God's word.

Yet, so was Hammurabi's code the word of Shamash, but the difference between Yahweh and Shamash, the sun god, separated Israel from Babylon with a chasm deeper than *el ghor* of the Jordan! Despite the highly personalized religion of the ancient Near East, Shamash remained a "power" subservient to Babylonian ritual, while Yahweh was truly a "person" who called Israel "my special possession, dearer to me than all other people" (Ex 19:5). Israel's law expressed God's personal wish for this beloved people; they must respond with loving faith.

Faith in God's personal care—an element unspoken, merely implied—such was Israel's obedience to God's law. The biblical law code did not lay out a blue print, determining in advance exactly what must be done inch by inch along the way. Casuistic laws provide only a "norm." The Chosen People must wait obediently, as God through priest or judge defines each new case. For guidance the priest or judge has the precedent of great leaders of old and their "casuistic laws." By studying their forefathers' humble obedience to God and by sharing God's kindly solicitude for His people, the judge will be able to hand down an equitable decision. Just as the judge may not approach a case with conceit or prejudice if his judgment is to be God's word, the people too must react with humble acceptance if they are to hear divine accents in human speech. With faith alive, the Chosen People, like Abraham, will be led by the power of the word. He who called Himself "The God of Abraham" will then discharge the promise of His name Yahweh, *He who is always there with you.*

THE WORD, A MAGIC FORMULA

God's word, like water, had fallen upon the land of Palestine and immediately a rich carpet of green spread across the countryside. The word was charged with such vitality and produced such abundance that men began to confuse the abundance with the life, the effect of the word with the word itself. Instead of listening to *God* as He spoke, Israel forgot all about God and concentrated upon His promises. The worshipper confused God and His gifts.

This change came so easily that few persons noticed what was happening. Blind trust in the power of God's word transformed that word into nothing more than an impersonal power at the service of man. Religion slumped into superstition. Israel's keen, generous faith had been so dulled by material interests and fleshly concerns, that the Chosen People were incapable of Abraham's heroic obedience and Moses' humble meekness before God's word. They were too dull to sense the mystery contained within the divine communication. "They grow powerful and rich, fat and sleek. They go their wicked way" (Jer 5:27-28).

The prophets alone detected this insidious state of affairs. They saw clearly that Israel's religion, founded upon the word of God, was being corrupted from within by a superstitious trust in the divine word. Amos, the first of the "classical prophets," was well trained to spot this cancerous condition. Years of pasturing sheep in the wilderness of Juda, not only sharpened his vision to spot a lizard silently moving across the sand, but it also made him sensitively aware of deep-seated human reactions. He was not fooled by the external grandeur, the elaborate ritual and the pompous behavior of Israel. He detected beneath the polished veneer the frustration, the bitterness, the infidelity of the people.

Standing before the crowd of worshipers at Bethel sanctuary, he caught their attention by condemning one after another of their enemies: Damascus, Gaza, Tyre and the rest. While the devotees were still clapping and shouting approval, the desert-trained prophet fiercely turned on them:

> For three crimes of *Israel,* and for four,
> I will not revoke my word (Am 2:6).

God's patience was exhausted; the number of offenses was complete. "The time is ripe to have done with my people" (Am 8:2).

> They sell the just man for silver,
> and the poor man for a pair of sandals (Am 2:6).

The wealthy would assure themselves and society that the poor acted justly. The law required that a man pay his debts. Lest this law be violated, the poor were sold into slavery to defray expenses. What they owed, however, was the price of a pair of sandals! These poor people must be sinners, so went the thinking of the times, because God's word had promised wealth and plenty to good religious folk.

> Son and father go to the same prostitute,
> profaning my holy name (Am 2:7).

God had promised to Abraham "descendants as the stars of the heavens" (Gen 22:17); and so in God's holy name the Israelites perform the fertility cult to consecrate their sex and their family to God. Amos labeled this religion "profanity" and its attraction lustful gratification. He would not even employ the technical word for temple prostitiute (*qedesa*); he called the girl a *na'ara,* a young female with sexual appeal.

The wine of those who have been fined
they drink in the house of their god (Am 2:8).

Strict justice inflicted fines upon transgressors, but the judges
used the proceeds to get drunk at sacred banquets! They
held both the fines and the sacrificial banquets to be God's
will, clearly legislated for in the Torah. God must have been
well pleased! In fact, He must have dozed off into sweet
slumber after receiving the gift of many flocks of sheep
and large casks of wine. In the popular mind, God had been
turned into an image of themselves, with animal lusts and
moral indifference. Externals were enough; wealth was the
sign of blessing. Little wonder Amos shouted "Woe!" at
"those who yearn for the day of the Lord" (Am 5:18).

God's word, evidently, no longer summoned worshipers
to faith. It was nothing but a magic formula to insure success. Once the sacred phrases were repeated in the temple
liturgy, the full effect of bounteous wealth *must* come. Man's
response was reduced to a superstitious trust in externals:
the externals of the liturgy and the externals of wealth. Lost
was the interior spirit of faith, whereby man could listen to
the mystery of God's love hidden within the word and make
an unconditional commitment of himself to the *person* of
God.

The change crept so slowly and so surreptitiously over the
faith of Israel that we almost question the fierce, uncom-
promising stand taken by the prophets. In defense of the
prophets we must admit that their holiness had bestowed
a sharpness of vision far more intense than their fellow
countrymen to pierce to the heart of the matter. What they
saw of Israel's hard arrogance turned them against God's
people. They witnessed the rejection of God's call. Israel
was flaunting God's love by abusing the gifts of His love.

God's goodness, it can be seen, was the occasion of this disastrous change. Was He too indulgent, too generous? No! but Israel like a spoilt child used God's gifts to turn against Him. Ezechiel presents the entire history of Israel in terms of such shameless ingratitude (ch 16).

God was continuously warning His people against this obsession with comfort and wealth, not only by the moral demands of the decalog but also by the punishment of evil. God even disciplined Moses, Aaron and Miriam. The Israelites, as the theological introduction to the book of Judges explained, "were quick to stray from the way their fathers had taken and did not follow their example of obedience. ... They would relapse and do worse" (Judg 2:17, 19).

The Deuteronomic ensemble of Josue-Judges-Samuel-Kings stressed repeatedly the evil effects of disobedience and infidelity. Lurking behind each word of this history, however, is the material attitude of a people too crass and too dull for this sublime teaching. The stories of Samuel, of Elias and Eliseus, of David and Solomon, all pulse with excitement over material gifts and marvelous deeds. Religion was following the quick, smooth road of the miraculous; the silent way of faith leading deep into the heart of God was too steep and forbidding and completely hidden by the bursts of splendor, wealth and prestige.

What could be done, when apostasy was being justified by the name of relgion? To David God had promised: "Your house and your kingdom shall be confirmed before me forever" (2 Sam 7:16). In dedicating the temple, Solomon declared that this tabernacle was the dwelling of God on earth, and therefore every prayer directed towards this place must be heard (cf. 3 Kgs 8:27-30). Later, when Jeremia flayed the people for their sins, they feel no need to reform their morals. They simply chant monotonously:

"This is the temple of the Lord! The temple of the Lord! The temple of the Lord!" (Jer 7:4). Possessing the temple, the Israelites say:

> No evil shall befall us,
>   neither sword nor famine shall we see.
> The prophets have become wind (Jer 5:12-13).

What was God to do, when faith in divine things was destroying faith in God? Was He to work more miracles and distribute more wondrous delights? Such action would only thicken the material spirit of their hearts. Yet, how could a people so dull, so "sleek and fat," be made aware of their apostasy from God?

THE PROPHETS, MEN OF THE WORD

God's answer to this seemingly hopeless situation was to raise up a series of religious leaders, the like of whom has seldom been equalled in any world religion, the prophets. The prophets, on their part, would simply speak *the word of God* and then wait for its full effects to be felt. Commissioning the prophets, God said:

> I place *my words* in your mouth! . . .
> to root up and to tear down,
>   to destroy and to demolish,
>   to build and to plant (Jer 1:9-10).

Before God's word would be able "to build and to plant," it must first go forth "to root up and to tear down." That is precisely what it had done to Abraham and Moses. It had *uprooted* the Patriarch from his native land that he might follow God's word into a strange land (Gen 12:1-3); it had *torn down* Moses' palace of Egyptian glory and *demolished* his pride through desert austerity, that he might lead the people to a covenant between themselves and God.

Consecration by God's Word

Unlike priest or king, the prophet did not receive his office automatically through membership in the sacred tribe of Levi or in the royal house of David. The prophet relied upon some other credential than noble blood. Neither did any public ceremony ratify and validate the divine choice.

The sacred oil which consecrated the prophet was different from the oil which anointed the high priest and the king. The oil which set the prophet aside for his special mission was the *word of God*. This all-powerful word, as Jeremia confessed, became "like fire burning in my heart, . . . I cannot endure it" (Jer 20:9). It had grasped the will of Jeremia and set his life upon a divine mission. Not matter how poignantly he longed "that I had in the desert a travelers' lodge that I might leave my people and depart from them" (Jer 9:1), still, he could not free himself from the strong grasp of God's word. On the day of his ordination, Jeremia received the anointing of this divine order:

> Behold I place my words in your mouth!
> This day I set you
> over nations and over kingdoms (Jer 1:9).

The prophetic consecration by the word of God was sollemnized secretly and mysteriously in Jeremia's soul.

If a prophet like Jeremia did belong to a priestly family, he disassociated himself from the privileged class. When he stood before the people, he did not attract atention with the solemn announcement: "Hear me, because I am a priest!" He said very simply: "Hear the word of the Lord" (Jer 7:2). Isaia may have taken advantage of his position at the royal court to speak freely before the king; he certainly put to use his excellent education as state advisor. Never, however, did he draw the power of his message from any of these class benefits, but rather from the interior conviction that "I have heard from the Lord, the God of hosts, the destruction decreed for all the earth" (Is 28:22). If, after the destruction is complete, "the Lord God will wipe away the tears from all faces," this too happens "because the Lord *has spoken*" (Is 25:8). The source of prophetic strength was the presence of God's word within the soul and upon the lips of the prophet.

The "classical prophets" even cut contact with the company of "professional prophets." Prophets like Amos, Osee and Isaia never joined the association of *nebi'im* nor did they follow a separate community life. They do not seem to have assembled even periodically with these groups, although saintly men like Samuel (1 Sam 9:20) and Elias (4 Kgs 2:3) lived at least intermittently among them.

The *nebi'im* (professional prophets, living for the most part in community) at first were fired with fervor and for a long time sustained the loyalty of God's people. In later times, unfortunately, these professional prophets were absorbed with selfish interests and used their reputation as a source of income. Michea said contemptuously:

> ...regarding the prophets
>   who lead my people astray;
> Who, when their teeth have something to bite
>   announce peace
> But when one fails to put something in their mouth,
>   proclaim war against him (Mich 3:5).

In the face of such a shameful reputation, it is little surprise that Amos snapped back at Amasia, the high priest of Bethel, when this gentleman ordered Amos to "flee to the land of Juda! There earn your bread by prophesying!" (Am 7:12). Amos resented the "accusation" of being one of the *nebi'im*. With a contemptuous twist of his mouth, he replied:

> I am no prophet,
> nor have I ever belonged
> to a company of prophets (Am 7:14).

Amasia's slur to "earn your bread by prophesying" portrays the professional prophet as an ecclesiastic using his spiritual office simply for material gain. In the case of the *nebi'im,* prophecy merely provided an opportunity to predict and thus achieve the victory and prosperity for their royal masters. In return, the prince provided his loyal seers with wealth and prestige.

Not even supernatural visions, granted personally to some of the "classical" prophets, were ever invoked as divine proof for the word of God. Amos (7:1ff) and Isaia (6:1ff) beheld a mysterious vision at the same time as God spoke His "consecrating" word. These inaugural visions, whenever they occurred, profoundly affected the prophets' character and deeply colored their thought. Isaia, ever after, reverently spoke of the "Holy One of God" and Amos preached with stern finality. In every instance, however, the prophet commanded a hearing from the people, not because he had seen a vision from God but rather because he could say: "Hear the word of God!"

For too long a time now the word of God was being silenced by the loud blasts of marvelous happenings. External wonders were distracting men away from God; bells and trumpets accompanying the magnificent ceremonies of worship substituted for good moral living. The people seemed almost to think that majestic ritual could blind God to the sight of their immorality and faithlessness. These people did not need more visions and more miracles, a fact very clear to the prophets. The land groaned under the scourge of a famine, but it was "not a famine of bread, or a thirst for water," declared Amos, but a famine "for hearing the word of the Lord" (Am 8:11).

The classical prophets, we must admit, worked miracles. As a "sign" to King Ezechia, Isaia commanded "the shadow cast by the sun on the stairway ... go back to the ten steps it has advanced" (Is 38:8). Earlier, Isaia had told Ezechia's father, King Achaz, to "ask for a sign from the Lord, your God; let it be deep as the nether world, or high as the sky" (Is 7:11). These marvelous occurences, however, were rare, and even when these wonders were offered, the prophet still insisted more emphatically upon interior faith. Isaia, in fact, had just finished saying to King Achaz:

> Unless your faith is firm,
> you shall not be firm (Is 7:9).

When Ezechia exhibited the wealth of his kingdom before the impressionable Babylonians, Isaia rebuked him for boasting of human greatness instead of trusting in divine strength. Faith was to be Israel's source of salvation.

Spirituality of the Word

Before investigating how the word of God developed a spirit of faith within the soul of Israel, we will look into the soul of the prophet for the effects of the divine word.

For Amos, dedication to the divine word was blunt obedience. A man of strong will, able to muster full strength to the duty at hand, Amos quickly marched north to Bethel at God's command: "Go, prophesy to my people Israel" (Am 7:16). Amos spoke without sympathy, coldly enunciating the devastating word of God. This word, which had transformed the shepherd into a prophet almost against his will, remained just as powerful in the announcement to sinful Israel: "I will crush you into the ground" (Am 2:13).

What was military obedience in Amos' disciplined soul was agonizing acceptance in Osee's sensitive spirit. Osee endured humiliation lower than the dirt on the street, as he retrieved "yet again" a wife who had become the "beloved of a paramour" (Os 3:1). Only thus will he be prepared to speak of God's infinite, forgiving love. God had been betrayed again and again, so that were a man in God's place, human anger would flatly declare: "So much, no more!" Osee, however, was thus to pour out the anguish of God's answer:

> I am God and not man,
>> the Holy One present among you;
>> I will not let the flames consume you (Os 11:9).

At the same time God's word, spoken by Osee, was deadly:

> . . .I smot them through the prophets,
> I slew them by the word of my mouth (Os 6:5).

God, however, destroys only what is evil and harmful, so that He can declare in the concluding message of Osee:

> I will heal their defection
> I will love them freely. . . .
> I shall be like the dew for Israel:
>> he shall blossom like the lily. . . .
>> I have humbled him, but I will prosper him.
>>> Os 14:5-6, 9).

No prophet, not even Osee, so laid bare the profound emotions of interior struggle as the one whose words are repeated by the liturgy of Passion and Holy Week. From the start, Jeremia begged God to send someone else because "I know not how to speak; I am too young" (Jer 1:6). The prophet's own weakness would reveal the source of his iron strength; his slowness in speech would prove God's statement: "I place my words in your mouth!" (Jer 1:9).

Only if they came from God could the words of such a diffident, fearful man become in later Israel the most popular of all prophetic scrolls and could men say of Jesus that He is Jeremia came back alive (cf. Matt 16:14).

God's words sunk so deeply into the soul of Jeremia, penetrated so thoroughly every pore of his mind and heart, and colored so profoundly every thought and reaction of the man, that it is often impossible to distinguish God's word from Jeremia's. This complete compenetration was achieved through years of interior struggle. Jeremia's first hesitation in accepting God's word was only the first of a series of tense arguments. Jeremia finally poured out words almost blasphemous in fury: "You have become for me a treacherous brook, whose waters do not abide!" (Jer 15:18). Divine obedience had led the prophet down a river bed whose waters vanished into desert dryness.

God's word, then, inscribed on the hearts of the prophets, was more than a truth to be believed; faith, we have already seen, was more than a response of the intellect! God's word, in the case of Amos, called for blind obedience. It ruthlessly cut into the heart and mind of Osee and Jeremia and slew whatever it could not conquer or did not want. It was ruthless, and yet, somehow or other, the all-powerful God felt "my heart . . . overwhelmed, my pity stirred" (Os 11:8). Even though Israel was "like a woman faithless to her lover," God begged her repeatedly: "Return, rebellious children" (Jer 3:14). God's word then came from God's deepest life and evoked the prophet's most intense emotion. God's word given and received was an interchange of life's love, hope and entire self.

To have promised wealth and to have worked miracles would have distracted the prophet and his listeners from God's spirit. This distraction is actually the worst of infidelities, because it uses God's gifts to purchase sinful pleasure. The prophets received the law of God's word on their heart, marking them out as God's very own. God chose them for this special mission, in order that they might share with all Israel this personal friendship with God. The prophets would perform their mission, exactly as God acted towards them, by announcing the word of God. That was also the way God had intervened in the lives of Abraham and Moses.

PROPHETIC WORD TO ISRAEL

The prophet thus continued the mission of Abraham and Moses by sustaining Israel's strong faith in a personal God. But many centuries had passed since God had first called Abraham and had directed Moses to the establishment of Israelite religion. The nomadic, patriarchical existence of Abraham and the austerer, desert wandering of Moses were gone forever, and yet the spirit of these extraordinary men must reappear in their descendants. One of the prophets exhorted the people:

> Look to the rock from which you were hewn,
>   and to the pit from which you were quarried;
> Look to Abraham, your father,
>   and to Sara, who gave you birth (Is 51:1-2).

In summoning a return to these heroes of the past, the prophets disregarded many details of Abraham's and Moses' lives. To express this truth more accurately, we can say that the prophets saw a *hidden, symbolic* meaning in their forefathers' external mode of life. To be like Abraham without homeland and citizenship; to be a wanderer like Moses through desert wastes—these circumstances became types or symbols of interior holiness, for they revealed an heroic dedication to God's word. By the word of God, once spoken

to Abraham and to Moses and now heard again in the
prophets, the spirit of the past will be reproduced in other
hearts. The deep, typical meaning will be fulfilled in other
lives.

Our present concern is to see how the prophets achieved
this reliving of the past. We will concentrate attention
upon three factors. First of all, in announcing God's word,
the prophets sounded no retreat from reality, but through
faith imparted a full meaning to reality. They did not issue
the impossible order of a return to the desert but they allowed the people to remain where they were. Yet the
prophets were not satisfied with conditions as they were!
God's plans were so vast and stupendous that the word will
create a new world of happiness upon earth. To remain
attentive to ordinary things, so the prophets declared, prepared Israel to witness wondrous things:

> . . .awesome deeds we could not hope for,
>   such as they had not heard of from of old.
> No ear has ever heard, no eye ever seen,
>   any God but you,
>   doing such deeds for those who wait for him (Is 64:2-3).

A new creation is the reward for humble, abiding faith in
God's word.

Besides an acceptance of reality and a belief in a new
creation, the prophetic message contained a third important
element. God, who spoke through the prophets, was no
stiff, faceless deity but a God personally interested in His
chosen people.

God's Word within Reality

The prophets did not summon any retreat from reality.
To be a loyal follower of Moses, the sons of Israel were not
obliged to dismantle their stone houses, abandon city life

and begin a nomadic wandering, pitching their tents wherever darkness caught them. Some fanatic Israelites, the Rechabites, did oblige themselves to this *literal* obedience to Moses. "All our lives," they confessed to Jeremia, "we have not drunk wine. . . . We build no houses. . . ; we own no vineyard or fields or crops, and we live in tents" (Jer 35:8-10). Never did the Bible commit Israel to such an inflexible observance of the law; the many adaptations incorporated into the Mosaic law, the modifications of later centuries, the existence of different applications, the very form of casuistic laws—all these features of biblical law rule out an obstinate, unyielding obedience to external rules. The stress is rather upon internal faith.

The prophets saw clearly that the cause of the nation's irreligious spirit lay basically not in the externals of civilization. There was nothing sinful about houses and crafts, architecture and music. All through her history Israel borrowed freely from her neighbors and yet maintained her own religious identity. From the Canaanites she learned farming; from the Philistines she received the secret of iron. Egypt contributed her wisdom literature; Ugarit, her religious poems; Tyre and Sidon, their architects and building material. Despite this unabashed copying of foreign culture, Israel remained religiously distinct. Her interior faith was never suppressed by all these external wrappings. Instead of that, her faith lived in and through these externals, harnessing them to the service of Yahweh.

Israel, therefore, was not obliged to flee to a never-never land of Shangri-La but rather to direct the penetrating power of faith upon the ordinary circumstances of life. Amos made that point very clear. Drought or locust plague; blight or searing wind; pestilence or death—all these circumstances are from God,

> Yet, you returned not to me,
> says the Lord (Am 4:6, 8, 9, 10, 11).

All these disasters were God's word, *acting* in their midst, calling Israel back to personal love and loyal faith. These calamities destroyed, only if they were not accepted as the word of God. In the depth of such darkness, faith became an act of heroic fortitude.

Monstrous Assyria, trampling like a lustful giant over the ancient Near East, was but exercising the will of God who was disciplining and so purifying His chosen people. Isaia, therefore, in speaking for God, called Assyria, "my rod in anger, my staff in wrath" (Is 10:5). When God's work was completed, the rod would be cast aside. Assyria would crash to destruction like a cedar on Lebanon toppling over a precipice (cf. Is 10:33).

How poignantly Israel wanted to escape into some other world, rather than recognize God's chastening hand in Assyria! Such an escape was as impossible as Jona's ridiculous attempt to flee across the sea from "the God of heaven who made the sea" (Jon 1:9). God clearly acted in every movement and change of Palestinian life, and consequently God could be found *only* in these earthly involvements.

When Habacuc complained about violence, ruin and misery, God replied that He will act—or speak—by "raising up Chaldea, that bitter and unruly people" to punish the wicked Jerusalemites (Hab 1:6). This answer provoked another question from the prophet:

> Why, then, do you gaze on the faithless in silence
> while the wicked man devours
> one more just than himself? (Hab 1:13).

This time God's answer would be so important that it must be written

> Clearly upon the tablets,
> so that one can read it even on the run (Hab 2:2).

The words of life, deserving to be chiseled by iron on stone tablets, are:

> The just man lives by faith (Hab 2:4).

Faith is life; without it, man is dead!

Israel had only one way of life at her disposal, that of faith. Every other way of living was a living death! She could not run away; she was obliged to find God by faith in all the human surroundings of contemporary Palestine. This demand of faith was heroic, because it compelled the wicked to accept the fire of purification, while it constrained the good to remain patient. God was not asleep but actively present in the storm.

Faith accepted the outstretched arm of God in all these events; it heard the saving word of God in everything. God's word acted and like rain it brought life. This sense of the divine presence in earthly involvements was the prophets' first great contribution to biblical life.

Creative Power of the Word

The life begotten of faith was actually a new creation. Here is one of those many conundrums of prophetic thought. In the midst of distress man wants to run away to a new creation of his own making, to an "unreal" world different from what he has at hand. The prophets forbade such a retreat from reality! By remaining humbly subject to God's world and word, the old was transformed into a new creation. What man strove to acquire for himself, by himself, God was waiting to give. Israel, however, must accept it as *God's* creation.

No prophet sang so lyrically of the new creation as Deu-

tero-Isaia (Is 40-55), and at the same time he is the prophet
who acclaimed with esctatic language the powerful word of
God. In speaking of the new creation, Deutro-Isaia will
move with the ease of a deft weaver, crossing one strand of
thought upon another. Each new idea, like a colored thread,
adds its own shade of meaning to the completed tapestry.

Crisscrossing through chapters forty to fifty-five are: 1) a
new creation, 2) extending throughout the universe, 3) by
which God cares for the poor and lowly, 4) and accepts the
suffering of the innocent in reparation for the sins of the
wicked, 5) but especially does His new creative act transform the lives of the children of Abraham, 6) whom God
will lead along a glorious exodus back to the Promised Land.
Each of these themes works in and out of the two great
strands of a *new creation* which the *word of God* will
achieve.

The two ideas of word and creation so delicately interchange in the majestic poems of Deutero-Isaia, the transition
from one to another is so spontaneous, that the reader might
almost miss their double presence. The quick movement
evidences the prophet's mastery of the Hebrew language.
Very frequently, for instance, creation is a participle de-
pending upon a verb *to speak.* In 42:5 four participles complete the idea of the principal verb:

> Thus says the Lord, the only God,
>   *creating* the heavens and *stretching* them out,
>   *extending* the earth with its covering of vegetation,
>   *giving* breath to the people upon it
>   and spirit to those who walk on it.

If creation is accomplished through the act of speaking, then
the wisdom of the divine word guides the act of creation.
God directs each act of nature, whether they be ordinary

acts of almost childish proportions like counting drops of
rain and weighing "dust on a scale" (Is 40:15) or grand
deeds of majestic splendor like marking "off the heavens
with a span" (40:12) and summoning the stars by name
(40:26). Small or mighty, each act is so truly from God
that the prophet exclaims:

> Who has directed the spirit of the Lord,
>   or who has instructed him as his counselor?
> Whom did he consult to gain knowledge?
>   Who taught him the path of judgment? (40:13-14).

Because creation is an act of God's word, it must orig-
inate, like the word, in the deep recesses of God's mind. It
is not so much the product of His hands as it is the thought
of His heart. It is not at all surprising, therefore, that
Deutero-Isaia is the prophet who sings exquisitely of the
personal bond of love between God and His people. He
wrote those touching lines so familiar to every Bible reader:

> Can a mother forget her infant,
>   be without tenderness for the child of her womb?
> Even should she forget,
>   I will never forget you.
> See, upon the palms of my hands I have written your name.
>   (Is 49:15-6).

With delicate finesse he arranges his sentence structure so
that the reader is intuitively aware of the presence of God.
Even the grammar of the Hebrew word is called into service,
so that the love of God may be presented in tones of beauty.
In one magnificent passage he juxtaposes over and over
again, yet never with monotony the personal pronouns: You
(Israel) and I (God). The Hebrew language easily adapts
itself to this procedure, but no Hebrew writer or speaker
has used it to such advantage as Deutero-Isaia.

> But *you*, Israel, *my* servant,
>   Jacob, *you* whom *I* have chosen,
>   offspring of Abraham *my* friend,
> *You* whom *I* have taken from the ends of the earth,
>   *you* whom *I* have summoned from its far-off places,
> *You* whom *I* have called *my* servant,
>   *I* have chosen *you* and *I* will not cast *you* off.
> Fear not, *I* am with *you*,
>   Be not dismayed; *I* am *your* God.
> *I* will strengthen *you*,
>   indeed, *I* will help *you*.
> Surely, *I* will uphold *you*
>   with *my* right hand of justice (Is 41:8-10).

The I-Thou exchange booms like a heavy drum, sounds deep like the great diapason tones of a pipe organ. The depth of sound comes from the infinite reserve of God's love. Because creation is so intricately linked with the act of God's speaking, Deutero-Isaia can present it as an act of God's knowning and loving.

To this divine word Deutero-Isaia attributes every saving work, even the redemptive role of the Suffering Servant. In many ways, the songs of the Suffering Servant bring the Old Testament doctrine of redemption to its point of fullest development. The doctrine of the expiatory suffering of the innocent is here presented with a clarity as startling as the tone of a tolling bell.

> He was pierced for our offenses,
>   crushed for our sins;
> Upon him was laid the chastisement of our peace,
>   by his stripes we were healed (Is 53:5).

This redemptive word could never have been spoken, had the Suffering Servant not been able to write:

> Morning after morning
>   he opens my ears that I may hear (50:4).

The Servant himself is swept forward into his redemptive
work by listening to the word of God. The Servant further
admits:

> The Lord has given me
> a well-trained tongue,
> That I may know how to speak to the weary
> a word that will rouse them (50:4).

And by uttering God's word the Servant gathers all others
into the redemptive design of God.

This divine purpose, enunciated by the word, is a new
creation. As always, Deutero-Isaia introduces the thread of
a new idea—here, the idea of sorrow and of the songs of
the Suffering Servant—only to enhance the depth of beauty
in the new creation.

> If he gives his life as an offering for sin,
> he shall see his descendants in a long life,
> and the will of God shall be accomplished through him.
> Because of his affliction
> he shall see the light in the fullness of days. . . .
> Therefore I will give him his portion among the great.
> (Is 53:10-12).

The word "creation" is not used, but the thought is present,
a new resurrection from the dead for the sorrowing people
of God.

God's Personal Concern

The prophetic message of the Word vibrated with the
tones of God's personal love. This feature of God's *personal* existence is the final notion in this chapter on the
prophetic mission of the word. It has frequently entered
the discussion, so that we can now be very brief.

By their emphasis upon the word of God, the prophets

kept the religion of Israel from destroying itself. God had revealed Himself to Abraham and Moses, it will be recalled, as a personal God who loved and cared for His people and wanted their loyalty and love in return. The early history of Israel recorded the great promises of God, and religion unfortunately centered more and more on what the people could get out of their worship. The momentum of the people's faith was an eager desire to receive more and more from God—a land, flowing with milk and honey; children, numerous as the stars in the heavens; a royalty, everlasting as God's fidelity; a temple where God answered every prayer. Without full consciousness of what was happening, Israel began to look upon God as wealthy benefactor, an indulgent Father, an extravagant Deity. Though God, He was helplessly bound to His promises; regardless of the people's sins He must be faithful to His word and bless Israel.

The prophets reversed this suicidal tendency in Israel's religion and brought the people back to a *personal* God who is strong in giving love and desirous of receiving the people's love. Listen once again to God's reply through Osee to a presumptuous people:

> It is love that I desire, not sacrifice,
> and knowledge of God rather than sacrifice (Os 6:6).

By His word, God destroyed everything which the people were substituting for Himself: land, city, temple, children, family ties, government, king and priest. The dreadful catastrophe of 587 B.C. could not be avoided once the prophets spoke the devastating word of God. Osee therefore uttered this sentence of doom:

> For this reason I smote them through the prophets,
> I slew them by the words of my mouth (Os 6:5).

This destruction, nonetheless, was meant to save the people. If, as Isaia taught, God smote the Egyptians in order to heal them (Is 19:22), how much more truly would the sorrows of His own people instruct them in the way of salvation? As Jeremia told Israel:

> Your conduct, your misdeeds, have done this to you;
>> how bitter is this disaster of yours (4:18).

The punishment was deserved and was necessary. A personally loving God, however, could react only with poignant sorrow, and plead:

> Return, rebel Israel, . . .
>> I will not remain angry with you;
> For I am merciful, . . .
>> Only know your guilt (Jer 3:12-13).

Israel must recognize what is destroying her happiness in order to find her way back to God. Jeremia's teaching rises in joy and merry-making in chapter thirty-one:

> I will turn their mourning into joy. . . .
> Cease your cries of mourning,
>> wipe the tears from your eyes.
> The sorrow you have shown
>> shall have its reward (Jer 31:13, 16).

Salvation, then, was the exhilarating knowledge of God's love. If God drives the people into exile, it is only that they may be forced to return to Him for help. *To return,* this word is one of *les mots-clés* of all the prophets. We meet it with a great variety of meaning in the Book of Emmanuel, chapters seven to twelve of Isaia. In Is 40:11 the thought of "return" is heard again in the tender strains of a new song. The return is to a personal God who will be satisfied only when His people enjoy in their heart the fullest possible happiness. Jeremia wrote of this religion of the heart:

> This is the covenant which I will make with the house of Israel after those days, says the Lord. I will place my law within them, and write it upon their hearts; I will be their God and they shall be my people (Jer 31:33).

Once this *cor ad cor* religion is established, God can trust His people with His gifts.

The conviction that the Lord loves His people induced the prophets to make high, moral demands. In other words, the prophets did not begin as moral reformers. Their primary intuition of faith glimpsed God's personal love and interest. Such a God could never be satisfied with external behavior; He wanted His people's love in return. Very similar, therefore, to the modern trend in moral theology, the prophetic movement stressed the primacy of charity, a supernatural, even mystical devotedness to God. From charity there was derived the standard for all other virtues.

Nowhere was the moral code so well expressed as in the *prophetic torah* of Michea:

> Will the Lord be pleased with thousands of rams,
>   with myriad streams of oil?
> Shall I give my first-born for my crime,
>   the fruit of my body for the sin of my soul?
> You have been told, O Man, what is good,
>   and what the Lord requires of you;
> Only to do the right and to love goodness,
>   and to walk humbly with your God (Mich 6:8).

If God were just an impersonal power or simply a distant governor, He would certainly be satisfied "with thousands of rams" and "myriad streams of oil." But if God is an interested Person, close to His people in a bond of love, then

He wants nothing less than the personal affection of His children. All the works of the flesh cannot compensate for the refusal of the soul to love. The beginning of such a love-bond between God and His chosen people is a recognition by Israel of how unworthy she is of God's attention. Humility not only attracts God's tender pity, but it also evokes from Israel a gracious gratitude for undeserved love.

Because the prophets grasped so clearly God's supreme personal love for Israel, they understood all other truths in their depths and expanse of meaning.

Jeremia and Ezechiel forbade the people to consider themselves just a mass of humanity, suffering indiscriminately for everybody's sins and finding peace in just anybody's virtue. Ezechiel expressed it this way: "All lives are mine; the life of the father is like the life of the son, both are mine" (Ez 18:4). God loves each one personally, individually. This prophetic doctrine of "personal responsibility" and all of its implications emerged from the prophetic understanding of God's personal love.

Messianism too developed vigorously through faith in God's personal concern for Israel. This growth is significant because the prophets so often saw Israel in a shambles of destruction and apostasy. Threat and doom explode again and again in prophetic preaching as the prophets condemn, argue, plead and finally give up! Isaia began his ministry with this discouraging prediction from God:

> You are to make the heart of this people sluggish,
>   to dull their ears and close their eyes;
> Else their eyes will see, their ears hear
>   their heart understand,
>   and they turn and be healed (Is 6:19).

To Jeremia God entrusted the dismal sentence:

> Behold, I make my words
>   in your mouth, a fire,
> And this people is the wood
>   that it shall devour (Jer 5:14).

Although looking out on such bleak infidelity, the prophets still foresaw a vista of future joy and light. Their staunch faith in God's infinite, personal love could enable them to predict such wonders as:

> ...songs of praise,
> the laughter of happy men (Jer 30:19).
> Fear not, O land!
>   exult and rejoice!
>   for the Lord has done great things!...
> The threshing floor shall be full of grain
>   and the vats shall overflow with wine and oil (Joel 2:21-24).
> There shall be no harm or ruin on all my holy mountain;
>   so the earth shall be filled with the knowledge of the Lord,
>   as water covers the sea (Is 11:9).

This messianic panorama of glory, like rays of sunlight, shines from the heart filled with the knowledge of the Lord, with the *word of God*. Knowledge, deep and personal, yet extending to every inch on the universe, catching up all things into the outstretched arm of God, into the depth of God's infinite life—this saving knowledge came from God in His word, reached other men through the prophets, and thus like rain and snow coming down from heaven achieved the end for which God sent it (cf. Is 55:11).

Conclusion

The word of God, spoken by the prophets, was alive with God's power. It was and remains the presence of God. True to their ancient Near Eastern background, the prophets could not consider the word just a "thought" or "concept" of the intellect. It was a thrust forward of all the powers of the one speaking. If the speaker was God, then it brought man into the dynamic, impelling presence of the Lord.

When God addressed Abraham, Moses, and His chosen people, He often left the most important part of His Message unspoken. Here entered *faith,* a strong, unconditional surrender of one's whole self to God. The word led Abraham forward to "the land which I will show you" (Gen 12:1). Abraham did not know beforehand exactly where the land was, and when he was assured that it was Palestine, he was not certain *when* or *how* it would be acquired.

The land was to be accepted as a gift from a personally loving God. Once the gift became a substitute for God, God summoned the prophets.

These men of God restored the faith of Abraham among the Israelites by calling out: "Hear the word of God." To hear this life-giving word, Israel must not flee into a dream world of unreality, but remain in her sorrowful situation. Only, Israel must humbly acknowledge her guilt and recognize her misery. In tender mercy God will then speak to the heart of His people. The prophets will be His spokesmen, but their word will be God's. The word will be God Himself, present to save and to make happy, creating a new wonder for His people. The greatest joy of this new wonder will be the personal bond of love between God and each of His servants.

> I will espouse you to me forever;
>   I will espouse you in right and in justice,
>   in love and in mercy,
> I will espouse you in fidelity,
>   and you shall know the Lord (Os 2:21-22).

Israel will know God when she receives this word of God in her heart. By their own strong dedication to a personal

God, the prophets prepared for the messianic glory of the word of God, the second Person of the Holy Trinity. This wonder, however, outwitted their most imaginative hopes (cf. Luke 10:23-24). It was the unspoken element in God's word to them as with faith they awaited the new creation which God promised through His prophet Isaia.

PART II

Now will I praise those godly men,
  our ancestors, each in his own time:
Counselors in their wisdom,
  seers of all things in prophecy (Sir 44:1, 3).

CHAPTER 2

AMOS,
DESERT-TRAINED
PROPHET

AMOS, according to modern tastes, was a poor choice for a prophet. A tough herdsman from the desert wilderness of southeastern Palestine, he had the coarse, harsh look of the desert in his leathery brown skin, long shaggy hair, and deepset, piercing eyes. His thoughts, too, were like the desert—dry, rough, and blunt. His voice roared with the terrifying sound of the desert lion.

In speech he was sharp and bitter. He called the aristocratic ladies of Samaria a herd of cattle, large and violent like the cows of the Bashan plateau: "Hear this word, women of the mountain of Samaria, you cows of Bashan" (4:1). He imitated their loud shout to their husbands: "Bring drink for us!" Amos showed them to be simply well-fed beasts who could turn with anger at the least irritation, then lazily roll over to crush their own weak and needy young. Could a man of God talk like this?

The men of Samaria also cringed under the stinging lash of Amos' ridicule. Amos mimicked their boasting when, with mock dignity and orotund voice, he declared: "Have we not, by our own strength, seized for ourselves (the fortress city of) Carnaim?" (6:13). Then with icy irony he caricatured these manly warriors, "stretched comfortably on their couches ... improvising to the music of the harp" (6:4-5). They pretended to be poets, he mocked—like King David, no less—and recited their verses unto boredom. Would a saintly prophet talk with such barbed words and curled lip? Would such words be inspired by God?

These are foolish questions because Amos, the inspired prophet, had no doubt that God spoke through him: "The lion roars: Who will not be afraid? Yahweh-God speaks: Who will not prophesy?" (3:8). Neither has the Church ever doubted that Amos' words belong to the Bible of inspired Scripture.

A very provocative question is why Amos adopted a style of speech so gruff and so sarcastic. How did he get that way? Amos would not have objected to our inquiries about him and his style of speech. He secretly delighted in putting the most embarrassing and exasperating questions to others, for he thus forced his audience to face up to reality. More than thirty times in nine short chapters does he propose nettling questions. His book moves forward on their momentum. To explain Amos' character and style we must seek him where God had found him.

From the Wilderness of Juda

Amos is introduced as "a shepherd from Tekoa" (1:1). The ordinary Hebrew word for "shepherd" is not used, for Amos belonged to a still lower class. He was one of the *noqedim,* poor herdsmen of a breed of desert sheep usually thin and undernourished, resembling the dry grass they lived on.

Amos pastured his sheep in the wilderness of Judah, that famished uninhabitable stretch of sand, rock and small patches of grass sloping some four thousand feet from the central mountain ridge of Palestine down to the deep gorge of the Dead Sea rift. In some spots the hills rise and fall with slow, undulating ease; at others they pull high and steep into the sky. Deep gullies cut through the hills to carry off the teeming rains from December to February. True, the rainy season covers the area with a maze of fresh green grass, but very soon the blistering summer sun burns the grass yellow and reduces the scrub bushes to stiff brown stalks. The river-beds run dry and become deep, merciless slashes hacking up the terrain.

In early morning Amos could stand and watch with wonder the sun suddenly rising over the purple plateau of Moab across the Dead Sea. At once it cast a panoply of color across the sands of Judah. Amos welcomed God's creature the sun, for it sent the prowling animals of the night back to the jungle of the Jordan. The night, with chilly driving winds, terrifying roar of lions and shriek of dying animals, was gone. All desert nights were nights of broken sleep because the shepherd had to make the rounds of his flock and keep the wood-fire burning brightly.

The heat of daylight turned the area into an oven. Amos the shepherd wore several layers of cotton cloth to insulate himself from the 110-120 degree temperature of the desert. He quenched his thirst sparingly because his goatskin water-pouch must last him a long time. Around noon he chewed on cucumber, melon, or herb, and toward evening he cooked some rice and vegetable.

Day, however, according to an exquisite song in the book

of Amos, "darkened into night" (5:8) and God once more "created the winds" to sweep across the moorland to "declare to man his thoughts" (4:13). A lonely life it was, so that Amos could ask: "Do two walk together unless they have agreed?" (3:3). Never in a desert! And a life of fear it was, for, "Does a lion roar in the forest when it has no prey?" (3:4). When the shepherd appeared to drive off the beast, he " ... snatches from the mouth of the lion a pair of legs or the tip of an ear of his sheep" (3:12). It was a hard life, lacking even necessities. A hardy shepherd despised those city-dwellers "lying upon beds of ivory, stretched comfortably on their couches. They eat lambs taken from the flock and calves from the stall" (6:4). Woe to such as these! "The Lord God has sworn: 'I abhor the pride of Jacob'" (6:1, 8).

Amos had only one necessity—God, and as the evening wind passed, it roared: "Yahweh, the God of hosts! He who made the Pleiades and Orion, who turns darkness into dawn, and darkens day into night; who summons the waters of the sea and pours them out upon the surface of the earth; who flashes destruction upon the strong, and brings ruin upon the fortress—his name is Yahweh" (5:8-9).

Amos made very few friends and saw these only on rare occasions. His occupation forced him to live alone with God. Alone, he knew none of the give-and-take of humans dwelling together. When he later spoke the word of God, he cared not a whit for other peoples' feelings. The desert had trained Amos to be as true and genuine as the naked realities of life, as hard as the rocks, as demanding as the weather, as tough as his leathery skin, as biting as wind-blown sand cutting down pompous pride. To keep alive in the desert was a mortal struggle, but Amos delighted in the fight, God was his reward.

The desert never tolerates "if's" and "maybe's." Its hard code of existence leaves no room for in-between, half-hearted, indecisive action. A man must choose life or death, to be for God or to be against Him, to give whole-souled dedication or to suffer total destruction. Amos knew no such word as compromise. He shouted that God would obliterate sinful mediocrity and religious forgery.

Amos saw that only a few, the "remnant," would be saved, and these he compared to a "pair of legs or the tip of an ear of a sheep" snatched from the mouth of a lion. Even here in a scene of sorrowful redemption he cast his prophecy in sarcasm, adding with disdain that the Israelites *may* also recover "the corner of a couch or a piece of a cot!" (3:12).

As "silence" is intoned over the haunted land of death, God gives the command "to shatter the great house to bits, and reduce the small house to rubble . . . Woe to those who yearn for the day of the Lord! What will this day of the Lord mean for you? Darkness and not light!" (6:11; 5:18).

Education

From the desert Amos learned the great truths that he handed down to the prophets of the Old and New Testaments: day of the Lord; remnant; darkness, not light, goodness, not might. Surrender all to God, he shouted, or all shall be destroyed. "Hate evil and love good, and let justice prevail at the gate. Then perhaps will Yahweh, the God of hosts, have pity on the remnant of Joseph" (5:15). This message will be echoed by another desert prophet, John the Baptist, and sealed by the Savior Himself, who prepared for His own ministry by forty days in the desert.

The book of Amos ranks with the golden literature of Isaia. The question naturally arises whether the prophet, like

Isaia, acquired his superb Hebrew style of preaching formally at the schools or inherently from the desert. Certainly Amos possessed extraordinary natural talent. Can we doubt that the harsh, lonely wilderness of Judah had not only trained him to think vigorously but also to speak powerfully? Certainly it made him keen to sense the silent slithering of a lizard across the sand or the dark hiding of a snake in the crack of a wall (5:19).

From the desert Amos gathered the images of lions, bears and snakes (3:4, 8, 12; 5:19), of snares for birds (3:5), of wagons loaded with sheaves (2:13), of locusts eating new grass (7:1-2), of fruit rotting in a basket (8:1-2). When he spoke of obese women, he used the cowherd's uncouth expression, "fat cows." Uncouth, yes; but somehow or other, of memorable literary value.

Shepherd life enabled Amos to speak with the melodious rhythm of the desert hills, the roaring blasts of evening winds, the cutting gashes of dry river-beds. His images burst with power, but the haunting sound of his words adds still greater power to those images.

We lose much of this thrust in the English translation. For instance: "And the most stouthearted of warriors shall flee naked on that day, says the Lord" (2:16). In the Hebrew original the verse moans with the ache and the shame of soldiers publicly stripped to the skin to be mocked and made sport of in their helplessness by gloating conquerors: *'arōm yanūs bayyōm-hahū ne'ūm-Yahwēh.* In other lines he will sustain the sound of i (pronounced ee), which in Hebrew often denotes the first person, "I." The opening word in 2:9, "It was I" (*we'anoki*), continues the sound and idea of "I, your God" in constant recurrence.

On another occasion he compares the tramp of exiles to the low groan of the creeking wheels of a heavily loaded wagon (2:13). These marching exiles were too sad and too weak even to cry; they can only moan and sigh. Amos uses the Hebrew sounds *me' ig . . . ta' iq* (pronounced *may-éek . . . tah-éek*). Again, when he states that "Gilgal shall be led into captivity," the Hebrew original reads: *hag-gilgál galóh yigléh* (5:5).

These are not isolated examples; all nine chapters are rich with such literary finesse. Did Amos absorb this power at the same time as the desert was also disciplining his character and sharpening his eyes? We think so.

Away from the Desert

Amos grew to love the desert. He was fascinated by its eternal expanse of sand and its infinite depth of sky, its monotonous sameness and yet its moving kaleidoscope of color, its manly challenge and its encircling warmth. It made of the prophet a man who despised the artificial and sought one necessity—God.

To earn food and clothing, however, the shepherd was forced at times to entrust his dwarf sheep to a friend, to leave the impoverished desert and to hire out as a "dresser of sycamore trees." These high, thickly-leafed trees—different from Western sycamores—never grew in the Judean wilderness but were found at the lower altitudes. Away from his desert home, Amos accepted a poor man's second job just to keep alive. He was not ashamed of this work; he openly admitted his profession, proud to be a common man (7:14). Amos spent hours silently pinching the sycamore fruit (something like a small fig) in order to hasten its maturity.

Amos also traveled to the markets of the large cities to barter his wool and cheese. One hour from Tekoa was the main road running north and south between Hebron, Bethlehem, Jerusalem, Bethel, Shechem and Samaria. The last city was almost fifty miles north, a two days' journey. Amos may have even offered his goods in the noisy bazaar of Damascus. On the road and in the crowed city-markets the thin, tanned shepherd of Judea mingled with foreigners: with Phoenicians, who often acted as middlemen for Egyptian wares; with Edomites and Moabites, who competed with their own wool and cheese but also offered Arabian spices and African delicacies such as peacocks and pet monkeys.

Amos saw the Arameans, whose bloody invasions once "threshed Gilead with sledges of iron" (1:3), so that an earlier prophet, Eliseus, wept at the mere thought of them (4 Kings 8:12). As Amos sat next to the Philistines he overheard their plans for slave-traffic. These men would haunt the battlefields to buy captive soldiers at the cheap price of a skin of wine. They would kidnap and whisk away poor helpless children. Each human experience was preparing Amos for his prophetic ministry.

Hear the Word of God

Later, when Amos began to utter his message at the Israelite sanctuary of Bethel, he shouted God's anger upon these crimes against humanity. Using a customary formula of the time, he roared the judgment of destruction upon Damascus, Philistia, Tyre, Edom, Ammon: "For three crimes . . . and for four, I will not revoke my word" (1:3, 6, 9. etc.). Three plus four is seven; the sacred number is complete. The time of patient endurance is at an end: "I will break the bar . . . I will turn my hand against . . . I will send fire . . . I will root out . . . (1:5-2:3).

This condemnation of Israel's enemies sent a thrill of fierce pleasure through the worshippers at Bethel. They were too dull, however, to realize that Amos was enunciating the universalism of God's love, of His interest and concern for *all* men. God wanted even these foreigners to be converted in order that they might be happy and at peace with Him. God would stop at nothing to save them.

Suddenly, while the Israelites were still applauding this "man of God," the prophet turned upon them and cried out: "For three crimes of *Israel*, and for four, I will not revoke my word" (2:6). They must cease their applause at their enemies' discomfort to listen as he excoriated their orgies of immorality under the pretense of sacrificial banquets, their demands that poor people pay the fines of justice so that the judge might afford to get drunk in the house of their gods, their "faith" in the blessing of a large family, exercised by a father's taking his son to the same prostitute who had served him. By this ostentatious but sensual worship "they trample the heads of the weak into the dust of the earth" (2:6-8).

No wonder Amos called these women devotees "cows of Bashan" and pictured the men driven away naked by foreign soldiers! Tough language! But God needed and therefore trained a desert herdsman to roar, to tear and to destory like a lion. If God *is* God, true and just, holy and compassionate, then He cannot tolerate forever the trampling of the poor and the persecuting of the innocent. He must exclaim: "I hate, I spurn your feasts" (5:21). God therefore answers: "Beware, I will crush you into the ground (*me'iq*) as a wagon crushes when laden with sheaves (*ta'iq*)" (2:13). "Punishment will never happen by chance! Is a bird brought to earth by a snare when there is no lure for it? . . . If evil befalls a city, has not Yahweh caused it? Indeed, Yahweh-God does nothing without revealing his plan" (3:5-7). After another series of divine, purposeful judgments, Amos bellowed the climactic line: "Prepare to meet your God, O Israel!" (4:12).

Go, Prophesy!

The prophecy of Amos concludes with a burst of glory as bright and colorful as the desert morning sun: "When the plowman shall overtake the reaper, and the vintager him who sows the seed, the juice of grapes shall drip down the mountain and all the hills shall run with it. I will bring about the restoration of my people Israel; they shall rebuild and inhabit their ruined cities" (9:13-13). These closing lines are probably a later inspired addition to the prophecy of Amos. They could have been written only because "the shepherd of Tekoa," like the desert-trained John the Baptist, had performed his job well and prepared the way for salvation.

Why did Amos speak so gruffly and so bitingly? He was a product of the desert. He was trained by the desert. Are his words inspired? Yes, because the need was for a prophet whose hard, biting words could incise and cut away the cancerous softness of a degenerate people. When suavity and literary phrasing were the best instruments, God opened the mouth of a Solomon. When hard blows and a blunt instrument were required, God raised up an Amos.

Amos' mission did not end with his life. Today we need to be shaken up by this plainspoken man of God, this Amos, the best choice possible for a prophet. God is still saying to him: "Go, prophesy to my people" (7:16).

CHAPTER 3 # OSEE AND THE MYSTERY OF LOVE

OSEE belongs to the early years of Israel's prophetic movement, but his ideas and, most of all, his spiritual attitudes
possess a maturity which we ordinarily associate with the
end of a long development. As we read his prophecy, we
sometimes wonder whether we have perhaps slipped ahead
into New Testament pages. Osee's heart seems to beat
sympathetically with the heart of Jesus and to suffuse His
warmth. We would never fully accept Osee's daring words
on the love of God if Jesus had not been even more daring
in transferring those words into action. Osee's message, like
Jesus' death, leaves no doubt that the most baffling mystery
about God is His love. That which brings God or any one
else personally close to us should be the easiest feature for
us to understand; yet it always remains wrapped in the greatest mystery. Friends, and especially lovers, can never ade-

quately explain how they feel towards one another, nor *why* they feel that way.

OSEE, HIS NAME AND MESSAGE

Could Beeri and his wife have suspected the future role of their infant son, when they gave him his name eight days after birth? It does not seem that they were more ambitious than any other new parents; Osee (or Hosea, in its Hebrew spelling still found in Jewish and Protestant editions of the Bible) was a common enough name in Israelite families. The last king of the northern country of Israel was called Osee. The parents of this child, however, truly deserved the honor of giving their son that name which would become the most sacred in the world. They called their child by a name almost the same as that which Mary and Joseph would use in addressing their son.

Name, Shared with Jesus

We like to think that God thus rewarded Beeri and his wife for the extraordinary love and exquisite kindness with which they reared their child. Osee owed it to his father and mother that he would one day be hailed "prophet of divine love." What they initially imparted, Osee transformed into an integral part of his character; and when later as a prophet he announced the gentle yet courageous and even agonizing nuances of divine love, he was but echoing the tones heard long ago in his parents' home. Osee's words were to be caught up and repeated by Someone whom Osee even now can look upon as his spiritual son and heir. Both were to carry the same name.

The name Osee, or Hosea, means "one who saves." It will be recalled that the famous warrior-conqueror, hand-picked by Moses to be his successor, and chosen by God to lead the

Israelites across the Jordan river and to wrestle the land of Palestine out of Canaanite control, was first called Hosea. In Num 27:16-17 we learn that Moses changed it to Yehosua ("Yahweh saves"—Josue in our Bibles). During the last several centuries before the birth of Jesus Christ, Yehosua became a very common name for Jewish boys. Spoken again and again in all kinds of situations, Yehosua was gradually clipped to a shorter form, Yesua. In the Hebrew language, the accent rested on the second-last syllable, the ū sound, and there it has remained as the name passed into Greek and many other European languages. In Greek it was spelled Jesōus or Jesus.

A Theme, Shared with Jesus

The similarity of Osee's name to Jesus' may have been a reward from God for his parents' and his own heroic love. Who can ever guess the secrets of divine Providence! There can be no doubt, however, of the intimate fellowship of thought between Osee and Jesus. Osee introduced a theme into biblical literature which Jesus will apply to Himself and transform into sublime fulfillment. Osee dared to call God the spouse of Israel, and Jesus braved ridicule in referring to Himself as the Bridegroom of His people.

A delegation once came to Jesus. These men, so proud of their piety towards God that they lacked the self-forgetfulness of genuine love, voiced a complaint. "The disciples of John [the Baptist] fast often," they said to Jesus, "and make supplications, and likewise those of the Pharisees, whereas your disciples eat and drink." In His reply, Jesus could have ripped away their pompous, pious attire with sharp satire. Instead, He spoke under the influence of the prophet Osee. With the poignant melancholy of a love ever kind but already rejected, He asked, "Can you make the wedding guests fast as long as the bridegroom is with them? But the days will come when the bridegroom will be taken away from them. Then they will fast" (Luke 5:33-35).

During the centuries separating Osee and Jesus, other prophets like Jeremia, Ezechiel and Deutero-Isaia further clarified this approach towards God; another biblical book, the *Canticle of Canticles* (also called, the *Song of Songs*), dramatized the love of God with a series of nuptial songs. The Christian liturgy quickly adopted this attitude of approaching God as Spouse of His people. Nowhere does the love bond between God and the Church reach a fuller expression then in prayer and especially in that supreme moment of prayer, the liturgy. The greatest act of the liturgy, the Eucharist, was re-enacted in a ceremony called *agape*, a Greek word meaning *love*. The image of God as Bridegroom constantly appears in the writings of the early Fathers and in the works of the later spiritual masters. Not only saints of southern lands like St. John of the Cross and St. Teresa of Jesus, but mystics of the Rhineland like Tauler and Ruysbroeck, structure their spiritual theology around the motif that God is spouse of the soul. To understand and appreciate this long tradition, repeatedly sanctioned by God over a three-thousand-year period, we must return to its source. There we will discover a vigorous expression and a personal intuition, fresh and appealing like new life, mysterious and attractive like pioneer adventure, tested and mature like battle scars. The Book of Osee, like the gospels and the crucifix, bears the marks of such a love and possesses the power to infuse a similar love in strong souls.

Osee's message, like genuine love, is very demanding, but it is also very encouraging. Presenting his ideas within the context of marriage, Osee plainly tells each reader that no desire, noble and true, is ever snuffed out unfulfilled. Mar-

riage being what it is, it not only satisfies man's deepest desires, but it also enables him to beget new life and more
love. By the very fact that God calls Himself the Bridegroom of each of His fellowers, He cannot destroy what is
consecrated to Him. He obliges Himself to fulfill and make
fruitful the love which He receives. We must return to this
point later, because it involves us in a mystery very apparent
in Christianity. Many Christians renounce the right to marry
by a vow of celibacy or virginity. There are others whose
initial joy in marriage is overwhelmed by a prolonged
separation. Death, (or what can even be worse, divorce)
has cut the bond. Still others proudly bear children, only
to lose them through the call of war or the forced migration of people or the stroke of mortal illness. Every
neighborhood holds lonely couples, aching for children yet
somehow unable to beget them. All of these cases exist in
Christian life, and each pounds out the hard sound of sacrifice. Even those who have freely given up their privilege
to marry, can never adequately perform their apostolic ministry, unless they be completely normal human beings, with
a genuine attraction towards marriage and parenthood.
What all of these have given to God must be given repeatedly, for the hardships and even the temptations of their
life are met over and over.

To each and all of these persons Osee declares: no desire,
true and good, will remain sterile and unfulfilled. To deny
this fulfillment is to substitute some lesser deity for the God
whom Christians worship. This God had pledged:

> I will espouse you to me forever: ...
> I will espouse you in fidelity,
>   and you shall know the Lord (Os 2:21-22)

God will be faithful to every promise, especially to those

which He placed deep within the nature of every human being. In the day of fulfillment, we shall truly *know* who is *the Lord*. To claim that God will leave good desires empty or only half fulfilled, reduces His love to something less abundant than what He expects of our generosity. Were it true, we would not be "like God" but more than God, and Eve should never have been punished for pretending that she could act the part of God better than He. God's measure of giving must exceed ours, which Jesus wants to be a "good measure, pressed down, shaken together, running over" (Luke 6:38).

A Mystery to be Experienced

This whole mystery of love can never be explained but only experienced. Osee's explanation does not remove the mystery; but to the person who has been open and generous with God and has willingly accepted the full demands of divine love, Osee speaks a message which spreads peace and understanding upon the soul. The prophecy of Osee records what has happened to a man intensely alive in God; such secrets will be shared only to the extent that the recipient, like Osee, lives in God. The law of communication always presumes this community bond, this sympathetic sharing, this experiential grasp of what the other is saying.

To transfer for a moment from the problem of Osee to a major problem of the modern world, can it not be said that excessive individualism is responsible for the poor communication between racial and national, religious and social groups, even between blood members of the same family? All this failure exists amidst unbelievable advances in the mechanical means of communication. When men are afraid to love and are hesitant about the outcome of love, they throw up defensive barriers to separate themselves from others. Someone like Pope John, on the contrary, who lacked most of the accepted means of communication, communicated most effectively. His rotund build and uneven gait, his wire spectacles and thumping feet, hardly won respect from a sophisticated world; his ignorance of modern languages and dependence on interpreters considerably slowed down the transmission of his thought to others. Yet, he was understood and appreciated by men everywhere because he communicated in charity, an instinct deeper than style and protocol, a rallying point where all men meet one another.

Osee also spoke in the media of charity, and though he dealt with mystery, the charitable man today nods in agreement and somehow understands. The charity, enabling one to appreciate Osee's words, impels one to know more and more about the prophet himself, about his early home life and education, his talents and ideals, his conflicts and problems, his whole environment and personality. Because these factors are deeply rooted in every human being, they strengthen the bonds of communication; they bring all men together in that one body and one soul which all possess as members of one human race, created by one God to His image and likeness.

We must be careful, however, not to overstress this 'oneness' of all human beings. Even if there is a basic unity, great differences also appear. Osee will undoubtedly appeal to all readers, but to some more than to others. If we make all men the same, we will confuse our knowledge of Osee and remove an important factor in communication, the different qualities by which men complement one another. Charity does not develop from a dull sameness but from a mutual respect.

INTRODUCING THE PROPHET OSEE

Each prophet, in fact, made his own unique contribution, and by separating them, one from the other, we not only better understand each one but we also appreciate all the varied ingredients, flowing together in different degrees, to form each human being. Each of us has a little of everyone, but each one is also a unique blend never again repeated by the Maker.

The Reverse of Amos

One way, therefore, of introducing Osee is to say that he is the exact reverse of the prophet Amos. Amos, we know, grew to manhood as a shepherd. As he led his flock across wide, sandy stretches for patches of tough grass or for wells of sulphurous-tasting water, Amos became as thin, wiry and tough as his desert breed of sheep. Like desert nomads of any age, Amos was fiercely independent. Accustomed to solitary life and seldom if ever craving for human friendship, yet intensely loyal to the friends of his choice, Amos bluntly spoke his mind and cared little how other people reacted. Never could his audience forget one occasion at the sanctuary of Bethel. The stylish women of Samaria had assembled very properly for worship, only to hear the uncouth Amos call them to their faces: "You herd of cows!" (Am 4:1). Amos was voicing the pent-up anger of countless poor whose families were crushed by all manner of social injustices, in order that their overlords might pamper these luxurious cows with soft delicacies. Amos also lashed at the men, those stalwart warriors who stretch out comfortably on ivory-embellished couches and sing their own poetry as though they were David! Here too is the voice of Everyman shouting down the sham and laying naked the shame which confuses sentimentality for culture and animal lust for human love. This voice, however, was not the voice of Osee but of Amos who asked no quarter and gave none.

Still other differences separated Amos and Osee. Amos was a southerner from the kingdom of Juda, whom God summoned to preach to the northerners of the kingdom of Israel. In this feature, too, Amos fulfilled a need felt by all men, the need for an outsider, cold and impartial, to clear away vague excuses and to hand down a clear judgment. Amos, though probably a young man, spoke like a gruff, elderly person whom the entire neighborhood respects but only the children love. The world always stands in need of honest, plain-spoken people like Amos. Such people attract only the innocent, but they still manage to salvage a great deal of goodness in others. The world, for the most part, consists of men and women who are no longer innocent; and even though they have regained their goodness, they cannot endure for long the cauterizing agony inflicted by an Amos. Truth, ironically expressed, sours the stomach of most people. They must also hear the sympathetic voice of an Osee and realize that here is a prophet agonizing with them.

Osee, we must admit, possessed all the ingredients which form an Amos; he was capable of anger, bitterness, and even satire, but in Osee the genes of character combined very differently. In Osee we detect not only the perceptiveness of Amos but also a strong admixture of sensitivity and warmth. Osee was endowed with a tenderness which thrived on love, with a glowing hope which had to be encouraged, with a simplicity which could be easily spurned and hurt, with an optimism which searched out the least speck of goodness in others. Osee was the kind of person which all of us, even an Amos, would like to be, for he activated our delicate and finest human qualities. All of us possess his traits of character, few of us, however, in exactly the same mixture, and even fewer still with the same courageous simplicity. No gift is more demanding of its owner than the grace to think kindly and to love tenderly. We can usually forecast the outcome of hate; seldom do we know exactly where love is tending.

Fully Human and Sensitive

Osee paid the heavy cost of such a sensitized personality. He was quite emotional, high strung, immediately reacting to what people felt and said about him. Loving greatly, he reacted at once to the least manifestation of friendliness or hostility. He was swayed quickly from one extreme to another. He was not the victim of irrational impulses, nor was he a pampered child who never grew up. He was an adult who *keenly* appreciated *all* the human involvements of life situations. In chapter two, for instance, he is the husband betrayed by an adulterous wife. He shouts angrily to the children:

> Protest against your mother, protest!
>   [Show her] that she is not my wife,
>   and that I am not her husband.
> Let her remove. . .
>   her adultery from between her breasts,
> Or I will strip her naked,
>   leaving her as on the day of her birth.

If he did not love so dearly, he never would have felt the agony so intensely. Here is a voice, shouting protest against life's vilest betrayal. True love, like a healthy body, battles fiercely against corrupting disease.

Gomer, the wife to whom he has entrusted the personal treasures of great love, was overheard to say:

> I will go after my lovers,
>> who give me my bread and my water,
>> my wool and my flax, my oil and my drink.

Sorrow floods upon Osee like a massive wave of ponderous water.

>> . . .she had not known
>> that it was I who gave her
>> the grain, the wine and the oil.

Gomer, evidently entertains her paramours with gifts which Osee had generously lavished upon her. Anger stirs, and quickly Osee's dejection explodes in outrage:

> I will take back my grain. . .
> I will snatch away my wool. . .
>> with which she covers her nakedness.
> So now I will lay bare her nakedness.
>> before the eyes of her lovers.

Osee, however, loves too dearly. Even if he flares up in rage at the betrayal of his affection, yet in the next instant he is again hopeful and forgiving. What other men would call groveling abjectness, in Osee's case is heroic confidence. We hear him say:

> Therefore, I will hedge in her way with thorns
>> and erect a wall against her,
>> so that she cannot find her paths.
> If she runs after her lovers,
>> she will not overtake them;
>> if she looks for them she shall not find them.
> Then she shall say,
>> "I will go back to my first husband,
>> for it was better with me then than now."
> So I will allure her;
>> I will lead her into the desert
>> and speak to her heart.

Such, then, is the character of Osee, swaying from one extreme to the other. Such quick transitions are not confined to any single chapter but are duplicated throughout all fourteen chapters. When, however, the love is most tenderly expressed, as in chapter eleven, the reversals are presented most dramatically. Speaking of God's love for Israel, Osee rises in idyllic hope—God is a father, fondling His child as He carries it in His arms—but these same hopes crash in anger—the sword shall begin with the cities of this child and cut a bloody swath even to desert solitudes. A gush of tears, it seems, almost overwhelms God, and He cries in agony:

> How can I give you up, O Ephraim,
> or deliver you up, O Israel?

Finally, a triumphant line rings out. For when human beings would stoutly declare: "So much, no more! I shall forgive no longer!" God's love sweeps forward from the sublimest of mysteries: "I am God and not man."

Osee, indeed, baffles us in his quick changes of mood, in his rapid swing from tender love to violent hate, from listless depression to aggressive anger, from a final verdict of punishment to the hope of a new beginning. There is no easy answer for the way Osee plummets to a deep area of the human heart, only to soar out of it and fall again into another. As a saint, he would have stepped beyond the scope of human psychology and would have been ranging through some of the incomprehensible sweeps of divine love. That fact of Osee's mysticism must always be kept in mind in any evaluation of his character and preaching.

Though at a loss for detailed reasons, we can vaguely make out some kind of consistency in Osee. He is always strong in his love. Osee faces all persons in such a way that they know beyond a doubt how greatly he loves them. Osee in some instinctive way is challenging them to love him in return or to hate him. Love always reveals the full virtuosity of another person's character. He can only eagerly accept or else stubbornly refuse.

Weakness, His Victory

Unless God had aided him, Osee could never have maintained his heroic, forgiving love over a long stretch of years. Though spirited by a divine power, however, Osee himself was not divine; and as a human being, he had his faults and failures. He groaned under the damaging effects of both original sin and his own personal sins. He had to battle upward against a load of evil tendencies: he was never able to direct activities from the serene heights of undisturbed holiness. Without reversing our judgment on the prophet's true greatness, we can still admit the presence of emotional problems, flowing particularly from his excessive sensitivity. Osee's occasional lack of balance, his frail emotionalism, his distorted tenderness—all these deviations show up in moments of stress; the prophet is reacting with strong love, and the victory of righteousness is won only after prolonged struggle. We on our part, therefore, receive no *carte blanche* from the Book of Osee to act like a prima donna, pouting over the least offense, exacting the most rigid protocol, always suspicious of a breach in etiquette. On the same score, Amos in no way justifies us in coldly spurning people or indiscriminately lashing them with a sharp tongue.

In every case, God made use of human beings with the widest variety of character. As each struggled against his own weakness and against the hostility of his environment, each received the help of God's spirit. Because of God's presence, each prophet manifested an extraordinary endurance, and lifted himself as well as his fellows to a super-human level of existence.

In these Old Testament examples, the divine was spiriting the earthly to enter combat with human weakness and thereby raise the human to a divine existence. All these cases prefigure the New Testament doctrine of redemption—resurrection. Osee, for example, exerts a divine power as he enlists in God's work all the talents and faculties under his command; but each of them must be mastered and controlled, for they are continually moving away. If he had been fortunate enough to live in New Testament times, he would have expressed the mystery of his life with these words of St. Paul: "that I may know him, [Jesus Christ, our Savior,] and the power of his resurrection and fellowship of his sufferings; become like him in death, in the hope that somehow I may attain to the resurrection from the dead" (Phil. 3:10-11). Yet with St. Paul he would also frankly remind us: "I do not accomplish the good which I wish to do but the evil which I do not wish, that I perform. . . . I see another law in my members, warring against the law of my mind" (Rom 7:20, 23).

A Disorderly Book

Still another weakness appears in the prophecy of Osee— the disorderly condition of the book. The lines follow no discernible pattern. Whoever was responsible for editing the book, Osee or a disciple, seems to have quickly dispatched the work by heaping everything together. We can spot only two breaks or divisions in all fourteen chapters. The Yahweh-Spouse theme is confined to the first three chapters; 14:2-9 marks the messianic conclusion. In between lies everything else! As though to warn the reader that this book is not to be read quickly or easily, a later editor added a final word, advising prayer and faith:

> Let him who is wise understand these things;
> let him who is prudent know them.
> Straight are the paths of the Lord,
> in them the just walk,
> but sinners stumble in them (14:10).

What other kind of book, though, could come from the highly sensitive character of Osee? A man whose ideas swing from one end of the horizon to the other should not be expected to think along straight lines nor follow a strictly logical sequence. All biblical writers, in fact, prefer a circuitous approach; they attack the issue first in one way, then in another. They are free of our more philosophical, more theoretical way of argument, but by that very fact they stayed closer to reality and remained more conscious of human complexities. No prophet allowed such uninhibited flow of thought as Osee; his words, like himself, rush from one emotion to another.

Osee can place some of the blame for the disorderly condition of his book with the chaotic state of his country's politics. We learn from the superscription over his book that he began to prophesy "in the days of Jeroboam . . . king of Israel" (1:1). During the long reign of this king (783-743 B.C.), the standard of living for the well-to-do rose to a peak of ivory luxury. Israel's boundaries spread out to embrace an area almost as extensive as David's domain. The social condition, however, was at the point of explosion.

Tirzah, one of the principal cities, was sharply divided between the very poor and the very rich. On one side of a thoroughfare, according to recent excavations, lay extensive holdings and palatial residences; just across the street were very small homes heaped one upon another. Osee called this condition "a hearth cake unturned" (7:8). This image comes from the Palestinians' practice of baking thin, round patties of unleavened bread on open stones which had been heated by the sun. When the bread is left unturned, raw dough appears on one side; the other side turns black and throws off smoke like charcoal. Israel was such a country of sharp differences. A few grew too rich and the rest stayed too poor. Homes and furniture were either decorated with inlaid ivory, or else were put together from unfinished wood. Religious ceremonies were elaborate and costly; the poor were forced to stay away. Politics degenerated into quick, selfish decisions, first in one direction, then a fast reversal in another. It was a nation overfed or undernourished; ornate or destitute; reeking with sacrificial smoke or coldly disdainful of religion's solemn mockery—"a hearth cake unturned."

Dark clouds were massing, a hurricane was being born. After Jeroboam II died, Assyria again asserted her rights of overlord; this demand for tribute and hostages bled the country of wealth and strength. The army revolted time and again, sweeping to power first an aggressive anti-Assyrian group, then a pacifist pro-Assyrian party. The poor joined each revolt, for they had nothing to lose. The wealthy proceeded to kill off their rivals, especially the remnants of the former royal family. In 732 B.C. the Assyrian army invaded the country. After allowing the soldiers to satisfy their lust for loot and pleasure, the Assyrian monarch sent the inhabitants of the northern section into exile. At times like these, the Assyrians were accustomed to march men and women naked! Between 724 and 721 B.C. Assyria suppressed another revolt, and this time she made sure that it would be the last. Nothing was left standing; the people, almost to the last man, were deported. Osee lived through these years of excessive luxury, senseless revolt, and final ruin—a hearth cake never turned. Always a man of exceptional sensitivity, Osee could not help but speak in a way reflecting the disorder and panic of his age.

This disordered state of Osee's prophecy provides a clue to modern art and music, literature and philosophy; these, in turn, enable us to understand Osee a little better. Contemporary culture is often an explosion of line and sound, hideous at times in its realistic portrayal of sex and hate, depressive in its use of heavy black lines. What might be unintelligible to an observer makes a great deal of sense against the background of two world wars, the forced migration and even the massacre of entire nations, the use of police dogs against racial minorities, the threat of nuclear holocaust, the disintegration of trust among nations, the massacre of a world leader. The most violent hate, however, usually produces the reaction of the greatest love; society raises up to cure itself. This fact shows that God is still present within His world. Osee proclaims that divine indwelling.

YAHWEH—SPOUSE OF ISRAEL
UNDERSTOOD THROUGH OSEE'S MARRIAGE

In the three opening chapters of his prophecy, Osee develops his extraordinary and unique theme of Yahweh-Spouse. To appreciate that exceptional intuition of God, we must observe the slow, agonizing process by which it emerged in the consciousness of the prophet. We are transported back to **Osee the** young man, loved by his friends for being idealistic, affectionate, enthusiastic, generous. Such a person, they knew, promised to be a kind, loving husband who would delight in his children and make his family his kingdom. Everyone remarked how fortunate would be the wife of his choice. Osee asked a girl named Gomer to share his life and thus to fulfill its hopes. He, in turn, promised to love her dearly. Osee

treasured this promise as his grandest opportunity. Although
we do not know how wealthy he may have been, there is no
indication of poverty. His was the joy of bringing many gifts
home to his wife.

Osee noticed that Gomer began acting in a strange way.
He could not believe what was happening; for the first time
in his life he felt suspicious of another. Was Gomer betraying his love? Once it became certain, the woman made no
attempt to conceal her adultery. She deserted Osee. As the
outraged husband looked back on the day of his marriage, he
felt that God had then ordered him: "Go, take a harlot wife
and harlot's children" (1:2).

Somehow or other, Osee recognized a demand to take the
woman back. He was convinced that this too came from God.

> Again the Lord said to me:
> Give your love to a woman,
>   beloved of a paramour, an adulteress (3:1).

"Again!" What agony is spelled out in that word! The other
men in town may once have pitied Osee at his broken marriage; but when he claimed his wife from the arms of a
paramour, and was willing to seek her out not once but again
and again, they scoffed: "That fool!" and added their own
expletives.

At other times Gomer came back of her own accord. She
no longer had any support from Osee who had stopped his
gifts. With nothing to flatter her paramours, she lost their
interest. They never cared for her anyway, but only their
own gain. Gomer, like any woman, could not compete in
the gamble of sexual promiscuity. Her lovers could go elsewhere and always find other women, younger and more
attractive, but where could she go? Her happiness, like every
woman's, depended upon marital fidelity. Fortunately for

Gomer, Osee was not only staunchly loyal to his marriage vows but also humbly forgiving towards his wife. She knew her man, so she reflected:

> I will go back to my first husband,
>   for it was better for me then than now (2:9).

When the second child was born, Osee named the daughter *Lo-ruhama,* which means "Without mercy" or "Without tenderness." How he would have loved to gather the child into his arms and press this part of his own flesh against himself. But did the child really belong to him? He could not be sure. When a son was born, he openly declared his name to be *Lo-ammi,* which means "Not my people." In chapter eleven Osee pictures God as a father, holding a child in His arms and drawing the little one "with bands of love." Yet the child was continually wandering off as if someone else were the father. This scene could easily have emerged from the tortured moments in Osee's own life.

Osee writhed in agony, victimized not only by a woman's infidelity but also by his own sensitive nature. During this dark night he was able to look far deeper into the heavens than had ever been possible during the distracting glare of the daylight. Loneliness turned his prayer into the challenge of another Job; Osee flung his plea against the boundaries of the divine. In the words of Job:

> I cry to you, but you do not answer me;
>   you stand off and look at me,
> Then you turn upon me without mercy
>   and with your strong hand you buffet me. . . .
> Of all my steps I should give him an account;
>   like a prince I should present myself before him.
> This is my final plea; let the Almighty answer me!
>   (Job 30:20-21, 37).

Does God give Osee the passion to love that He might torture it with another's crude unworthiness? Does God impart high ideals for the sole reason that He enjoys their violent disintegration? Is this Providence, only to make sure that men suffer from the excess of their goodness? Osee, seemingly deserted by God, hurled questions close to blasphemy against the heavens. Each time he sharpened the intensity of his words. God had left him alone to search the darkness and to stumble against its hazards.

God finally gave an answer. It probably did not happen by direct revelation; later we shall see that several factors in Israel's religious heritage converge in the formulation of Osee's message. Perhaps—we can never be absolutely certain in matters of great psychic and mystic depths like this— as Osee was questioning God, and by this attitude whirling ever more desperately into the mystery of God, he saw himself directly confronting God. His own dark image seemed to be thrown upon the brightness of God, so that light and darkness manifested one another. Sharp differences showed up, but these differences resulted from the close union of one with the other. God's light gradually transfigured Osee's darkness. Through the struggle of his own love, Osee experienced sympathetically something of God's thoughts and love. Love, human and divine, fidelity accepted and betrayed, sympathy turned into anger and ending in compassion, a power human in experience and divine in endurance—all of these actions, reactions, and counteractions mingled in the dark night of life in God. Then it was that the answer broke through to consciousness and Osee could never forget it. It was as simple and as mysterious as is God: *"Thus the Lord loves the people Israel"* (3:1).

This answer, like God's response to Job, necessarily came at the end of a prolonged ordeal. The strongest faith always exists on the brink of the deepest cavern of unbelief. Faith is not a lesson to be learned from books; for nothing human, not even the most sublime expression of human words, can capture its contents. Faith does not find its security in anything human, but in God. Osee must experience the agony of a love more than human before he can faintly grasp the meaning of God's love. This love was thoroughly divine, yet known only through its total involvement in human existence. It expressed itself in great redemptive acts like the exodus out of Egypt and the conquest of Palestine; as human, therefore, as mass migration and military conquest. This human, earthly shape of the divine love made it possible for man to betray God's love with selfish interests. Israel could use human means to rebuff God. God's people could prefer other human pleasures to God, yet be forced back to God for the reason given by Jeremia:

> Your own wickedness chastises you,
>   your own infidelities punish you.
> Know then and see how evil and bitter
>   is your forsaking the Lord your God (2:19).

This mystery of divine love eluded all human explanation. Osee had searched its meaning in the experience of the dark night. He could now become God's spokesman, never removing the mystery with his human language, but somehow or other always able to allow the echo of the divine to sound within the tone of his voice and to be heard between the words of his sentence. Osee's message would communicate to the degree that others like him had undergone the same agony of love. Communication meant a power to help others find their way out of frustration or agony and to recognize the divine meaning of it all. Osee was leading others to the most intense form of life in God and thereby became a human instrument in the communication of divine life.

Religious Influence of the North

We can trace, therefore, the origins of Osee's message to the intensity of his love for Gomer and to the strength of his faith in God. If he had never loved Gomer so passionately, he would never have missed her so much; if he had never trusted God so completely, he would never have been tempted against Providence so crucially. There were still other factors helping to forge Osee's message about God, Spouse of Israel. Each of these influences were impressed upon Osee because of the geographical location of his home. He belonged to the northern kingdom of Israel. We will delay upon three factors of "northern" thought: convenant theology; Deuteronomic approach towards law; fertility worship.

At the northern sanctuary of Sichem, the Mosaic religion was interpreted along the lines of covenant theology. The independent studies of Mendenhall in this country and of Baltzer in Germany have proven that the covenant-bond was not a distinctly biblical idea, nor was it revealed immediately to Moses. It had been the method of regulating treaties in the kingdom of the Hittites during the two centuries before Moses, 1400-1200 B.C. (The Hittites had migrated from Europe and occupied the central area of modern Turkey.) In the covenant treaty an overlord enumerated his many benevolent acts towards his vassal, who, in turn, was expected to preserve peace and to obey a series of laws out of gratitude to the stronger power. This form of agreement, technically known as the Hittite-suzerainty treaty, shows up in ancient documents unearthed in Syria and is closely paralleled in the Bible: i.e., Ex 20-23; Deut 5; Jos 24. What may have been a farce among the Hittites, who claimed that the people conquered by them reacted gratefully, reached its finest and truest expression in the Bible. The suzerainty treaty initiated a covenant theology among the people of God—an insight into God's great redemptive acts and into the meaning of law. As a result, religion was explained on God's part as free acts of affection in favor of His chosen people and on Israel's part as obedient acts of gratitude for God's great goodness. Covenant-theology, which originated and developed in the homeland of Osee, certainly stressed the primacy of love in the acts of religion. So, too, did Osee.

The northern kingdom of Israel also produced the law code of Deuteronomy, a book which was certainly one of Our Lord's favorites. Deuteronomy interprets law and history according to the principle: if you are faithful, God will bless you; if you are disobedient, God will allow your sins to punish you. But as punishment drives you to tears of compunction, God cannot listen unmoved to your cries for help. He shall send a deliverer. This view does not consider sorrow as the mighty revenge of God's justice but as the divine means of healing the effects of sin. Sorrow turns Israel's attention once again to God. Osee was born and grew up, not only physically but also mentally and spiritually, in the land of Deuteronomy. The roots of his prophecy lay deep in the past, drawing their strength not only from the *Shema prayer* (Deut 6:4-9) but also from other passages like this one:

> You are a people sacred to the Lord, your God; he has chosen you from all the nations on the face of the earth to be a people peculiarly his own. It was not because you are the largest of all nations that the Lord set his heart on you and chose you, for you are really the smallest of all nations. It was because the Lord loved you and because of his fidelity to the oath he had sworn to your fathers. . . . Understand, then, that the Lord, your God, is God indeed, the faithful God who keeps his merciful covenant down to the thousandth generations (Deut 7:6-9).

Deuteronomy, like the prophet Osee, belonged to the north, to a kingdom, therefore, which had rebelled against the Davidic dynasty at Jerusalem after the death of Solomon in 931 B.C. The northern kingdom of Israel even set up its own sanctuaries at Dan and Bethel in opposition to the Jerusalem temple. Jerusalem, of course, looked upon the north first as rebels and later as heretics. The south, we have to admit, remained the center of orthodoxy and unity. Jesus was to be born from the family of David; and not only did He worship at the Jerusalem temple, but He also answered the Samaritan woman who questioned him whether or not "Jerusalem is the place where one ought to worship." "You worship," He said to her, "what you do not know; we worship what we know, for salvation is from the Jews" (John 4:20, 22). These facts are true, even though many other details about the northern kingdom of Israel and about the Samaritans who later occupied the area, remain wrapped in oblivion.

What is also undeniable, however, is that the unorthodox north contributed to the Bible and to Christian spirituality not only some of the most perceptive insight into the mystery of God but also an insistence upon "the more excellent way" of "charity" (1 Cor 13:1). In the spirit of Osee we can make this observation upon the contemporary religious scene. No religion, then as now, can afford to reject offhand the teaching and the spirit of any other sect on the assumption that they are unorthodox or outside of unity. In Old Testament times such a tight-fisted, defensive pose would have expunged from the Bible the book of Deuteronomy and the prophecy of Osee.

The religious society of the kingdom of Israel impressed upon Osee a special regard for charity. This same insistence, however, left the northern kingdom vulnerable to the excess of love. It was here in this country that the Mosaic religion was corroded and corrupted by the degenerate rites of the fertility cult. Osee felt the influence even of this religious practice. Fertility worship begged God (or the gods) to bless the family with many children, the livestock with great increase and the lands with bumper crops. The worshipers sought to achieve this blessing by dedicating their sexual activity to the gods. Intercourse with the temple personnel channeled the abundant vitality of the divinity through the bodies and property of the worshipers. The sanctuaries, accordingly, were staffed with hierodules of either sex. Religion thereby sanctioned sexual activity of every sort, natural as well as unnatural. The fertility cult was a common feature in all Near Eastern religions, and it eventually spread to Greece and Rome. It was vigorously condemned by only one religion, that of Moses (Deut. 23:18-19). The God of Israel, alone among all the gods, is never portrayed with a mate. The stricture against sacred prostitution occurs, as we might expect, where the danger was most imminent, in the north. The law code of Deuteronomy, in fact, calls the despicable hire collected by the male prostitutes "a dog's price." Although this sensuous routine was carried on at times even in the precincts of the Jerusalem temple, the most devastating erosion ate into the north. (Gomer incidentally, may have attached herself to a nothern sanctuary as one of the *qadeshah* or "sacred prostitutes.")

Braving this depraved culture, Osee called Yahweh "the Spouse of Israel." The abuse of love never blinded Osee to its nobility. Neither Osee nor any other prophet to appear later ever crusaded for a complete withdrawal from the current civilization and contemporary problems. Osee never preached the impossible message that God's people must dynamite the past and present, and begin all over again.

Accepting the people as he found them, with their desires and ambitions, thought patterns, work, and recreational habits, Osee sought to remove the impulsive pride, the false emphases and the narrow-mindedness. He would help them to arrive at honesty by facing up to their pride, at true marriage by witnessing its disintegration, at a kindly disposition by confessing their selfishness.

Only by courageously working with reality, even though the real was depraved and corrupt, could God's people find Him. Osee was thus able to show them that what they genuinely wanted was already waiting for them in God, through charity, justice and chastity. Every sin is like the first sin of mankind. Eve wanted to acquire a God-like status but independently of God. God, nonetheless, had already created her and Adam to His "image and likeness" and was planning to make them even more fully His children by enlarging their share in His divine nature (cf. 2 Pet 1:4). To people panicking in a futile search for security and joy, and descending to the crude excesses of the fertility cult, Osee speaks of the true and faithful Spouse:

I will espouse you in fidelity,
On that day I will respond, says the Lord;
    and you shall know the Lord.
    I will respond to the heavens,
    and they shall respond to the earth;
The earth shall respond to the grain, and wine, and oil,
    and these shall respond to Jezrael.
I will sow him for myself in the land,
    and I will have pity on Lo-ruhama.
I will say to Lo-ammi, "You are my people,"
    and he shall say, "My God!" (Os 2:21-15).

GOD'S SURPASSING LOVE

God, Spouse of Israel—that phrase expresses in very human words what is most divine about God. It provides the human mind with an insight into the inmost being of God, where God thinks and loves, where God, if we may hazard the statement, is most truly God. Eternity will never exhaust the full implications of this bond of love and of this communication of life between God and man, uniting God and man in the uniquely personal elements of each one's existence. To live conscious of love such as that will be eternity's greatest joy. For men on this side of eternity, the grandest opportunity exists in searching out the implications and consequences of that love. Osee is our best guide.

God's Initiative

Osee, first of all, shows God taking the initiative. In the lines just quoted, God is heard to say: "*I* espouse you. . . ." Our Lord phrased the same idea just a little differently: "You have not chosen me, but I have chosen you" (John 15:16). These words touch the heart of every vocation, whether it be a calling to the priesthood, the religious life or the consecrated life in the world or whether it be a vocation to marriage, family and the lay apostolate. When someone is asked why he married or did not marry, perhaps, the impatient answer which immediately comes to mind is: "Isn't that my personal business?" The truer answer, coming from the book of Osee, acknowledges: "That was God's business!" Every vocation is a call from God; He takes the initiative, drawing, attracting, pulling in that direction where the person's talents can be exploited to his own fulfillment and to the benefit of others. Because a vocation is a directive of divine providence, the first determining factor is not a person's capability nor his worthiness, but the will of God for him. Talents, desires and stamina also come from God and are, therefore, an indication of God's will, but those qualifications must always submit to God for the final verdict. Vocational guidance dare not remove the mystery of God's love in this matter, but ought to be controlled by an attitude of faith. Faith recognizes a strong bond of co-consecration: God, dedicating His love and strength to His chosen one; man, consecrating himself unconditionally to God's will.

Mutual Trust

This mystery of vocation brings up another factor in Osee's teaching about God, Spouse of Israel. Mystery, as just pointed out, involves trust, especially when the mystery is none other than the wonder of marriage. Husbands and wives, genuinely in love, trust one another completely. If a husband must report to his wife all his activities from the moment he leaves the house until he returns in the late afternoon, their marriage is not established on love but on suspicion. The "ideal couple" do not feel obliged to give ten reasons for every action; instead, they speak frankly and act spontaneously. They banish that sophisticated air which must always be correct, exact and all-knowing.

As Spouse of Israel, God acts on the presupposition that there exists a love-bond between Himself and His people, stronger than that between husband and wife, for He is "God, not man" (Os 11:9). At times He acts without providing the reasons. If God had to supply a list of explanations for every request, He would be insulting our love for Him. He would be reducing it to suspicion or, at least, to a cold sophistication. Before man obeys God or accepts His providential arrangements, he is not entitled to sit back and square off with Him: "Now, that's unreasonable! Why did You do that? Explain yourself!" Such an attitude is blasphemous from a creature. Osee, however, prefers to call it a hateful violation of the love which spouses owe one another.

Marriage is a mutual contract, a two-way agreement; what is true for one party is true for the other. God dares to oblige Himself by such an agreement. He always remains God, and we keep our place as creatures, just as in marriage—to draw a weak parallel—the husband is the head of the home!/ It is also plain that while God appears good and dependable, the creature's reliability is spoiled by original sin. In many respects, however, the trust which God requires of us He also grants to us. God, in fact, regards us with a strong trust and a total confidence, for He is "God, not man."

In other words, God is not scrutinizing our daily actions to find as many faults as possible, neither is He suspicious that we are always on the point of betraying Him. God trusts us! Osee is here providing one of the most effective cures for scrupulosity. We insult God's love, which Osee recognized as the love of a spouse, if we never feel at peace in His presence. Love does not exist in a climate of suspicion or fault-finding. In a happy marriage each partner not only gives the other the benefit of the doubt but also laughs away many small grievances. Osee teaches us to think that way of God. In a later section of the Bible, chapters forty to fifty-five of Isaia, composed under the influence of Osee's Yahweh-Spouse theme, God is heard to address Israel in these playful terms of endearment:

> Fear not, O worm Jacob,
> O maggot Israel;
> I will help you, says the Lord (Is 41:14).

Mysterously Personal

The tone of one's voice and the light within one's eyes can change those words of Isaia from charm and trust to shame and contempt. Love, however, can take that chance. It thrives on puns; jokes are possible only between friends. Two persons in love will laugh and giggle over the most meaningless remarks. Love has its own language, deeply personal and far beyond the wave length of everyone else. In many ways this aspect of marriage can be applied to the bond between God and Israel. This thought can be stated in the form of a warning: no one has a right to pass judgment on his fellowmen for the unique manner in which they show their love for God. To some a longer fast is a showing of love; another prays longer; yet another performs some tiring act of zeal—nurses a neighbor back to health or cares for an aged relative. To no man is granted the privilege of judging who it is who loves the more deeply. God asks and the soul responds with very personal expressions of love.

It can also be maintained, as we think about the very personal form of married love, that no one can model himself on any other human being. Transferring this idea to the bond of love between God and His people, we find that God will expect sacrifices from and will grant joys to one person and not another. No one is entitled to criticize God as unjust. God loves each person individually. Finally, if love is deeply personal, then each one must take for granted that there will be secrets between himself and God which can never be adequately explained to anyone else, much less appreciated by them. These secrets may even remain a baffling mystery to one's self. Such was the case of Osee, spending hours and days in search of an answer for what was happening in his life and at the end finding himself in the mystery of God.

Betrayal of Love

Because God is the Spouse of His people, Osee enables us to learn still more about God from human love in marriage.

Marriage is one of the most serious undertakings on this earth, for the partners not only share wealth and years, but they even allow one another to glimpse into the depth of their personality. Everything lies open for the other to see and (God grant) to respect and love. Precisely here is the chasm separating the true expression of love from the mere exercise of sex. Sex is for the moment and is quickly over with; it is satisfied with physical and emotional excitement. Gomer's paramours wanted only sex; they were afraid of love. This fear forced them eventually to abandon her. Love transforms sex into a lasting experience, a full sharing of all one's self. Love is courageous enough to gamble a lifetime and even to allow the possibility of the other's discovering one's faults and weaknesses. Love is trustful and expects to be trusted; it is forgiving and expects to be forgiven. All this, of course, makes it such a serious matter. Only one fault, however, is unpardonable. Seldom, if ever, do men forgive the betrayal of love. They call it adultery.

Here too there is a parallel with the love-bond between God and His people. \Sin betrays that bond of love. Because sin strikes at a love greater than marriage, sin must be ranked at least with the heinousness of adultery. Sin is adultery to the extent that a person maliciously turns against God and uses His gifts to obtain unlawful pleasure. Sin, therefore, must not be guaged according to a legal yardstick; the external act, able to be measured and judged by human eyes, is not sinful, unless it is impelled by hatred for God; this no human vision can see. God is offended when His love is ignored and violated.

For this reason a "small" sin in a person trusted with special gifts from God can be a greater crime than a "great" sin in someone else less favored. To take an impossible situation as an example, the least sin in Jesus Christ—just the shadow of a deliberate, resentful thought against another —would have been far more serious than all the human crimes perpetuated since the first sin in paradise. To transfer back to the real, we must admit that we ourselves can be hurt more by a cross look from someone we love than by a kick from a total stranger.

Osee, therefore, is asking us to form a judgment about sin, not by analyzing ourselves first or the circumstances of the act, but rather by fixing our gaze first upon God, Spouse of His people. Osee leads to a conclusion which borders on the heretical. This juxtaposition of truth-error should not surprise us; we have already seen that the most heroic faith exists on the edge of apostasy. Sin, according to the prophet, injures a love equal to and greater than the love between husband and wife; Osee puts it down as adultery. How, we ask, is God affected by sin? Can the unhappiness and the tragedy of man's adultery cloud His eternal joy? Can God lose and regain His joy in us? Here words stop at the threshold of mystery. Within Osee's words we sense a struggle of divine passion, a tension within God, a surge of His anger, a return to love. We hear the cry of "divine passion" within the books of Osee:

> How could I give you up, O Ephraim,
>   or deliver you up, O Israel?
> How could I treat you as Adama,
>   or make you like Seboim?
> My heart is overwhelmed,
>   my pity is stirred.
> I will not give vent to my blazing anger,
>   I will not destroy Ephraim again;
> For I am God and not man... (11:8-9).

A prophet of the Babylonian exile composed lines which

appear to be a meditation on the words of Osee. If not that, then they ponder the identical mystery of divine love in confrontation with sin. Deutero-Isaia overhears God saying to Israel:

> You burdened me with your sins,
>   and wearied me with your crimes (Is 43:24).

The word "burdened" reads literally in the Hebrew: "you made a servant [or slave] out of me." Here is the mystery which no words, even of an inspired prophet, can solve: God enslaved and wearied by man's sins. God took that chance when He loved man as dearly as husband and wife love one another. We have always been told that God is unchangeably joyful. Without denying that truth, Deutero-Isaia and Osee remind us that no rigid formula about God can remove the mystery surrounding His love. On God's part, sin is not simply a vitiated human act to be measured and punished; it is an affrontery to His love and an attack upon a human being whom God loves more than spouses love one another.

Osee brings to our startled attention the ugly malice of sin. Sin is blacker than adultery. Another aspect lies in the divine forgiveness. Osee forgave Gomer again and again, and finally God revealed to him: "thus the Lord loves the people of Israel" (3:1). Osee, in fact, sought out Gomer and brought her home again; God will do the same. God says about His chosen one, Israel:

> So I will allure her!
>   I will lead her into the desert
>   and speak to her heart.
> From there I will give her the vineyards she had
>   and the valley of Achor as a door of hope.
> She shall respond there as in the days of her youth,
>   when she came up from the land of Egypt (2:16-17).

These lines show that God not only forgives but He also removes the effects of sin. Israel has returned to the golden joys of the Mosaic days when she was young, attractive and pure. The whole land of Palestine then lay before her, the home prepared by God for His spouse. Israel was at the "door of hope" in "the valley of Achor." As in the time of Josue, Israel was stepping into her new home for the first, ecstatic time. Centuries later divine forgiveness enables her her to relive the joy of the first moment of her love. This absolute forgetfulness of every betrayal is humanly impossible. Seldom if ever can the scars of adultery be forgotten, much less removed. Osee, however, never lets us forget that God *is* God, not man!

Fulfillment of Love

At one extreme of marriage lurks the sinister possibility of adultery, but the true direction of married love lies in the fruitful begetting of children. Marriage cries out for children and is never complete without them. When Osee likens the bond between God and His people to that of marriage, he reminds us that God's love in us must be fruitful, productive of more love and more goodness in others. Osee clearly enunciates the purpose of divine predilection. God does not love Israel that this people might wrap themselves cozily in soft contentment and ignore the rest of the world. From the daily scene of married life Osee draws the conclusion that God's love must be fruitful, before man can have a sign that he possesses it. The more selfishly a married couple live just for themselves, rejecting children, the more quickly their love tires and destroys itself. Love can never exist in a selfish home. God's love, therefore, cannot remain locked up within a proud Israel. Israel must continually seek to share with many others her divinely bestowed knowledge and goodness.

The missionary interest of Israel began in the earliest days with God's words to Abraham: "Through you all nations will be blessed" (Gen 12:3). Osee restates it with renewed vigor and fuller insight.

Here is the purpose, then, as Osee saw it, of the love granted to us by God. God loves us in order that we may share His love and His goodness. In order that there may be a continual increase of life, God chooses some for marriage, some for a dedicated apostolate in the world, others for the priesthood and the religious life. We can easily see the transmission of life through marriage, but unfortunately the call to consecrated virginity and celibacy can appear barren of life. Too often it is explained as a sacrifice undertaken out of love for God. Undeniably, it is a sacrifice—and as such a loss and a hardship—for these persons who deprive themselves of marriage, home and children; but this loss is only temporary.

On this earth, priests and religious expend their life, imparting a genuine, wholesome appreciation of God; they seek to help men and women find their joys and their sorrows caught up in the sufferings and the triumph of Jesus Christ. As all men are aided in identifying themselves with Jesus and as they find in Him their salvation in distress and their fulfillment in hope, they are growing in life. They are developing in that center where they are truly themselves and no one else, where they think, struggle and decide, where they love, seek and attain. This life is often called their life of faith and charity, a life shared with them by God, a life which will withstand the tomb and exists eternally with God. Priests and religious devote themselves to propagating this eternal life. Parents, of course, seek to impart these same spiritual benefits to the children whom they have begotten in the flesh, but ordinarily their sphere of opportunity is much more limited; the full-time apostle possesses a greater liberty of action.

The results, however, can never be tallied up on earth, and heaven will spring many surprises. Jesus hinted at this when he said: "The last shall be first, and the first last" (Matt 20:16). The apostolic opportunities of married people have been greatly underrated; they have a role in the neighborhood and community, in labor and business, in government and education, which no priest nor religious can assume. There will always be need, however, of priests and religious, consecrated to God by celibacy or virginity. To the reasons already given, one more may be added to show this necessity. Both Osee and Jeremia (cf. Jer 16:1-3) reveal the holiness which blossomed in them, not only despite but also because of the loss of wife and children. In every age there will be spouses who lose their partners, parents separated from their children. Of every Christian in the married state God at times asks heroic sacrifice; how else can heroic love be fully expressed? Words are not sufficient to advise and console these many disconsolate, despairing persons; only the example of peace and hope in similar situations can ever help them. Priests and religious should supply this example.

When the final age has come, when death shall be no more and the universe will be completely transformed into the home of God's elect, when all who are saved have risen to eternal life through the power of Jesus' resurrection, then each one will look around with wonder and overwhelming gratitude. Each will be especially attracted to those who have communicated this life of God to them. Groups will gather together like families; these men and women will recognize a common bond of life, uniting them to one another and to the one who formed their character on earth. Then it will be realized that just as parents impress their own physical features upon the faces of their children, teachers and apostles impress upon souls their own understanding of God, Jesus Christ, His Blessed Mother, and the way of salvation. This interior formation of character has opened the soul to the blessings of God and the gifts of Jesus Christ. It has made possible the supreme gift of the resurrection, reuniting body and soul for eternal happiness.

While on earth, those whom God calls to the specialized vocation of celibacy and virginity, must trust that the message of Osee is true. Osee never proved it; he only stated it with strong conviction. Because his own unhappy marriage seemed to reduce his life to frustration and barrenness, Osee was forced to question God for the meaning and the purpose of his own existence. Finally he was able to preach forgiveness and fulfillment to a sinful people; he was able to impart the eternal life of knowledge and love to generations of Israelites, even to us right now. He became a prophet, exhorting Israel to ponder her vocation as God's beloved, and in that divine love find the sacredness and nobility of her existence. Osee exclaims these extraordinary facts with strong, moving language. Because what he states is really true, his words become powerful instruments for settling the needs of many other persons. Somehow or other, when Osee's words are heard, people admit that the prophet is enlivening their faith in God and clarifying its meaning for them.

Osee assures each one that no desire, true and noble, remains unfulfilled. The necessity to love and be loved; the longing for children—these deepest needs of human beings cannot be frustrated without tearing apart the human nature created by God. These desires will not be destroyed in solemn holocaust; God will fulfill them through the power of His love. The prophet declares:

> The number of the Israelites
> shall be like the sand of the sea,
> which can be neither measured nor counted.
> Whereas they were called,
> "Lo-ammi,"
> They shall be called,
> "Children of the living God."
> Then the people of Juda and of Israel
> shall be gathered together;
> They shall appoint for themselves one head
> and come up from other lands,
> for great shall be the day of Jezrael.
> Say to your brothers, "Ammi,"
> and to your sisters, "Ruhama" (2:1-3).

Conclusion

Because love is the great mystery of human life, divine love is the great mystery of the Bible. Without resolving the mystery, Osee enables us to live in faith and trust. As a spouse of God, we love God and God loves us: with trust, with loyalty, with fruitfulness. To refuse such love is to commit adultery! But God, deeply affected by such betrayal, shall forgive and even remove the scars and bring us back to the moment of espousal. Osee uses daring language, strange to modern ears, but God's love too is daring in the chances which it takes. Strange, even ridiculous language passes between those who are in love; Osee's words lead into the mysterious realm of God's most personal life. Osee has already gone the full way and can help us as an excellent guide. For this reason we must return repeatedly to his prophecy. If we live courageously and study his prophecy prayerfully, then we fully accept the conclusion which a scribe appended to his book:

> Let him who is wise understand these things;
> let him who is prudent know them.

Straight are the paths of the Lord,
  in them the just walk,
  but sinners stumble in them (14:10).

CHAPTER 4 JEREMIA,
SUCCESSFUL
FAILURE

JEREMIA is certainly to be ranked among the holiest of the prophets. At the request of God he never married, so that he could consecrate himself unreservedly to God's work (Jer 16:2). From beginning to end he was heroically dedicated to God's holy will. Preaching God's word made him look foolish at times, but he humbly admits: "I allowed myself to be duped" (20:7). After the fall of Jerusalem in the summer of 587 B.C., the Babylonians offered Jeremia the luxury of preferential treatment in the land of exile, but he deliberately chose to remain among the charred ruins and the discouraged populace of Palestine. This prophet from the town of Anathoth was commissioned to speak God's word. Yet he was to influence the Israelite people much more by the example of his holy life than by the eloquence of his preaching.

After his death, the scrolls containing his words as well as the story of his life were frequently in the hands of the chosen people. We find Daniel meditating on his words (Dan 9:2). Other books of the Bible show how the people spontaneously opened the Sacred Scripture to the words of Jeremia (cf. II Par 36:21; I Esd 1:1; Sir 49:7; II Mach. 15:14). And when our Lord asked St. Peter: "Whom do men say the Son of Man is?" Peter replied: "Some say John the Baptist; others, Elias; and others, Jeremia or one of the prophets" (Matt 16:13f). The prophecy of Jeremia had become such a commonplace in Jewish life that a tradition arose demanding that he return. The people must hear the prophet's message from his own lips, as it is formed once again in a heart burning with zeal for God. They looked back upon his life as a magnificent success.

Jeremia's Life as Jeremia Saw It

Yet, how did Jeremia look back on his own life, when his tired soul and toil-worn body were nearing the end of their earthly pilgrimage? The prophet's words to his faithful companion Baruch are an extract from his own heart. He dictated them after completing the first edition of his prophecy. They express very well what the old man thought about himself: "Alas! the Lord adds grief to my pain; I am weary from groaning, and can find no rest ... (But thus) says the Lord ... Do you seek great things for yourself? Seek them not! I am bringing evil on all mankind, says the Lord, but your life I will leave you as booty, wherever you may go" (45:3-5).

Baruch at once remembers these other words of Jeremia, his master: "My heart is broken within me" (23:9).

Now that he was close to death, Jeremia could boast of no great accomplishments. There remained only his life,

and even that would soon be violently snatched away as he
died a martyr's death. No man's life ever seemed to turn
into the cold ashes of dead failure as did Jeremia's. God
had set him "over nations and over kingdoms . . . to destroy
and to demolish (1:10)." No kingdom was so torn and
demolished as that within his own soul. This collapse of
what he considered his mission in life almost drove him to
despair, although he had felt convinced from the very beginning that his work would end in frustration. He had
begged God to send some one else. Yet, as always, he sub-
mitted to the summons of God's holy will. This timid, fearful man would soon stand up before the jostling crowd to
speak God's word. Often he pleaded with outstretched arms:
"Return, rebellious, and I will cure you of your rebelling"
(3:22). On other occasions he hurled angry threats against
distant mountains: "Hear, O nations! and know, O earth!
. . . See, I bring evil upon this people, the fruit of their own
schemes" (6:18f). But the people kept shrugging their
shoulders with playful indifference, or, as time went on,
they spit their angry insults at this meddlesome "friar."
Always Jeremia failed.

His unswerving efforts could not prevent the siege of
Jerusalem. When the Babylonians encircled the city, the
prophet entreated Sedecia, the Israelite king, to surrender
and to save the scraps. In retaliation, the prophet was jailed
for being a traitor. After the total destruction of the city
and temple, he urged the remnant left behind in Palestine to
settle down and live peacefully. Instead, the ones who first
pretended to honor and consult Jeremia fled into Egypt and
dragged him along against his will. Finally, according to
Jewish tradition, they turned on Jeremia and stoned to death
the sorrowful old man. Not even his empty life was spared
him. The silence of Egyptian sand would have consigned

this prophet to oblivion had not his faithful friend Baruch
written down an account of his words and life.

A Soul Laid Bare

Jeremia left behind no monument of external wonder, but
he did fulfill his vocation in life. He accomplished what
God wanted him to do. He achieved success, we might say,
through failure, repeated failure. Jeremia is important, not
so much for the conversions he made nor for the eloquence
of his speaking, nor for his messianic prophecies, but he is
important simply for what he was. The great wonders of
his life were not outside him but within the silence of his
lonely soul: wonders of energetic obedience and humble
submission to God's will. For this reason, perhaps, the prophecy of Jeremia is reserved by the Church for the liturgy of
Passiontide. Jeremia prefigures the silent Sufferer of Calvary
and thus conditioned his fellow Israelites to recognize the
power of divine redemption in the "weakness" of a God-
man put to death by His enemies.

This example of suffering and resignation would rise from
the tomb of Jeremia and preach a sermon which would re-
echo through the cities of the Jews, swelling in crescendo
with the passage of time. The words of Jeremia which
Baruch gathered passed from Egypt to Palestine and from
there to other distant groups of Jews. The Israelites, exiled
in Babylon recalled still other words of the prophet and
proceeded to add these to Baruch's collection. Yet Jeremia
never heard this echo of his voice. He died, haunted by the
whispering, static repetition: "Denounce him! Denounce
him!" Pathetically, he had once considered these accusers
"my intimate friends" (20:10).

Jeremia did not easily accept this vocation to be a failure.

Struggle, entreaty with God, questioning, alarm, complaint—
these and other reactions stir within those passages
called "The Confessions of Jeremia" (11:18-12:6; 15:10-21;
17:14-18; 18:18-23; 20:7-18). In these sections especially
the soul of the prophet is laid bare before our eyes. Like
Hamlet, who climbs a high turret away from the clamor of
the court and the muted connivings of his uncle, Jeremia
steps aside from the noise and ritual of the temple and its
courtyards, from the muffled intrigue and harsh shouts of
his enemies, to close his eyes for a moment to the make-
believe world of irreligious people whose proud self-reliance
was raising a tower of Babel in defiance of God; and in the
style of a soliloquy he pours out the deepest secrets of
his soul.

> Woe to me, mother, that you gave me birth!
> a man of strife and contention to all the land!
> I neither borrow nor lend,
> yet all curse me.
> Tell me, Lord, have I not served you well?
> Have I not interceded with you for my enemies
> in the time of their misfortune and anguish?
> Remember me, Lord, visit me,
> and avenge me on my persecutors.
> Because of your long-suffering banish me not;
> know that for you I have borne insult. . .
> Under the weight of your hand I sat alone
> because you filled me with indignation.
> Why is my pain continuous,
> my wound incurable, refusing to be healed? (15:10-18).

Perhaps Jeremia at times carries this introspection to extreme. He is unable to suppress the "I" as he records the
word of God, and so his personal reflections intrude within
the phrases of the divine message. He speaks these words
of God:

> Like a woman faithless to her lover,
> even so have you been faithless to me,
> O house of Israel, says the Lord.

Immediately, Jeremia interposes:

> A cry is heard on the heights!
> the plaintive weeping of Israel's children. . . .

At once, however, he returns to the message of God:

> Return, rebellious children,
> and I will cure you of your rebelling (3:20-22).

Since Jeremia was a man of uncommon sensitiveness and strange melancholy, some may feel that God's word is prejudiced by the prophet's interruptions, which at times seem downright revengeful. Let us not be hasty, however, in our judgment. A *temptation* to get even must not be confused with a coldly calculated determination to revenge oneself. Jeremia was too honest not to voice those temptations embarrassing and humiliating to him. So much had the prophet been transformed by God's grace that the personal "I" of Jeremia was identical with God's reaction. If Jeremia was extremely sensitive and gloomy in outlook, he had no other character to live and work with than the one given to him by God. In this humble acceptance of himself with his limitations and liabilities, Jeremia is an example for each one of us.

The personal confessions of the prophet can teach us very much. We too begin our lives with great hopes and ambitions. We will leap across every barrier and with strenuous perseverance arrive at the goal of our desires. As fathers or mothers, we will do so very much for God, if only He will give us the opportunity: a large family of children, trained to be obedient and God-fearing; ourselves devoted to Catholic action in the parish or school. If we are priests or religious, then our ideal is to set up a dynamic Catholic parish, charged with enthusiasm and charity. We will train active lay-leaders in the class rooms; we will nurse them back to health in our hospitals; we will have homes for their orphan children or aging relatives.

The Peace of Surrender

But as obedience shifts us from one place to another, or business forces a change of residence, we never seem to stay long enough to accomplish any lasting good. If we do remain in one place for a number of years, then life settles down to such a dull, monotonous routine that we almost live by habit rather than by free determination. We find ourselves getting older, less enthusiastic; the hopes of raising great monuments to God's glory vanish.

There is heard the rumbling of a clash of interests; what we want to do for God runs head-on against what God wants us to do for Him. Mothers find it hard to see greatness in washing dirty dishes and faces, answering telephones and doorbells, picking up toys and spilled food. Or there may be the frustration of being able to have only one child, or even no children at all. Fathers may find it necessary to be away from home for days at a time. Economic situations may force them to look for a second job in the evening or on week ends. They ask themselves; "Where is this ideal family life I dreamed about before marriage?" Religion teachers are often tempted to think that little good comes from all their efforts, since their rowdy groups of boys and girls grow up and act as though they had never been to a Catholic school. Teachers are inclined to fear the worst, for seldom do they see what kind of man the child becomes. Zealous priests may be assigned to office duty, with hours spent at the desk, adding up numbers and filling in reports, when they long to be calling on their flock, visiting the sick, and helping the unfortunate. Jeremia reminds us that a vocation is whatever God wants. It is accepting ourselves just as He made us, with our talents, dispositions and character, or with their lack. God may give one talent for teaching and five talents for sickness. He may move us like pawns on a chess board. His demands may be so ordinary, so common, that they stir little response or awaken slight eagerness. Yet in God's will alone can we find peace—not the peace won by a victorious army which carries with it a pride that may be its future failure, but the peace of submission and surrender to the conquering forces of God's will, which, though hidden even from us, can be only success.

An Eternal Vocation

As Jeremia dragged out the final day of his life in the foreign land of Egypt, how frequently he must have glanced back over the day of his youth. Elderly people are accustomed to do this. We can picture him sitting alone in his home in Egypt. The heaviness of the summer heat has stifled every sound. Not even the sycamores and cypress trees have the energy to rustle their branches. Jeremia has only to close his eyes and he is back again in the past. He is now able to relive those early days with a deeper sense of their meaning. A lifetime of devoted service with years of suffering, contradiction, and failure, have imparted a mellowness of character which humbly accepts what has happened without wanting to know the reason why. What he once performed with earnest but unfruitful zeal he now relives with deep understanding.

Just to close his eyes is enough to sweep him back to the

land of Palestine, back to that day forty-three years ago when God first called him to be a prophet. He was a young man then, just past his nineteenth birthday. That afternoon he had walked the two-and-one-half miles from Jerusalem to his own village of Anathoth. He had left the city by its northern gate, and entered the central plateau section of Palestine. The land was like the top of a table covered with a soiled cloth which rose and fell in soft folds. The hills were drab and dreary, yellow with dried-up grass and with the stubs of a former wheat crop. The sight of it left Jeremia sad and melancholy. Later on his words manifest the influence of the land upon his thinking, as when he says:

> The portion that delighted me they have turned
>   into a desert waste. . . .
> They have made it a mournful waste,
>   desolate it lies before me,
> Desolate, all the land,
>   because no one takes it to heart. . . .
> They have sown wheat and reaped thorns,
>   they have tired themselves out to no purpose (12:10-13).

Behind him is Jerusalem, a city dead from sin and already in the process of decay. He passes through fields, dry, famished, and thirsting for the autumn rains. Once at home, he sits down to watch the sunset. He wonders how such a colorful panoply of peace and glory can rest upon such a sordid earth. Thus he muses, as he awaits the evening meal.

Suddenly he is hearing clear, distinct words spoken within him. He is startled and surprised. Who can it be? Then he knows. This is the first of many messages which he is to receive from God. The words of God are consoling and reassuring. He can recall them with all the distinctness of a bell ringing out its tones:

Before I formed you in the womb, I knew you;
before you were born, I consecrated you for my service (1:5).

Jeremia realizes that he is not forgotten by God. The future prophet can say of himself: "From all eternity God has been thinking of me." He is overwhelmed with the thought. God's concern in creating the universe—in piling up mountains, in digging out oceans and river beds and filling them with water, in ornamenting the sky with stars and planets, and in covering the earth with trees and flowers, in all the involved and intricate governing of nations and the thousands of people in each of them—in all of these elaborate cares God could not forget me. This reaction of Jeremia is twin brother to the cry of St. Paul, who will write many centuries later: "God loved *me* and gave Himself up for *me*" (Gal 2:20). This love, centered upon the Apostle of the Gentiles, like that centered upon Jeremia, stretched back into eternity, for St. Paul will also write: "Blessed be the God and Father of our Lord Jesus Christ, who has blessed us with every spiritual blessing on high in Christ, even as He chose us in Him before the foundation of the world" (Eph 1:3-4). Before his birth, therefore, Jeremia was already set apart for a special work. From all eternity God possessed the secret of who he is to be and what he is to do. Who was more suitable than Jeremia to introduce into the Hebrew religion the theology of the individual?

A Consecration

God is speaking to each of us today what He once said to Jeremia: "Before you were born, I consecrated you and set you apart for My service." The hands of a priest are consecrated with sacred oil and thus set aside for placing God's blessing upon marriage and children, upon repentant sinners and the dying. Similarly, each one's life has been consecrated by a sacred oil, the oil of God's will. This anointing has been made from eternity. To use the sacred vessel of one's life for anything other than for what God wants it, is a worse desecration than to spit upon the hands of a priest. Hands are material and will crumble into dust, the anointing oils forgotten; but souls are spiritual and will endure forever, the anointing oils shining in glory.

A truth such as this has many implications. For instance, it is not for parents to decide what vocation their children are to follow; the parents' roles are guide and counselor, to direct along the way of God's holy will. For everyone subject to authority, an act of obedience touches their life with the oil of consecration. To revolt is to "follow a thing of nought" (2:5), since disobedience is a blind rush towards empty meaninglessness.

This elementary demand of God, that we conform ourselves to His will, was burned deeply upon the soul of Jeremia. He quickly condemned anyone for "walking in the hardness of his evil heart instead of listening to God" (16:12). On one occasion he solemnly declared:

> Pay attention to this,
>   foolish and senseless people
> Who have eyes and see not,
>   who have ears and hear not.
> Should you not fear me, says the Lord,
>   should you not tremble before me?
> I made the sandy shore the sea's limit,
>   which by eternal decree it may not overstep.
> Toss though it may, it is to no avail;
>   though its billows roar, they cannot pass.
> But this people's heart is stubborn and rebellious;
>   they turn and go away (5:21-23).

In these words Jeremia is calling on the sea and stars and seasons of the year to witness against the Israelites. "Be amazed at this, O heavens, and shudder with sheer horror, says the Lord" (2:12). As we read his prophecy today, this same sea and stars and seasons call out against each one of us. The elements of nature shout: "We cannot know our maker as you can, yet we obey. You can know His excelling love in Christ Jesus, yet you rise up defiantly against His will and disobey!"

To Wreck and to Ruin

The first words spoken to Jeremia are consoling: from all eternity God set him aside for a very special work. Then there follow bewildering words:

> A prophet to the nations I appoint you, ...
> To root up and to tear down,
>   to destroy and to demolish,
>   to build and to plant (1:5, 10).

Though still quite young, Jeremia knows at least vaguely the kind of future God is laying out before him. Like Someone to come after him, whose life Jeremia foreshadows, this young man of Anathoth is also being "destined for the fall and for the rise of many in Israel, and for a sign which shall be contradicted" (Luke 2:34).

Humble, timid, and afraid, Jeremia has no ambition for such a mission; in no way does he desire to preach God's message to his fellow Israelites. Nothing pleases him more than to be a Mr. Nobody, unnoticed by the Jerusalem populace and ignored by the ruling clique of royal counselors and priests. How contented he can be to live in the tiny world of his own heart! Furthermore, the Jerusalem aristocracy are determined to tolerate no interference from the priestly family of Anathoth. Solomon had banished Jeremia's ancestors to this insignificant village and placed full control of the Temple in the open hands of the rival priestly family of Sadoc (3 Kings 2:26). Now Jeremia must turn to face Jerusalem, to brave an angry gale of furious wind and ominous black clouds. In the days of Moses, God Himself called this nation "a stiff-necked people" (Ex 33:5). Six hundred years later they are still under the spell of a "heart . . . stubborn and rebellious."

Jeremia also knows only too well that there has been no prophet whose ministry was not a source of sorrow. Amos was told bluntly: "Off with you, visionary, flee to the land of Juda . . . Never again prophesy in Bethel" (Amos 7:12-13). Osee endured the excruciating sorrow of having an adulterous wife (Osee 3:1). Michea was made a ridiculous spectacle, mimicked by people who likened his words to spittle: "Do not keep on dropping words! They are dropping words! They should not be dropping words about such things!" (Mich 2:6).

God is summoning Jeremia from his plain country hideaway to the gorgeous Temple which stands like a glittering jewel in the setting of Mount Sion, on the northeastern heights of Jerusalem. He must watch until a group of inquisitive worshippers gather around him, then he is to proclaim the word of God:

> What right has my beloved in my house,
>   while she prepares her plots?
> Can vows and sacred meat turn away
>   your misfortune from you?
> Will you still be jubilant
>   when you hear the great invasion?
> A spreading olive tree, goodly to behold,
>   the Lord has named you;
> Now he sets fire to it,
>   its branches burn (11:15-16).

Richly clad priests and perfumed devotees stiffen with sublime indignation at these "sacrilegious words." Yet Jeremia must continue: "Put not your trust in the deceitful words: 'This is the Temple of the Lord! the Temple of the Lord! the Temple of the Lord!'" (7:4). The worshippers pretend that pompous bearing, rotund voices and repetitious formulas can transform the dirt of sin into the gold of righteousness. Jeremia replies:

> Small and great alike, all are greedy for gain;
>   prophet and priest, all practice fraud.
> They would repair, as though it were nought,
>   the injury of my people:
> "Peace, peace!" they say,
>   though there is no peace (6:13-14).

The final Hebrew phrase is dramatic: "Shalom! Shalom! we-en Shalom!"

These people are worms, crawling in and out of the dirt of sin. When the sabbath begins, they stand erect with stiff dignity and wrap themselves in robes of vaunted holiness in an effort to hide their naked foulness. The glare of the sun, reflected from the marble walls and the golden roof of the Temple, the piercing sound of trumpets and bells, the rolling cadences of chanted psalms—all these accessories of worship are to make God blind and deaf to daily immorality. Jeremia must rip off this sham of externalism and exclaim:

> "Can a man hide in secret
>   without my seeing him?" says the Lord (23:24).

Jeremia is being appointed to root up this proud spirit of self-complacency, to tear down this sham of ritual and lavish worship. He must destroy and demolish, before he is able to build and to plant. Not even infinite power can erect a lasting temple of holiness upon foundations of rotten wood.

Muffled Te Deums

When Jeremia receives notice of his eternal vocation, he remonstrates with God in friendly simplicity: "Ah, Lord

God! I know not how to speak; I am only a boy" (1:6). Each of us can sympathize with the newly-consecrated prophet, because Jeremia is Everyman and Everywoman.

The day of ordination to the priesthood, of religious profession, of marriage vows rings with bells of joy. Hearts are bubbling with enthusiasm. The *Te Deum* of thanksgiving must continue forever. Jeremia says to the Israelites in the name of God:

> I remember the devotion of your youth,
>   how you loved me as a bride,
> Following me in the desert,
>   in a land unsown.
> Sacred to the Lord was Israel,
>   the first fruits of his harvest (2:2-3).

Yet life muffles the *Te Deum*. Perhaps the scandal of someone's bad example was enough to pull down our own ideals, to become an excuse for demanding that much less of ourselves. The priesthood or religious life may stretch through a desert land of trifling necessities and day-by-day routine, and the whisper of temptation can be loud: "Why did God bring me here?" Marriage may turn into the doldrum of petty jobs, the frustration of "doing the things that never stay done," the taxing weight of tiredness and sickness. Jeremia is Everyman and Everywoman, feeling a clash of interests. What God wants done clashes with what we want to do for Him! How easy we forget the true nature of vocation—the fulfillment of God's eternal plans.

Spirit of Revolt

This rebellion against God's will expresses itself in many different ways: we become jealous, develop inferiority complexes, or inflict on others our anger, moodiness, revenge, or despondency. Envy invades the mind of a person when he sees that another succeeds where he had failed. Why are these others the popular ones, able to lead the conversation with witty remarks? The family next door has none of his troubles, and yet they never thank God for their benefits, while his home is plagued with sickness and doctor bills despite many prayers! From the seed of envy there grow the tendrils of discontent: "Would that I could be that other person, rather than the person God has made me!" As this vine wraps itself around the soul, the deadening effects of inferiority benumb the spirit: "If I were that other person, then I could do so much. But as it is, I fail so often, so what's the use of even trying?"

To us, as to Jeremia, God is saying at each moment of the day, but especially at the moment of prayer and Holy Communion: "Have no fear . . . because I am with you" (1:8). Loving obedience to God's will strikes a fire of zeal which will burn away envy and revenge and light up our dark despair and despondency. When Jeremia experienced this same frustration and inferiority at the sight of seeming failures, he confessed to God his bewilderment: "All the day I am an object of laughter; everyone mocks me" (20:7). But even as he inveighs against failure, he grows strong in his resolve.

> I say to myself, I will not mention him,
>   I will speak in his name no more.
> But then it becomes like fire burning in my heart,
>   imprisoned in my bones;
> I grow weary holding it in,
>   I cannot endure it (20:9).

Reactions of anger, moodiness or revenge are actually manifestations of a hidden revolt against God's providence. Like a small child unable to control the actions of grown-ups, we stamp our feet and pout in a corner. Once again our actions are speaking to God, louder than any words: "Why didn't you arrange it differently? It is all your fault." Jeremia draws his strength from the reassuring promise of God: "When the time comes, you will fully understand" (30:24). These words of God are enough for any man of faith. Like a symphonic theme repeated lightly in times of joy, ponderously in moments of sorrow, Jeremia hears God saying to him: "I am with you ... to deliver you" (30:11). As if stating the impossible, God exclaims:

> If the heavens on high can be measured,
> or the foundations below the earth be sounded,
> Then will I cast off the whole race of Israel
> because of all they have done, says the Lord (31:37).

The saints have understood God's plan. Often, when St. Paul of the Cross met with trouble and contradiction, he doffed his little skull cap, bowed his head, and whispered: "Fiat voluntas tua" (Thy will be done).

Kneeling in Gethsemani

These words of St. Paul of the Cross remind us at once of a Gethsemani where the souls of God's saints often knelt in dark desolation. Jeremia is often found, alone with God in prayer, talking about himself and hearing God's answer. Here we find him expressing the doubts and difficulties disturbing his life. As we read the record of his interior trials, we feel how much like ourselves is this holy man of God.

In his great grief over constant failure and in his inability to shake the people loose from their sinful habits, he bemoans:

> Oh, that my head were a spring of water,
> my eyes a fountain of tears,
> That I might weep day and night

> over the slain of the daughter of my people!
> Would I had in the desert
> a travelers' lodge!
> That I might leave my people
> and depart from them (8:23-9:1).

Like us he wanted to run away from it all. Alone with God, he pours out his anguish:

> Remember me, Lord, visit me,
> and avenge me on my persecutors. . . .
> Under the weight of your hand I sat alone
> because you filled me with indignation.
> Why is pain continuous,
> my wound incurable, refusing to be healed?
> You have indeed become for me a treacherous brook,
> whose water do not abide (15:15-18).

In these words we can sense the clash and tension within his soul. Jeremia is close to blasphemy, when he asks if God's will is not like the waters of a treacherous stream. Long ago he had abandoned himself to God's demands; that surrender to God is now leading him down a dried up river bed, with a searing sweep of sand on every side. The desert will swallow him as it did the water.

God's only answer is:

> Though they fight against you,
> they shall not prevail,
> For I am with you,
> to deliver and rescue you, says the Lord (15:20).

A Tree Planted near the Water

To us, at times, God gives no other answer than: "I am with you." One word from God creates light and beauty. Even if the interior of our soul revolts, and we find ourselves sitting alone under the mighty demands of God's will, still we must trust. Only in trust will we find peace.

God has left us the divinely inspired message of Jeremia to remind us that struggle should not surprise us. There is never victory without pain. Temptation to revolt is not sin if we quell the rebellion. The only way to react is to bow our head and whisper: "Thy will be done." Jeremia expresses it very beautifully:

> Blessed is the man who trusts in the Lord
>   whose hope is the Lord.
> He is like a tree planted beside the waters
>   that stretches out its boots to the stream;
> It fears not the heat when it comes,
>   its leaves stay green;
> In the year of drought it shows no distress,
>   but still bears fruit (17:7-8).

Even if the blight of desert dryness surrounds our life, Jeremia tells us to sink our roots deep in the will of God. The heat of the scorching sun may bear down upon us; the blasts of desert heat may blow upon us. But our lives, like the leaves, "stay green." Living with God, the soul drinks in the life-giving strength of God's grace and never ceases to bear fruit.

Raise a Peal of Gladness

It was the same with Jeremia. His life of many failures leads to a glorious finale. He never realized it while he lived. We who can read the last chapter of his life know it to be true. In the midst of his book we find the magnificent chapter thirty-one where the prophet speaks so intimately of the love of God that his words slip beyond the border dividing the Old Testament from the New and belong to the Incarnate Word whose life revealed the excelling love of God.

Jeremia is a shadow cast by Christ upon the ages before

His birth at Bethlehem. The light responsible for this shadow was God's will. As the luminous brightness of this divine light fell upon Christ, the inevitable result was a dark shadow of obscurity. The noonday sun throws the heaviest shade. Men without faith could not see the light of God's will but only the darkness of seeming failure. They ridiculed Christ for His "weakness" and "foolishness" (1 Cor 1:17-18). He was a scandal to these wise and powerful people. Yet never did Jesus waver from what He clearly knew to be the will of His heavenly Father. Struggle against temptation racked His soul in Gethsemani, but deep within that soul always lay the peace of surrender. Never did a moment of hesitation compromise His heroic consecration; from all eternity He had foreseen and embraced this vocation to humiliating death. However, was it really death? Yes, it was, since His human soul was torn from His body by scourges and nails. At the same time this death was life, since it was on the cross that His life of loving consecration to His eternal Father expressed itself most vigorously.

The portrait of no other Old Testament prophet is better suited for Christ than Jeremia. We are tempted to think that the Second Person of the Trinity could have stepped into that external form or portrait, animated it with His divine life, and begun His ministry. No, not quite! There is someone else, still more capable of preparing the human nature of Jesus Christ, someone else who was called to live in the greater obscurity of Nazareth and to give up the dream of all women of her race, the dream of being the mother of the Savior. Her *fiat* to God's will continued even to the sacrifice more heroic than the renouncing of motherhood, for she abdicated her mother's rights in handing Christ over to death upon the cross. But next to the hidden maid of Nazareth ranks Jeremia. In this prophet, total consecration

to God's will is in reality the fulness of love. His failures
are not the result of placid inactivity. He struggles and
fights. With violence to his natural inclination, he stands
before jeering crowds and temporizing kings, the mobs and
the Pilates of his own day. As in the case of Christ's death,
Jeremia's too is a burst of life, a flaming torch of love.
Jeremia's fire of love is fed by the wood of His cross of
suffering. His cross can never be consumed, for the life of
Jeremia "stands forever" in the Bible as the word of God
(Is 40:8). The cross of Calvary has at its center the broken
heart of the Son of God, pouring out its love. At the center
of the book of Jeremia is chapter thirty-one where the prophet's heart breaks, not in death but in ecstatic love.

At first, these words of the prophet fall on deaf ears;
their reception is the dull thud of a ball hitting a pad of
stuffed wool. The prophet's death brings his message to life
and it begins to be clearly understood. Like Christ, Jeremia,
too, must die before his message from God can make sense.

> With age-old love I have loved you;
>   so I have kept my mercy toward you....
> Carrying your festive tambourines,
>   you shall go forth dancing with the merrymakers....
> Shout with joy for Jacob,
>   exult at the head of the nations;
>   proclaim your praise and say:
> The Lord has delivered his people....
> They departed in tears,
>   but I will console them and guide them;
> I will lead them to brooks of water,
>   on a level road, so that none shall stumble....
> Cease your cries of mourning,
>   wipe the tears from your eyes.
> The sorrow you have shown shall have its reward....
> My heart stirs for him,
>   I must show him mercy, says the Lord (31:3-20).

At the close of his life Jeremia could ask of God, not for his own sake since he already knew the answer, but for our sake:

Ah! must—
Designer infinite!—
Ah! must Thou char the wood ere Thou canst limn with it?

The Law of Love

Jeremia concludes his "gospel message" of divine love with the assurance: "I will place my law within them, and write it upon their hearts; I will be their God, and they shall be my people" (31:33). What God demands is an interior covenant of love. He will be satisfied only when charity is as personal as our heart's deepest thoughts. Each new seeming failure in the following of God's will should convince us that God does not want something outside of us so much as He wants something within. He wants a gift of that part of our being which we call "I myself." As our Lord said to Sister Josefa Menendez: "I have no need of your strength, but I do need your surrender." If love produces the trust of blind obedience, then God can write the law of His love upon our heart. "I will be their God, and they shall be My people." We do not send good works or mighty accomplishments as ambassadors. We come ourselves.

Jeremia learned the lesson of success by the way of failure. Only when the externals crumbled and fell apart so that nothing remained but his heart, did he realize that, really, his heart was what God wanted. Though his life was surrounded by desert dryness, his heart had sunk its roots deep in the divine will. His message, which became his very life, has never ceased to bear fruit. As each generation of Jews and Christians read the book of the prophet of Anathoth, they can hear Jeremia speaking to them in person. He is saying:

Seek that good for which God has set you apart and has consecrated you from all eternity. Act with zeal and energy. But most of all equip yourself with a heart completely surrendered to God. This surrender may not bring the consolation of conquering nations and kingdoms, but it actually provides a more heroic opportunity—the conquest of yourself. Once God possesses your heart, He can write the law of His love upon it. "The sorrow shall have its rewards." God will give you something greater than a universe of wonders. He will give you the wonder of wonders, Himself. "I will be their God."

CHAPTER 5

FIRST ISAIA AND THE EMMANUEL PROPHECY

To LISTEN to Is 7:14 is like standing beside "the waters of Siloe." Isaia reminded his audience of those silent, mysterious waters, in the same context and in almost the same breath that he pronounced the "Emmanuel Prophecy." In chapter 8, verse 6, we read:

> ...These people have spurned
> The waters of Siloe, that flow gently, ...
> Yet, his outspread wings shall fill the breadth
> of your land, Emmanuel (8:6-8).

The clear, fresh waters of Siloe are an overflow from the spring of Gihon, in the Kidron valley, on the east side of Jerusalem. These shallow waters move so silently and so unperturbedly, that no motion can be seen, no ripple heard. Its gentle current can only be felt against the legs of someone standing within its stream. Isaia, in effect, was admitting that his prophecy of 7:14 was just as mysterious at the silent waters of Siloe, but that each contained within its gentle flow that name of salvation, *Emmanuel,* which means *God with us.* How fitting, then, that the Emmanuel prophecy reach its fulfillment when a saintly girl was alone, gently wrapped in silent prayer! We are tempted to think that the silent whisper of God's words in Is 7:14 has been shouted down by the long, loud succession of one interpretation upon another. Hölscher put it succinctly: "So viel Köpfe, so viel Meinungen!"—"as many heads, so many opinions!" Steinmann added his own "Amen!" when he wrote: "On the sense of each line of this celebrated text, the grandest confusion reigns among critics." A new exegete cannot restrain that discouraging lament: "Why try? My effort will simply mean another opinion to be itemized, or, worse still, another head to be lopped off!" True, no single attempt will ever satisfy everyone, but repeated efforts at least serve the purpose of keeping these gentle waters of Is 7:14 from running unnoticed and thus believers are introduced again and again into the presence of *Emmanuel, God with us.*

In this present study we seek to identify the Mother of Emmanuel in Is 7:14. To do this, however, we must direct most of our attention to her royal son. The *Almah* (for thus she is called in the Hebrew text of Is 7:14) stands silently at His side. Her entire life is absorbed into the life and work of her son, just as he before his birth had been hidden within her. To know the mother we must first become acquainted with her son, but at once we are caught in a series of circles. Each sweeps us onward to a deeper knowledge of the other.

Is 7:14 is one of the earliest biblical texts calling attention to the mother of the Lord's Anointed. At the same time, as Jean Steinmann has remarked, "in this oracle there are found the essentials of all the other messianic ideas, later to be developed by Isaia." One of the safest ways, therefore, to unravel the ideas tightly entwined in the words of 7:14 is to study the main doctrinal trends woven into the sixty-six chapters of the book of Isaia.

Our plan, consequently, calls first of all for an aerial view of the general lines of thought stretching through the entire expanse of the book of Isaia. After that quick survey, we will narrow our sights to chapters seven to twelve, usually called "The Book of Emmanuel." Only with this general and specific background shall we advance any opinion on God's thought behind the words of 7:14 and seek to identify the Mother of Emmanuel in the famous prophecy:

> Therefore the Lord himself will give you this sign:
> the maiden (*ha 'alma*) shall be with child,
> and bear a son,
> and name him Emmanuel.

In the Book of Emmanuel (Is 7-12) there is a line addressed by Isaia to King Achaz, which haunts every sermon of the Prophet and which echoes in the words of his disciples. It provides the most important clue to the mystery of 7:14.

> Unless your faith is firm
> You shall not be firm (7:9b).

ISAIA, PROPHET OF DIVINE FAITH

Faith was certainly the watchword of Isaia. It endowed the prophet with a vision so keenly supernatural that things were constantly being turned inside out and viewed in their deepest point of existence. Isaia was never fooled by a glitter of splendor on the outside. He searched deep to the very heart; sham appearance of greatness melted before his eyes, and he saw each man or each event in their naked truthfulness. As we read his sermons, we sometimes suspect him of marshaling a series of contrasting ideas just for literary effect. But no! Faith alway acts that way. It pulls down the great and lifts up the poor, as the Mother of Emmanuel was later to sing in her *Magnificat.*

Isaia of Jerusalem

There are many examples of how Isaia's strong faith overturned earthly standards of greatness. He ridiculed King Achaz for playing the part of a manly king (3:1-12). As he watched Achaz making decisions quickly and acting independently, Isaia quipped:

> My people! babes are their masters,
> And women rule them (3:12).

Achaz tried to wrap his childishness in the heavy robes of royal manliness. While Isaia saw a child pretending to be a man, he took occasion to speak of a man, the "Godlike hero" and the "Father forever," who will conceal his regal might beneath a lowly appearance:

> For a child is born to us, . . .
> And the government is upon his shoulder (9:6).

The prophet's faith was truly turning things inside out, in order that nothing be hidden beneath wrapping of pretense.

Isaia made strong demands upon the faith of Achaz, demands too strong, in fact, for the wobbling king to carry. We can cite the instance of the Syro-Ephramite war. Caught within the grip of advancing, hostile armies—from the north, the combined forces of Syria and Israel; from the west, the Philistines; and from the south, the Edomites—Achaz was told by Isaia to do nothing, only to trust in God. What strength of supernatural character was needed simply to do nothing! Achaz, however, lacked the prophet's spirit of faith.

This supernatural faith had produced in Isaia the conviction that *God alone saves;* all that man can do is humbly to believe, staunchly to trust, silently to wait upon his Lord. The prophet expressed this message of *salvation through God alone* in many different ways. We will cite some of these examples, and in this way condition ourselves for the mysterious message of faith in 7:14.

Isaia found "Emmanuel," "God with us," not in the mighty waters of the Euphrates, that is, not in the colossal strength of Assyria, but in the gently flowing waters of Siloe, that is, in the divine promises to little Juda (8:5-8). If God alone saves, then, as Isaia warned in ch. 8:

> Plan a plan, it shall come to nought;
> Speak a word, it shall not stand!
> Because God is with us—Emmanuel (8:10).

In ch. 9 he proclaimed that only "those who dwell in a land of deep darkness" shall see "a great light"; in ch. 11, the life of the new David is said to spring from the seeming dead root of Jesse, hidden beneath the ground. Light out of darkness, life out of death—such was his mysterious teaching of faith.

Because this call for heroic faith was rejected by his hearers, Isaia realized that his preaching was intended by God for future generations of believers. God had already given notice in the prophet's inaugural vision that the people of his times would:

> Keep on hearing, but understand not;
> And keep on seeing, but know not! (6:9).

Deutero-Isaia

In order to prepare for the future, Isaia disclosed: "I will bind up my testimony, and seal my teaching in the heart of

my disciples" (8:16). One of the greatest of these disciples
was a prophet of the Babylonian exile, whose sermons of
golden oratory were to be attached to the scroll containing
the preaching of his master. Those sermons now constitute
chapter 40-55 of the present book of Isaia. Not only
were his words absorbed into the book of his master,
but even his name was forgotten and he is known to us as
Second Isaia or Deutero-Isaia. No one can help us more in
understanding the mysterious message of faith in 7:14 than
this most perfect of Isaia's disciples.

Pulsating energetically within the message of Deutero-
Isaia is the power of faith to turn things inside out. Because
there is nothing impulsive about his way of speaking—actually, he uses the tools of language most adroitly—his
words are all the more forceful. He exclaimed on one
occasion:

> Bring forth the people who are blind, yet have eyes,
> And are deaf, yet have ears (43:8).

In one sense, God's servants are blind, because they have
no eyes to behold despairingly the bleak picture of Palestine,
devastated and abandoned, or the oppressive scene of the
exiles, scattered in the work areas of Babylon. But God's
children, though blind, have eyes of faith by which they
can look deep into the *meaning* of sorrow and suffering.
They must be blind and deaf to human ways of happiness,
if they are to see the redemptive purpose of God and to hear
His call of salvation. Again, light shines within darkness,
life bursts from death.

Deutero-Isaia enunciated his message of faith in a figure of
speech which is of special help in understanding 7:14. He
pictured Israel, no longer a driven victim of foreign oppression, no longer widowed and deprived of children. Israel,
instead, appeared as a joyful mother, looking with amaze-

ment at the fullness of her messianic glory. With arms outstretched she cries with astonishment:

> Who can have borne me these (children)?
> I am bereaved and barren, exiled and banished,
> So these—who can have reared them?
> See! I have been left alone,
> So these—whence can they have come? (49:21).

The same faith which gave sight to the blind now enabled the barren and the lonely to produce life. That the Jewish commonwealth could be re-created out of the broken, charred and scattered pieces of the Babylonian exiles intrigued Deutero-Isaia and absorbed his thought. From the prospects of such a renewal he constructed his theology of creation. He reasoned that if God can create Israel out of the chaos of the exile, then He must have been powerful enough to create the universe "in the beginning." In each case the doctrinal theme of his master and namesake comes clearly to the surface: *only God can save,* and He does so in the most secret of ways.

On many occasions Deutero-Isaia became ecstatic at the thought of Israel's recreation. And here we notice a concatenation of ideas with 7:14. Especially at the beginning of ch. 54 he described the new birth of Israel with ideas drawn from the marvelous births of sacred history, from Isaac, Samson and Samuel, who were born of barren women:

> Sing, O barren one, you who have borne no children;
> Break into singing, and cry aloud, you who have not travailed!
> For more are the children of her that is desolate
> Than the children of her that is married (54:1).

No virgin birth is predicted in ch. 54. In fact, Deutero-Isaia seems to be moving in the traditions of Osee and Jeremia, which portrayed Israel as the spouse of God. In that same ch. 54 Israel is addressed: "Your husband is your

Maker" (54:5). But added to the note of personal love, so evident in the Yahweh-Spouse theme of Osee and Jeremia, is the Isaian emphasis upon a new family of children created by God alone. This stress is but a repetition of the familiar doctrine: *only God saves,* and to convince man of this doctrine, God will save in the most undreamed-of ways, almost as if he were creating children out of nothing.

Here, then, is the general Isaian background for appreciating 7:14. Isaia's entire message of salvation can be summarized in the statement: only God saves, and to prove it, he saves the most baffling and in the most marvelous of ways. To teach that the rebirth of the Jewish commonwealth will be due, not to human merit, but solely to God's powerful love, Deutero-Isaia used the biblical metaphor of a barren woman's giving birth to a large family. The same notion of a woman's giving birth is found in the mysterious text of 7:14. Again it has the same general connotation: God alone saves, in the most marvelous of ways. Deutero-Isaia takes us no further. Whether or not the earlier prophet, "First Isaia," had already taken the step of proposing a "virgin-birth" awaits further investigation. But he certainly proposes a message of salvation which rests upon faith.

> Unless your faith is firm
> You shall not be firm (7:9b).

Isaia, like Moses, rejoiced to see the messianic day, because nowhere will he find this surrender of faith more heroically present than in the future Emmanuel and in his holy Mother.

THE DOCTRINE OF FAITH IN THE
BOOK OF EMMANUEL

An accurate exegesis of 7:14 requires something more than the general background of Isaia and Deutero-Isaia. The theme of salvation through God alone, the call for faith, the penchant for literary contrast—these Isaian characteristics will show up in a *very specific* way in the Book of Emmanuel (ch. 7-12). This book is one of the earliest collections of the prophet's preaching; it must now be examined more closely, if we are to identify the Mother of Emmanuel.

Political Crisis

The Book of Emmanuel, with its message of faith, is intricately involved in the politics of the year 736 B.C. The secretary or redactor, who prepared the biographical sketch of ch. 7, sensed the need of some kind of historical introduction. He opened the section, therefore, with ideas borrowed from the Fourth Book of Kings (16:5-9). It was the time of the Syro-Ephramite league, when a coalition had been formed against Assyria by Phacee, King of Israel (737-732), and Rasin, King of Damascus (740-732). Juda, at first under King Jotham (740-736) and soon afterward under the young twenty-year-old King Achaz (736-716), chose neutrality (4 Kgs 15:37; 16:5f). As Phacee and Rasin braced themselves for the inevitable Assyrian invasion from the north, they wanted no neutral, and perhaps hostile power to the south. They decided to whip Juda into line with them. In their war against Juda, they burned cities, slaughtered inhabitants, deported naked men and women (cf. 2 Par 28). Once they captured Jerusalem, they were determined to place an Israelite landowner from Transjordan upon the Davidic throne.

Jerusalem was tightening her defenses for the siege. Everyone was fearful; "the heart of the people," as Isaia remarked, "shook as the trees of the forest shake before the wind" (7:2). As the king darted from one part of the city to another, the prophet Isaia was told by God: "Go out now to meet Achaz." Isaia found the king "on the highway to the fuller's field," inspecting the water-supply of the capital. The prophet was accompained by a very young son, Shear Yashub (= "a remnant will return"). Isaia tried to reassure the frightened king. It was unreasonable, the prophet said, to panic and to "be afraid . . . because of these two tails of smoking firebrands" (7:4). These words of Isaia likened the kings of Israel and Damascus to flaming torches which have almost destroyed themselves. The prophet offered a miraculous "sign" that God would preserve the Davidic dynasty and save His people. But before Achaz could ever detect the hand of God in such a sign, the king had need of faith. The prophet, therefore, addressed the king very solemnly:

> Unless your faith be firm,
> You shall not be firm (Is 7:9b).

Achaz, on his part, had already abandoned his faith. He was determined not to entrust the security of his throne to Yahweh, the God of Israel. He had, in fact, openly apostasized, by sacrificing his first-born infant son to the Canaanite gods (4 Kgs 16:3; 2 Par 28:3). By killing and burning the heir-apparent, Achaz had entreated the god Moloch for the continuity of his dynasty. An apostate from the God of the chosen people, Achaz had nowhere to turn, except to the King of Assyria.

The king replied to Isaia, however, with pompous religiosity. Choosing his words from the sacred scroll of Deuteronomy, he announced: "I will not test the Lord by asking" for a sign (Is 7:12; cf. Deut 6:16). Isaia replied with the Emmanuel prophecy of 7:14.

Rejection of Achaz

We will sidestep the Emmanuel prophecy and examine another idea, already hinted at, which is basic for understanding this prophecy and for recognizing the mother of Emmanuel. Put simply, it is this: Achaz, in repudiating faith in Yahweh, tore to shreds his only title to the throne. The mother of Emmanuel, who will return that title to the true Son of David, by contrast with Achaz, must be a maiden of heroic faith.

A legitimate title to the Judean throne had to be traced not only through blood descent to King David, but also through divine promise back to God. The *divine* right to the throne derived from the oracle of the prophet Nathan, in which God had said to David and to all his descendants:

> I will be a father to him,
>   and he a son to me;
> If he acts wickedly I will chastise him
>   with the rod men use,
>   with blows the sons of men give.
> But my covenant-love shall not be taken from him. . . .
>   your throne is set firm forever (2 Sam 7:14-16).

Achaz, abandoning faith, cast off his divine "sonship"; he no longer occupied the privileged place of being God's special representative over the chosen people. He was no longer king! Just as the vocation of the Israelite nation was a call to faith in Yahweh's promise to redeem, likewise, the Davidic royalty rested on the same faith. Only one detail was added: the king would have a prominent place in this divine work of salvation. In appealing to Assyria rather than accepting Isaia's advice of trust in Yahweh, Achaz was destroying himself. Isaia, whose eyes pierced to the inner truth of things, saw the end of Davidic rule. In the verses following 7:14, the prophet described the royal dynasty, covered with darkness and oblivion.

Isaia predicted the dreadful invasion of Judean territory by Assyria, the colossal power in which Achaz trusted.

Assyria's policy, like that of Communist Russia today, was calculated to inject agonizing fear and trembling weakness into every nation. When Tiglath-Pileser III conquered Syria in 732 and thus ended the Syro-Ephramite threat, the buildings of Damascus were looted and demolished, the chief men were executed and their heads collected for war trophies, the populace terrorized before being bundled together for deportation, the king burned alive on a funeral pyre before the temporary throne of the Assyrian monarch.

Isaia saw this same force storming into Juda. He said sternly about Achaz and the house of David:

> Behold! the Lord raises against them
> The waters of the River, great and mighty,
> Even the king of Assyria. . . .
> It shall rise above all its channels, . . .
> It shall pass into Juda,
> And flood it all throughout (Is 8:7-8a).

Isaia concluded this prophecy with the words:

> It shall spread its wings the full width
> of your land, Emmanuel (8:8b).

Again, we meet the mystery of Isaia's preaching. In the midst of such devastation there would be the presence of *Emmanuel, God with us.* Emmanuel in this case seems to be Ezechia, the son and heir of Achaz, during whose reign Juda was swept with the roaring waters of destruction (cf. Is 10:5ff) but in the end miraculously delivered (cf. Is 36-37). Emmanuel, however, is not only the name of the royal heir; it is also a symbolic message of faith. Out of this destruction will come salvation.

The Messianic King

At his birth and during his lifetime Emmanuel would look out upon cities, smashed and deserted, upon farmlands, running wild with weeds. The surviving inhabitants would be forced to follow an austere, pastoral existence. Their food, according to Isaia, would be "thick milk and honey," that is, the natural products of an uncultivated land, the food of wandering nomads. Very soon after his birth—or, to use the language of Isaia, "before the child knows how to refuse the bad and to choose the good" (7:16)—the two kingdoms of the north would be wasteland. Eventually, that same flood of destruction would sweep into Juda. Again, to quote Isaia:

> Thick milk and honey will be the food of everyone
> who is left in the midst of the land (7:22).

Within all this murky darkness, however, light would shine.

> It shall spread its wings
> The full length of your land, Emmanuel (8:8b).

At this point, Isaia passed from the contemporary scene around him and peered into the distant future. Up till this time, as Coppens has remarked, "messianism had been a program for the encumbent king." At each coronation, the oracle of Nathan to King David was chanted. The people sang enthronization hymns like Pss 2 and 109 (110), which repeated God's promise first spoken by Nathan. Little did the assembly know, but that *this new* king may be the chosen one to achieve the divine promises of a prosperous God-fearing nation. Now, in the preaching of Isaia, God made it clear that the nation must wait through a long stretch of darkness (cf. Is 30:15). During this period of trial, the country was to be engulfed in chaos of tribulation (Is 9:8 —10:34). The root of David was to remain buried and forgotten. But in the time to come, as formerly at the creation of the universe, the spirit of God would rest upon the land

and would create light and beauty. At the same time this same divine spirit would bring new life from the root of Jesse; the small, tender sprout, the son of David, would be born of a mother, hidden and unknown. From such an obscure origin the child would rise to power over a paradise of idyllic peace (Is 11:1-9).

A similar transition from dense darkness to beaming light, from death to life, appears in Is 9:1-7. Heralding the glorious era of prosperity and justice is the coronation of a Davidic King, who will be endowed with the wisdom of Solomon, the bravery of David, the religious virtues of Moses and of the Patriarchs. Although many phases of this section were borrowed by Isaia from the Hebrew ritual for the coronation of a king, still the general context sweeps us far off into the future messianic age, beyond the darkness of the moment to the dawn of new light.

Isaia, in the Book of Emmanuel, has silently slipped from the contemporary scene into the remote future. No longer seeing the figures of Achaz' son and the boy's mother, he was looking at the future Emmanuel and His Mother. The most prominent feature of the Messias and His Queen-Mother was to be their spirit of total surrender to God's will. In them the Israelite would find his most perfect model, and yet this very fact would make King and Mother very unique. Never will any of God's people have shown such unselfish and sinless consecration to God.

As the *perfect* representative of all God's people, they will rise above everyone. Theirs will be a pre-eminent spirit of faith. This spirit might be called the "spirit of virginity" —a strong, devoted, single-minded consecration to God. In the Book of Emmanuel as in the entire book of Isaia, we find enunciated not a virgin-birth but rather this virginal spirit of faith. Seeing such holiness in Emmanuel and in His Mother, people will spontaneously exclaim: *God is with us.*

EMMANUEL AND ALMAH OF IS 7:14

We have seen that there are two great themes treading their way through the entire book of Isaia: God alone saves; man receives salvation by humble faith. When we narrowed our sights to ch. 7-12, it was found that Achaz had thrust aside this faith when he had decided to find salvation through an appeal to Assyria. Because of this apostasy, a sentence of doom was leveled upon him and upon the House of David. Mysteriously enough, Emmanuel was to be present in the midst of this destruction. But again, only faith could assure anyone that destruction and lowliness held within themselves *Emmanuel, God with us,* the Giver of life and peace.

These conclusions are quite certain, and in the light of them we now endeavor to study more closely the text of 7:14. We have already insinuated the interpretation which, we think, best agrees with the total context. Stated very briefly it is this. The Emmanuel of 7:14 is an heir to the Davidic throne to be born to Achaz, most probably the future King Ezechia. The *Almah* is Achaz' new bride. Later as Queen-Mother, she would exercise a strong influence over state policies. Ezechia and his mother, Abia, however, seemed to fade away and upon their faces there appeared the likenesses of the future Son of David and of His Mother. In the *literal sense,* accordingly, there are present by prophetic *compenetration* both Ezechia and his mother, as well as Jesus and His saintly Mother Mary. The sign of Achaz does not consist so much in the birth of the Davidic heir as in other events associated with the child. These other events were a sign to Achaz that *only God saves.* How marvelously will this sign of *salvation through God alone* reappear in Jesus and His Mother! From the Isaian point of view, this sign will be manifested in them through their humble trust in God and through their total surrender to God's will. From the New Testament viewpoint, this sign will show up ever more wonderously in the virgin-birth.

No single interpretation of 7:14 will ever satisfy everyone, and this for many reasons. First, we must keep in mind that exegesis begins with a damaged text. Almost every line of the Hebrew text needs correction, and the poor condition of the ancient Greek Septuagint provides little assistance. Second, chapter 7 did not come directly from Isaia. It is the work of a redactor or collector who reshuffled oracles and events to accord with his own private plan. Notice the repeated introductions, always a mark that we are dealing not with a continuous narrative but with an assembly of parts: "*once more* the Lord spoke" (7:10); "*Then* said the Lord" (8:1); "*Once more* the Lord spoke" (8:5); "*Thus* spoke the Lord" (8:11).

In order to regain Isaia's point of view, some interpreters rearrange the order of verses; Feuillet, for instance, places the first part of 7:14 at the very end of the chapter. Such manipulations always risk being subjective. After all, it is our present Bible which is the ancient inspired document, and therefore we must give serious consideration to the redactor's point of view.

The redactor has not made our job easy. Unwittingly he has strewn difficulties in our way. He has mixed plural and singular verbs. He was not consistent in naming the sign: first, it is *Emmanuel,* but toward the end of ch. 8, *Isaia's children* are called "signs and symbols." In 7:14 and 8:8 he used the word Emmanuel of a person; in 8:10, of God's power to save. The literary and textual links in the chain of thought are so weak, that no explanation will be strong enough to hold the consent of all.

We have said the Emmanuel and the Almah of 7:14 refer directly and immediately to Ezechia and his mother Abia. Because 7:14 is such a battleground of controversy, this opinion must be defended!

(A) The first reason, already developed in the preceding section is the setting of Is 7-12. Unless it can be proven otherwise, each verse of these chapters must be considered integral parts of the general thought-progression. In the Book of Emmanuel the principal plot portrays Achaz frantic about the security of his throne. All Jerusalem, we are told, is trembling "as the trees of the forest shake before the wind" (7:2). We know from the Fourth Book of Kings that Achaz has even proceeded to the frightful excess of sacrificing his first-born infant son to Moloch, god of fertility. So tense was the atmosphere of 7:14.

Isaia not only solemnly promised an heir to Achaz, but also declared that this young son would be a *sign* to the apostate king that he should have trusted only in Yahweh. The sign, therefore, consisted not just in the birth of a royal successor. Circumstances attending the boy's life would feature even more largely in the sign. The child would witness the hectic foolishness of Achaz' policy. The Syro-Ephramite league would crumble very soon under Assyrian attack (734-732) and not long afterward, before the child reached full maturity, Samaria would be leveled to the ground (722-721 B.C.). This same child would even live to see an Assyrian expedition launched against Juda. This Assyrian invasion during Ezechia's reign is actually described in the book of Emmanuel (10:5-19, 24-34).

Achaz' appeal to Assyria was thus proven to be wholly unnecessary, even deadly. But the flood waters of Assyria, sweeping irresistibly into Juda, would also wash the country clean and thus prepare for the golden Messianic age of *God with us.*

The general context of ch. 7-12 gives to 7:14 an urgent concern over royal succession along with the answer that security was to be achieved by faith in God's power to save.

(B) Still another argument that Emmanuel is a future son of Achaz, and *"Almah"* a new bride of the king, is the *stylistic formula* employed in 7:14. If Isaia created the language for this one occasion, then there would be better reason to press a special meaning from each word and possibly to arrive at a virgin birth prophecy. If, on the other hand, he makes use of a familiar, set formula, which like a proverb can fit many different occasions, then his words are not to be searched so literally for each and every shade of meaning.

The Hebrew formulary of Is 7:14 occurs elsewhere in the Bible. In fact, it is identical with the angelic words announcing the birth of Ismael. The angel said to Agar, one of Abraham's secondary wives:

> Behold, you have conceived (Hebrew *hara*) and you shall
> bear a son;
> You shall call his name Ismael (Gen 16:11).

Twice in the Samson story does the first part of the same formula occur:

> Behold, you will conceive (Hebrew: *hara*) and you shall
> bear a son (Jgs 13:5, 7).

After Samson's birth the stylistic phrase is slightly modified to fit the laws of Hebrew prose, and we read:

> And the woman bore a son,
> and she called his name Samson (Jgs 13:24).

This same formula reappears in the Annunciation scenes of St. Luke's gospel.

Isaia adds to the common biblical formula the words *Almah* and *Emmanuel*. *Emmanuel* rings symbolically like the name Ismael, given to Agar's son. Both names end with *El,* the Hebrew word for God. Isaia chose a name symbolic of his doctrinal theme and proceeded in ch. 8 to explain its meaning (8:8,10). *God is with us* in the devastating events accompanying the child's life.

Although *Emmanuel* is found nowhere in the Hebrew Bible outside of Isaia, *Almah* occurs possibly eight times. *Almah* would not be a difficult word to explain, had it not been for the Septuagint and the Christian interpretations of Is. 7:14. It is generally agreed that the Hebrew word *"almah"* designates a maiden of marriageable age. Even though the technical word for virgin is *betula,* nonetheless, an *almah* is a maiden not yet married, and therefore presumably (but not necessarily) a virgin. But the word *almah* says nothing directly about virginity. Its whole meaning centers on a girl who is attractive to young men and ready for marriage (cf. Prov 30:19). In some ways, we might compare *almah* to the modern word "young lady"—a girl mature enough for marriage, presumably a virgin, but virginity remains beyond the thought-range of the word.

It is likely that Ugaritic (Canaanite) literature influenced Isaia to insert *almah* into the biblical formula for birth-announcements. The annunciation formula plus *almah* has been found in the Ugaritic text, "The Wedding of Nikkal and the Moon God." The verse reads:

> Behold, an *almah* shall bear a son.

Also very noticable in Ugaritic myths, like the Danal cycle, is another feature observable in Is 7: anxious concern over

dynastic succession. Without discussing the Ugaritic material
at length, we will note in passing: the words of the annunciation formula were most probably a *liturgical,* and certainly
a *set* phrase at Ugarit: there is not the least hint of a virgin
birth.

In fact, we fully agree with Gerhard Delling that the idea
of a virgin birth would never have been borrowed by Isaia
from pagan sources. The idea, no matter what its origin,
would have been repellent to Isaia. Because of pagan theol-
ogies of his time, a virgin conceiving by the power of
Yahweh could have meant nothing else to Isaia than carnal
union between Yahweh and a divine goddess. The Israelites
borrowed words and stories from their neighbors, but they
violently rejected pagan theology.

Both within and without the Bible the stylistic formula of
7:14 presages a birth of special religious significance, but
not at all a virgin birth. Neither Agar nor Manue, the
mothers of Ismael and Samson, conceived virginally, but their
children were to perform a special role in God's plan of
salvation. Neither does the phrase, "almah conceiving,"
in any way imply a virgin-birth. Rebecca is called an *almah*
before marriage. Isaac could have said of her before their
marriage what Isaia spoke in Is. 7:14: "Behold the almah
will conceive and she will bear a son." Finally, the statement
that the *almah* will name the child in no way even hints that
the boy is without a human father and therefore divine. We
are dealing with a stylistic formula. Both Agar and Manue
are said to have named their child. Furthermore, the Hebrew
reading of 7:14, "*she* shall name him," reads differently in
the Greek version (manuscripts B, A) and in the Isaia
scroll found at Qumran (1Q Is^a).

The stylistic formula of 7:14, therefore, was too commonly used, for it to throw any mystic aura around the

prophecy or for it to lift the prophecy out of the general context. Knowing as we do the plot and the actors of the Book of Emmanuel, we must conclude that this child is a son and heir of King Achaz and that the *almah* is Achaz' new wife. There is, indeed, a messianic role given to Emmanuel and the *Almah,* but not because of the language used in 7:14.

(C) Besides the arguments of stylistic formula, there is still another reason why Isaia would refer to the mother of the next king. This reason has been greatly responsible for originating the formula here employed by Isaia. We are referring to the honor paid by the royal court of Jerusalem to the queen-mother, called the *gᵉbira.* This subject has been handled at length in other sources and so we will omit many historical details on the origin and development of this office of Queen-Mother.

The Mosaic religion, as we well know, tolerated a royal harem. Even David, as he rose in importance, took many wives to himself. These wives were often just ornamental signs of dignity and affluence. Even though the king surrounded himself with a large number of wives, he could, of course, have only *one* mother, who became the *gᵉbira* of the court. The king's wives, even his favorites, remained within the enclosure of the harem and seldom swayed policies of state; the queen-mother was liberated from the strict seclusion of the harem and appeared publicly at royal functions.

The queen-mother possessed great power and privileges, not only because she alone of all the former king's wives had given birth to the heir and successor, but also because of the peculiar nature of the Judean royalty. The two Hebrew states of Juda and Israel developed along different traditions. The northern state of Israel remained more faithful to the older idea, found in the Book of Judges. In *Judges* we find that leadership was not passed down from father to son but was a charismatic office, given immediately by God. In the northern kingdom of Israel, therefore, a national decline made the people think that the divine spirit had withdrawn from the king. Military revolts swept away the incumbent royal family in a tide of blood.

In Juda to the south, kings were assassinated, but the throne always remained within the Davidic family. The prophet Nathan had promised that through the Davidic king God would fulfill the promises made to the patriarchs and to Moses. Not only did the nation feel that its national well-being rested with the Davidic family, but a superstitious confidence developed whereby the people felt that, despite their sins, God's word to David made the kingdom indestructible. Juda's security for the present as well as all her hopes for the future were linked to the family of David. Each new king received these royal prerogatives through his father and queen-mother.

When Isaia stood before King Achaz and spoke the Emmanuel prophecy, the prophet's hopes for the future quickly passed over the apostate king and rested with the heir and the queen-mother. The wife, who would bear the royal successor, seemed much more important than Achaz! She would also later stand beside the child as queen-mother. This same child, however, would live to see Juda swallowed up in darkness. The thought of devastation induced the mind of Isaia to leap forward into the Messianic future.

Since salvation must still come through the Davidic family, another Queen-Mother would give birth to another *Emmanuel,* who will be *God with us.* At one and the same time, Isaia beheld the present and the future Mother of Emmanuel. This "prophetic compenetration" of the present with the future brings us to the last detail in this study of 7:14.

(D) The Messianic future has already been brought to our attention by the general context of ch. 7-12. There are two other biblical texts which help us to appreciate the full, Messianic meaning of Is 7:14; two texts which likewise underline the role of the Queen-Mother. We are referring to Mich 5:2 and Gen 3:15.

Michea, a contemporary of Isaia, also spoke of a mother who was about to give birth to a Davidic heir. Again, black clouds of destruction are to be seen lowering over the mighty city of Jerusalem (Mich 4:14). In the midst of the darkness God's promises are moving toward a definitive fulfillment. Michea's vision looks both to the past and to the future, widening into an endless expanse of time. The origins of the child reach back into a past, covered with the haze of centuries, back to David some 300 years ago, to Moses over 500 years ago, to the Patriarchs at the dawn of biblical history. Time again stretches into unknown reaches as Michea looks to the future. The sorrow of the present moment will end because hidden within this sorrow is the Messianic Deliverer. The child's coming forth from the seclusion of his mother's body symbolizes the emergence of the Davidic dynasty from near extinction. Because this child will be a Davidic king, Michea spoke explicitly of his mother, the *g^ebira*.

The manner in which Michea quickly moved into the unknown future brings another Scriptural text to our attention, Gen 3:15. We ask if the Protoevangelion, like Michea, corroborates the Isaian tradition of a queen-mother closely associated with her royal son?

The Protoevangelion occurs in what is called the Yahwist or "J" tradition of the Pentateuch. This "J" tradition contains Mosaic narratives which circulated in the southern kingdom of Juda and which were redacted during a great religious reform. The reform of Ezechia bids high for this privilege of editing the Yahwist traditions. Henri Cazelles writes: "It is very possible that he (the Yahwist) has seen in the salvific maternity of Eve the Prototype of the royal maternity."

From Gen 3:15 and more clearly for Mich 5:2 we receive corroboration that Isaia quickly passed beyond Ezechia and his mother Abia to a King and Queen-Mother of the messianic future. The point of departure, however, has been the crisis which Achaz saw endangering the Davidic dynasty and the temporary solution of this crisis during the reform of Ezechia. The king and queen-mother occupied attention and held power during these days.

Is 7:14 originated during the dynastic crisis threatening Achaz and his successor. But the present danger merged into the future by a process which we call "prophetic compenetration." All three traditions—the Isaian, the Michean and the Yahwist—expected the king and his queen-mother to govern a land of Paradise. The roaring waters of the Assyrian invasion have become the cleansing and fructifying waters of tribulation, washing the world clean, and, like the four great rivers of Paradise, transforming a devastated country into a garden land of all good things (cf. Gen 2; Is 11; Mich 2:3-4a).

This habit of the present or the near future quickly slipping into distant, Messianic glory became ever more noticable with biblical writers after Isaia. Deutero-Isaia sang of the return from exile with the rapturous language of the Messianic age (Is 40-55). He called Cyrus, who freed the Jews, God's Anointed (Is 45:1). In the midst of another trial, two other prophets, Deutero-Zacharia and Daniel, predicted the end of sorrow as though heralding the final "Day of the Lord!" (Zach 9-14; Dan 7-12).

The message of Isaia can be distilled in the few, clear words:

> Unless your faith be firm,
> You shall not be firm (Is 7:9b).

Isaia gave a sign to Achaz to prove that the abandonment of faith was self-destruction. Yet, even in the roaring waters of divine anger, there would live *Emmanuel, God with us.* Surely, *only God can save* in such a mysterious way as that; only faith can detect the presence of God in chaotic destruction and exclaim: *Emmanuel.*

Even though Achaz haughtily rejected this first sign, Isaia gave him another. Yahweh would preserve the dynasty, despite the threat of the Syro-Ephramite forces, but Achaz' son and heir, Ezechia, would live through days of sorrow and darkness, brought on by his father's perfidious appeal to Assyria. Ezechia may have been fervent enough to instigate a reform, but he evidently could not be the fulfillment of God's promises.

If not immediately, then with time, Isaia realized that the true *Emmanuel* of the Davidic line would be crowned only in the distant future. Chaos would envelop a faithless society. Yet, from a root hidden deep in the ground a sprout would spring and the spirit rest upon it (Is 11). A Davidic king would be enthroned; he would be a "Wonderful Counsellor, Godlike Hero...." (Is 9). This Davidic Savior would come from obscurity and lowliness—surely a sign that *only God saves.* The figures of Ezechia and Abia have faded away; the future Emmanuel and His Mother appear in their places.

Giving birth to a royal heir and standing beside her Messianic Son, would be the *g^ebira,* His Queen-Mother. Because her Son would be born in obscurity, she would be a humble, lowly handmaid of the Lord. The faith which Achaz repudiated would be her source of pre-eminent holiness. This faith would produce a virginal spirit of desiring God and His holy will even more than the honor of giving birth to the Messias. "How will this be, since I remain a virgin?" (Lk 1:34—Kleist-Lilly tr.).

Isaia never dreamed of a holiness so exalted, of a faith so transcendent. But it was exactly this humble faith of Mary, totally surrending her to whatever God wanted, which brought the response to her lips: "Let it be done, I pray, according to his words" (Lk 1:38). "And the word was made flesh and dwelt among us" (Jn 1:14). Faith in God's word brought the sign of Isaia to a fulfillment far more magnificent than the prophet ever envisaged: *only God saves,* even to the extent of a virgin conceiving and bearing the Savior of the world.

To say that the Mother of Emmanuel is directly and immediately Abia, the mother of Ezechia, also reserves for Mary the exalted title of *g*e*bira* or Queen-Mother, actively beside her royal Son in the rule of His kingdom. To deny a virgin-birth prophecy in the strictly literal sense is not to deprive Is 7:14 of apologetical use. Is 7:14 predicts a Davidic Savior, arising out of obscurity, ruling a kingdom of happiness and peace, associating with Himself the Queen-Mother of ancient tradition. The denial of the virginal birth in 7:14, however, shifts attention from a physical miracle to a marvel still more supernatural, Mary's *virginal spirit* of sanctity.

For Isaia, and most certainly for later generations, all hopes centered on the future, messianic age. The devout Israelite longed and prayed, sometimes with agonizing desperation, that God would send the promised Emmanuel. But first, of course, there must be the sign that God alone saves—a maiden lost in obscurity and absorbed in humble faith. *The Mother of Emmanuel in Is 7:14,* begged of God by centuries of prayer, was the poorest and the most humble of God's handmaids: *Mary, the Virgin Mother of Jesus.*

CHAPTER 6 DEUTERO-ISAIA
LOOKS TO THE
NEW CREATION

THE true Israelite was forever conscious of his total dependence upon God. He had no other claim to greatness. The Hebrew people could not look back upon a distinguished blood or a racial background. When the Bible, in chapter ten of Genesis, lists the nations of the world, Israel is tucked away and almost overlooked in the general context of humanity. There is nothing fundamentally outstanding about her natural capacity or her inherited nobility which would immediately set her apart from the rest of mankind.

One of the earliest liturgical creeds in the Bible begins with this humble confession: "My father was a wandering Aramean who went down to Egpyt with a small household, and lived there as an alien" (Deut 26:5). The prophet Ezechiel energetically deflates the pretentious pride of his fellow-countrymen, by telling them: "In origin and birth you come from the land of Canaanites. Your father was an

167

Amorite, and your mother a Hittite" (Ez 16:3). Israel's glory and renown are to be attributed not to racial stock nor to earthly renown but rather to her special election by God. Ezechiel expresses this divine vocation very well: "Then I passed by you . . . I bathed you with water and washed your blood from you; and I anointed you with oil. I clothed you with embroidered robes . . . I adorned you with ornaments . . . Your beauty was perfect, because of the splendor which I had bestowed upon you" (Ez 16:6-14).

From these words of Ezechiel there can be deduced the two fundamental norms governing biblical theology and especially that part of biblical theology to be dealt with in this chapter. *First,* if we expect to appreciate the religious culture of Israel, we must never separate the children of Abraham from their ancient Near Eastern background. We are not to treat them as citizens of our modern world. A mixture of Semitic and non-Semitic blood flowed in Israelite veins. The folklore and ancient traditions, the laws and religious practices, the language and the patterns of thought came to the Hebrews by blood inheritance from their ancestors in the Fertile Crescent, for his father was an Amorite, and his mother a Hittite. *Second,* whatever greatness Israel attained, as well as her mere survival as a nation, was the work of God, personally intervening in her history. So desperately did Israel depend upon God that many times she would have died, naked and bare, weltering in her blood—as Ezechiel put it—if the divine Good Samaritan had not passed by, stopped and bandaged her wounds. With each new redemptive act, God could repeat: "I bore you up on eagle wings and brought you here to *myself . . . my special possession,* dearer to me than all other people, though all the earth is mine" (Ex 19:4-5).

This chapter investigates the development of the theology

of creation in the Old Testament, giving special attention to the contribution made by the prophet Deutero-Isaia. This "Great Unknown," as he is sometimes described, composed chapters forty to fifty-five in the book of Isaia. It is the general position of contemporary Catholic biblical scholarship that this prophet is distinct from Isaia of Jerusalem, an earlier prophet, who lived around 700 B.C. Deutero-Isaia belonged, however, to a school of thought, inaugurated by the Jerusalem prophet; he adapted the message of this earlier prophet to the vastly different conditions of the Babylonian exile, 587-538 B.C.

The two basic factors, which we have just considered sustained the creation-belief of Israel and carried it forward to future development and greater precision in the preaching of Deutero-Isaia. The biblical theology of creation rests solidly upon: (1) the ancient Near Eastern origin of the Hebrew people; (2) Israel's special election by God, manifested in great redemptive acts. The first factor, origin, maintains both the *antiquity* of Israelite belief in creation and the specific coloration by which creation is considered a struggle against chaotic forces. The second factor, redemptive acts, points out the *historical* or experiential quality of this belief. Not by philosophical abstraction did the Israelites come to know ever more clearly the creative power of God, but by personal experience of his protection and help. It was particularly God's redemptive acts during the historical period of the exile, and the impact of these mighty deeds upon the great unknown prophet of this time—for want of any other name history calls him Deutero-Isaia—which achieved a notable advance in Israel's creation-theology. God's historical intervention imparted a momentum and character to biblical religion which kept its theology outside an abstract philosophical synthesis and totally within the phenomenological framework of history.

A consideration of the *heritage of biblical faith* relative to God as Maker and Lord of the universe will indicate some of the attitudes and doctrines which were traditional in the nation and formative in the thought of Deutero-Isaia. We shall then be able to specify more accurately, in the second part of this chapter, *the personal contribution* of Deutero-Isaia to the biblical theology of creation. Because creation occupied such a prominent place in his teaching, this chapter will impart a general orientation towards chapters forty to fifty-five of the book of Isaia.

INFLUENCING FACTORS

As we seek to separate the chief elements influencing Deutero-Isaia, we recognize that belief in the creative power of Yahweh lies deep in sacred history. It did not flash upon the Israelite mind with the sudden brightness of a desert sunrise. Reading Is 40—55, we can see that the prophet quietly takes for granted that agreement exists with his fellow co-religionists upon the basic truthfulness of this doctrine.

Creation-belief goes back deep within the history of all other nations in the ancient Near East. The creation-myths of the Fertile Crescent come from a very early age. One of them, *the Enuma elis,* is usually assigned to the old Babylonian period, in the first part of the second millenium. In Egypt the text of the creation of Atum was carved inside the pyramids of Mer-ne-Re and Pepi II already in the twenty-fourth century before Christ. A hymn to the sun, coming from the reign of Amenophis III (1406-1370 B.C.), addresses the solar disc with these words: "O Creator of what the earth brings forth." Ugaritic texts, originating in an area north of Palestine several centuries before Moses, address the bull-divinity El: "Creator of creatures." We possess still other texts from Ugarit in which creation is presented as a struggle between the gods Baal and Yam.

It took time for these creation stories of neighboring peoples to be incorporated into Hebrew religion. Israel was jealous lest her own basic intuition of God, as a personal being who had intervened in the lives of her fathers, be contaminated by the sensual nature-deities of other nations. Even though the Israelites were slow in accommodating the Canaanite creation accounts to their religious traditions, nevertheless, the *idea* of the world's dependence upon God occurs in some of the most ancient texts of the Bible. In the Song of Debora God commands *the stars* to fight against the invading army of Sisara (Judges 5:20), while in Gen 49:25 Jacob prays: "By the God of your fathers, may he bless you . . . with the blessings of *the skies above.*" The earliest form of chapter one of Genesis can be traced to a very ancient period and witnesses to the Hebrew belief in Yahweh's power over the cosmos.

Deutero-Isaia was acquainted with these traditions which taught that Yahweh triumphed over chaotic forces and now controls the universe. He refers to Eden and paradise (51:3); he speaks of the Canaanite deity Rahab (51:9). He refers to the *depths* or *abyss* of hostile waters, the same word found in the creation story of Genesis (1:2) and possibly in the Babylonian epic of creation. He employs the rare Hebrew word *tohu* (40:17,23) which in Genesis describes the world before creation. Although Deutero-Isaia did not startle the exiles with any revolutionary ideas, this "Great Unknown" was responsible for a notable advance or development in the biblical theology of creation. In order to appreciate his special contribution, we must know what elements of biblical tradition pervaded his thinking. It appears that there were three decisive factors in the formation of his creation-theology. *First,* there was *the polarization of biblical faith around the great redemptive acts of God* in the experience of the Israelite nation. *Second,* he was greatly impressed by *the historical fulfillment of the word of God,* as spoken through the earlier prophets. And *last, the hymns and liturgical songs* of his people induced an awareness of God's creative action.

Salvation History

Israelites in the days of Deutero-Isaia inherited this truth as one of the basic tenets of their religion: Yahweh was no nature god, immersed in the awesome and mysterious forces of the physical universe. God was a *personal* Being who had freely, and therefore lovingly, intervened in human history to make the offspring of Abraham "my special possession, dearer to me than all other people" (Ex 19:5). The earliest confessions of faith in the Bible tell of God's redemptive acts in Israelite history:

> You shall go to the priest in office at that time and say to him: "Today I acknowlege to the Lord, my God, that I have indeed come into the land which he swore to our fathers he would give us. ... My father was a wandering Aramean who went down to Egypt with a small household and lived there as an alien. But there he became a nation, strong and numerous. When the Egyptians maltreated and oppressed us, imposing hard labor upon us, we cried to the Lord, the God of our fathers, and he heard our cry and saw our affliction, our toil and our oppression. He brought us out of Egypt with his strong hand and outstretched arm, with terrifying power, with signs and wonders; and bringing us into this country, he gave us this land flowing with milk and honey. Therefore, I have now brought you the first fruits of the products of the soil which you, O Lord, have given me.
>
> And having set them before the Lord, your God, you shall

bow down in his presence. Then you and your family, together
with the Levite and the aliens who live among you, shall make
merry over all these good things which the Lord, your God,
has given you (Deut 26:3-11).

The redemptive acts of God whereby He personally intervened in Israelite history are the most frequent motive of
praise or intercession in the psalms, while "creation and
nature" constitute the theme of only a small number of
hymns. And even in Psalms 8 or 28, two most typical of the
cosmic hymns, historical motives also occur. Ps 8 seems to
reflect Israel's struggle against enemy forces at the same
time that it speaks of creation:

> You have exalted your majesty above the heavens.
> Out of the mouths of babes and sucklings
> you have fashioned praise because of your foes,
> to silence the hostile and the vengeful.

Ps 28:11 ends with the request:

> May the Lord give strength to his people;
> May the Lord bless his people with peace!

Although Yahweh is known primarily by the revelation of
Himself in history, rather than from the study of His attributes reflected in the material universe, history always draws
attention to Yahweh's power over the cosmos.

God cannot act within history without involving Himself
in space and time. Mighty deeds of history automatically
become mighty deeds of nature. From the earliest traditions
of the Bible Yahweh is seen as Master of the Universe. He
makes use of the elements: sun, rain, dew, lightning, thunder and every other force of nature, to accomplish His purposes in history. He blessed Abraham with material riches,
multiplied the flocks of Jacob, revealed the years of drought
and prosperity to Joseph, divided the waters of the Red Sea,

and, in the desert of Sinai, nourished His people with Manna from the sky and quenched their thirst with water from the rock. The blessings and curses, recounted in chapters twenty-seven and twenty-eight of Deuteronomy, declare that God would so reveal Himself forever.

As the years coursed by, there evolved an ever clearer realization of God's mastery over nature. His power was seen to extend to every moment of time and to every point in the universe. The prophecies of Amos and Osee conclude with a promise that God will transform this earth into paradise for His chosen ones. With the plowman overtaking the reaper and the treader of grapes him who sows the seed, God's chosen people will dwell "upon their soil which I have given them" (Am 9:15). During the invasion of Sennacherib, Isaia of Jerusalem corroborates the promise of God's protection by resolutely acknowledging His power over nature *from long ago*. The prophet declares to King Ezechia: "You made a reservoir between the two walls for the water of the old pool [to sustain you in time of siege], but you looked not to him who planned it long ago" (Is 22:11). Jeremia frequently extols the sway of God over the obedient forces of the cosmos. Yet, he always closely linked the manifestation of this divine power with Israelite history. God is asking through this prophet:

> Should you not tremble before me?
> I made the sandy shore the sea's limit,
>   which by eternal decree it may not overstep.
> Toss thought it may, it is to no avail;
>   though its billows roar, they cannot pass over.
> But this people's heart is stubborn and rebellious (Jer 5:22-23).

Or again: "Tell your masters: Thus says the Lord of hosts, the God of Israel: It is I who made the earth, and man and beast on the face of the earth, by my great power, with

my outstretched arm; and I can give them to whomever I
think fit" (27:4-5).

In these words, Jeremia is looking upon creation, not as
the basic cause of all things, but as the beginning of sacred
history, the first of those acts of "my outstretched arm" by
which God redeemed Israel. Another of these acts, as we
already saw in Deuteronomy, was the moment "He brought
us out of Egypt with his strong hand and *outstretched arm.*"

If creation, however, is an historical event, contrariwise,
history is a continuation of this creative power of God. Isaia
and Jeremia use such terms as *to make* and *to form* in describing God's intervention in Hebrew history. Through the
events of history, therefore, Yahweh is forming, making or
creating history. The theology of history and the theology
of creation contributed to each other's development.

Fulfillment of the Prophetic Word

A second, formative element which influenced the thinking of Deutero-Isaia on creation was *the fulfillment of the
prophetic word.* Although King Achaz pretended that a
royal command would nullify the words of Yahweh spoken
by the prophet, Isaia of Jerusalem, although priests and
noblemen had thought that ridicule and chains would silence
Jeremia or that Egypt would bury his words in her silent
sands, the prophetic oracles came thundering back in dreadful fulfillment during the terrible days of 588-587 B.C.
"Only when the hour comes—and it is surely coming!—shall
they know that there was a prophet among them" (Ez
33:33).

Living during the long discouraging days of the exile,
Deutero-Isaia had time for thought. When he reviewed the
past and recalled the words of the prophets, he realized that
not a single syllable of God's words had fallen to the ground

sterile. What had been predicted was accomplished. Deutero-Isaia declared on the part of God:

> Things of the past I foretold long ago,
>> they went forth from my mouth, I let you hear of them;
>> then suddenly I took action and they came to be (Is 48:3).

That this idea is linked with the notion of creation is shown from the words which immediately follow:

> Now that you have heard, look at all this;
>> must you not admit it?
> From now on I announce new things to you,
>> hidden events of which you knew not.
> Now, not long ago, *have they been created* (48:6-7).

God's words produced their effect in a way beyond human vision. This appreciation of God's omnipotent word came to Deutero-Isaia not only from the fulfillment of the prophetic word, but also from the spirit and teaching of the prophets before him.

First of all, there was the common Semitic use of *dabar,* a Hebrew term which can refer either to words or to actions. In Gen 20:19, for instance, *dabar* is translated: "What had you in mind in doing *this thing?*" Words were thought to possess a dynamic as well as an intellectual element. The notion, that God's word always accomplishes just what it says, can be detected in the early patriarchal blessings and curses. Once spoken, these cannot be reversed, for already they are in the process of fulfillment. In fact, the future can be explained only with the postulate of an earlier blessing or word (cf. Gen 9:25-27; 12:1-3; 16:11ff; 25:23).

Secondly, the power of the divine word is one of the most distinguishing features of the great prophets. While the earlier prophets, like Elias and Eliseus, relied greatly upon prodigious works and extraordinary means of knowledge, the later, "writing" prophets based their strength upon the enunciation of the word of God. Isaia of Jerusalem, the prophet whose teaching was sealed up in the heart of his future disciple (cf. 8:16), possessed an enduring faith in the power of God's word; and he demanded the same unquestioning faith from his hearers. His own eyes of faith had recognized a divine energy hidden beneath the most unpretentious exterior. Astonishing effects were to emerge almost out of nothing, simply because God's words had promised that they would happen: new life for the Davidic dynasty sprouting from a dead root (11:1); victory over the Syro-Ephramite league by belief in that victory (7:1-9); the tremendous roar of God's power, not in the mighty Euphrates but in the silent waters of Siloe (8:5-8). Faith in the power of God to fulfill exactly what His prophet declared was an integral part of the message of Isaia of Jerusalem. Deutero-Isaia will further develop this prophetic teaching as he proclaims *the creative power* of the divine word.

The Influence of the Liturgy

The Old Testament liturgy is the *third* and final element of importance in shaping the thought and style of Deutero-Isaia on creation. This influence must be considered because the early use of the Hebrew word *bara'* (to create) seems confined to liturgical texts. Even though at this moment we are investigating the background and formative factors of Deutero-Isaia, we will here pause to analyze the style or literary genre of chapters forty to fifty-five in the book of Isaia to establish a liturgical influence upon the author. Two reasons can be advanced: the melodious style of Deutero-Isaia's writing; and a common bond of ideas with the earlier worship.

The ancient hymns of Israel are like distant background music in the poems of Deutero-Isaia. The familiar songs of his people were humming in his mind as he addressed his own religious rhapsodies to dejected Jews. The elaborate care and the many technical devices used to produce harmony of sound and force of ideas show that these chapters were originally written, not oral. Yet, like the earlier songs which inspired them, these poems of Deutero-Isaia were *written to be sung aloud,* not to be read privately.

Deutero-Isaia's very frequent use of the active participle manifests a characteristic feature of liturgical hymns. Participial constructions refer to a continuous state, to an action of indefinite duration. Such a word, therefore, as $w^e go'alek,$ customarily translated "I will redeem you" (41:14), carries the fuller meaning: God is ever busy at His task of love, redeeming His people; never beginning, never stopping, just redeeming. Redemption is not an event of the distant past nor of the far-off future; it is an act in the very process of accomplishment, in this moment of worship and adoration.

The liturgy of the chosen people left its mark not only upon the style of Deutero-Isaia but also upon his *idea of creation.* As mentioned earlier, reminiscences of the early creation hymns are present in chapters forty to fifty-five of the Isaia book. A possible dependence of ideas shows up in Deutero-Isaia's frequent use of the Hebrew word *bara'* (to create). The prophet most probably took the word *bara'* from the liturgical language of the hymns, and then by his habitual use of it deepened and at the same time restricted the meaning of the word.

A slow but steady development is noticeable in the biblical use of *bara'.* At first, it had a wide general meaning—any wondrous, mighty, *historical* act of God. We are told in a section commonly called the "The Decalogue of Worship": "Here, then, ... is the covenant I will make. Before the eyes of all your people I will work such wonders as have never been *created* in any nation anywhere on earth, so that this people among whom you live may see how awe-inspiring are the *deeds* which I, the Lord, will do at your side." This *historical* motif will cling to *bara'* in its later uses. Yet, a possible transition from an *historical* theme to the notion of *power over nature* may be perceptible in Ps 88:12-13:

> Yours are the heavens, and yours is the earth;
> the world and its fullness you have founded;
> North and south *you created*.

It is possible that Deutero-Isaia accepts *bara'* from a liturgical hymn like Ps 88 and then proceeds to transform it into a technical word for the exclusively divine act of creation. The liturgy of Israel thus influenced Deutero-Isaia: certainly in his style; also in the manner of acclaiming God's powerful sway over nature; and possibly in the use of *bara'*.

Here, then, are the important elements in the religion of Israel which contributed to Deutero-Isaia's theology of creation: the great, historical redemptive acts of God; the fulfillment of the prophetic word; and the expression of Israelite faith through liturgical songs. Deutero-Isaia was a true Israelite. His faith was rooted in the history of his people. His faith also told him that Yahweh was a *living God*, whose power was not exhausted by the great deeds of His outstretched arm in the past. This past was ever being repeated, even in his own lifetime, when the word of God was re-creating the Israelite commonwealth out of the chaos of the Babylonian exile. The very first moment of creation is happening all over again, for the exodus from Babylon is nothing other than a triumph over those deities whom the

Babylonians venerated not only as their protectors and military leaders, but also as the creators of the cosmos.

DEUTERO-ISAIA'S CONTRIBUTION TO THE THEOLOGY OF CREATION

We will now examine how Deutero-Isaia took the faith of his fathers into his heart and made it glow with greater intensity. The fire of divine inspiration, the warmth of personal holiness, and the consummate skill of poetic genius all contributed to the development of his theology of creation. We will study four features of Deutero-Isaia's creation-theology: the more technical or specialized use of *bara'*; the creative power of the word of God; creation in the beginning of time; and the eschatological meaning of creation. This investigation will prepare us for a better understanding and appreciation of all that Deutero-Isaia wrote. J. Begrich recognized over twenty years ago that the major themes of Deutero-Isaia can be traced to his belief in creation.

Bara' Becomes a Technical Term

We have already seen that from the earliest days of biblical religion Yahweh was worshipped as Lord and Ruler of the material universe. God's power over nature, however, was never in the forefront and cannot be classed as a focal point of Israelite religion. The true Israelite reacted violently against any form of "nature religion"; he repudiated the impersonal nature gods of the Canaanites. The chosen people adored the God of their fathers, who had *personally* intervened by *historical* acts of wonder and never ceased performing similar marvels with his "outstretched arm." It is no matter for surprise, therefore, to learn that *bara'*—the word associated with material creation in Deutero-Isaia—occurs only three times in earlier traditions (Ex 34:10;

Num 16:30; Ps 88:13), and the first two of these cases are doubtful. Furthermore, each of these examples is in the context of a mighty *historical* act.

In Deutero-Isaia *bara'* continues to emphasize what has always been the most characteristic feature of biblical religion: God's personal historical acts of love and power towards His chosen people. God alone is the one acting in these events described by *bara'*, for these deeds are beyond the dreams of man. In the future God will make use of human instruments but only to accomplish what man could never achieve by himself:

> Now, not long ago, they are *created,*
> and before this time you did not hear of them,
> so that you cannot claim to have known them (48:7).

What are these "new things" of history (42:9) which the word of God is announcing? They are none other than the wonders of a *new exodus.* Leading His chosen ones out of the "Egypt" of the Babylonian exile, God slakes the parched tongue of the thirsty; He opens rivers on the bare heights and springs in the folds of the valleys; He plants in the barren wilderness cedars, acacias, myrtles, oleasters and cypresses:

> That all may see and know,
> observe and understand,
> That the hand of the Lord has done this,
> the Holy One of Israel has *created it* (41:20).

Like Osee or Jeremia, Deutero-Isaia overlooks the weary, monotonous hardships of an eastern caravan as it slowly advances across desert land or through hostile territory. With ecstatic joy he envisions God's people returning to the Land of Promise along a miraculously prepared highway, called the *way of the Lord* (40:3). He calls upon deaf ones to hear and blind ones to see (42:18), for this stupendous prodigy will overcome all natural obstacles and be performed especially for the sake of the *anawim* (the poor and lowly). Yet, even *his* poetical soul realized that this new exodus is no trail through golden clouds but a march upon earthly clay. The return to Palestine remains an *actual historical fact,* witnessed by the heavens above and consummated upon the earth below.

> Let justice descend, O heavens, like dew from above,
>   like gentle rain let the skies drop it down.
> Let the earth open and salvation bud forth;
>   let justice also spring up!
> I, the Lord, have *created* this (45:8).

True, the event surpasses all earthly powers, for "I, the Lord, have created this"; still, the earth is the theater of action and men are the actors. "Let *the earth* open and salvation bud forth." The process of emphasizing *material* creation in the word *bara'* is now in progress.

This development in the theology of creation will be further advanced by the fact that the exodus was a devastating blow at Babylonian *nature*-gods. Occupying a rank of importance in the pantheon of Babylon were the hosts of the heavens and the chaotic forces of the depths of the earth. When Israel was led into exile, her tiny nation was caught in the grip of these monstrous powers. The dark waters above and below the firmament, worshipped by the Babylonians, submerged the chosen people in a whirl of confusion and sorrow. The days of the primal deluge returned, and with good reason! As in the days of Noe, sixth century Israel "was corrupt in the sight of God and filled with violence" (Gen 6:11). Deutero-Isaia saw that it was the sins of the chosen people which caused "the fountains of the

great deep to burst forth and the floodgates of the heavens
... [to be] opened" (Gen 7:11).

Sin always begets suffering, sorrow and chaos, but God
uses this sinful brood as obedient servants for washing away
the filth of evil and for creating a new people. "It is I also
who have *created* the destroyer to work havoc," God declared, "and no weapon fashioned against you shall prevail"
(54:16-17). Concerning these forces of nature before which
the Babylonians burned incense, Deutero-Isaia has this to
say:

> I am the Lord, and there is no other;
>   I form the light and *create the darkness,*
> I make happiness and *create woe,*
>   I, the Lord, do all these things (45:6-7).

If God creates darkness and woe, He never intends such
sorrowful conditions to endure for long.

> The creator of the heavens,
>   who is God,
> The designer and maker of the earth
>   who established it,
> Not creating it to be a waste,
>   but designing it to be lived in (45:18).

This bleak state of chaos is no longer the insolent and
massive violence of sin. Deutero-Isaia pictures it as a re-
grettable situation to be controlled and turned into good.
God looks again at the flood waters of chaos and says:

> I clothe the heavens in mourning,
>   and make sackcloth their vesture (50:3).

About man He says:

> Who among you fears the Lord,
>   heeds his servant's voice,

> And walks in darkness
>   without any light. . . ? (50:10).

So man invokes God:

> Awake, awake, put on strength,
>   O arm of the Lord!
> Awake as in the days of old,
>   in ages long ago!
> Was it not you who crushed Rahab,
>   you who pierced the dragon?
> Was it not you dried up the sea,
>   the waters of the great deep? (51:9-10).

This new creation, therefore, is an *historical* act of God, accomplished upon this earth over the powers of *nature*. *Bara'* continues to *denote* an historical event. At the same time Deutero-Isaia gives the word an added meaning; it now *connotes* or implies a power over *nature*, that is, over the material cosmos. Heaven and earth emerge from the chaotic seas, as the Israelites receive back again their Promised Land. By reducing chaos to order and beauty, Yahweh dispossesses the other Semitic nature-gods: Rahab, the dragon, Tiamat, Marduk, the hosts of heaven. The defeat of Babylon was an annihilation of Babylonian gods. The creative powers which the Chaldeans falsely claimed for their idols are attributed to the one and only true God.

> Thus says the Lord, Israel's King
>   and redeemer, the Lord of hosts;
> I am the first and I am the last;
>   there is no God but me (44:6).
> For your sakes I send to Babylon;
>   I will lower all the bars, . . .
> I am the Lord, your Holy One,
>   your King, who is creating Israel (43:14-15).

Deutero-Isaia ridicules the Babylonian New Year festival,

when the *Enuma Elis* was chanted and the creation gods
were carried through the streets in solemn procession:

> They are without knowledge who bear wooden idols,
> and pray to gods that cannot save. . . .
> Who announced this from the beginning. . . ?
> Was it not I, the Lord,
> besides whom there is no other God? (45:20-21).

About the stars Yahweh exclaims:

> Lift up your eyes on high
> and see who has created these:
> He leads out their army and numbers them,
> calling them all by name (40:26).

Not only does Yahweh claim the stars as His creatures but
the entire heaven and earth. He is the one . . .

> Creating the heavens and stretching them out,
> Extending the earth with its covering of vegetation (42:5).
> The Lord is the eternal God,
> creating the ends of the earth (40:28).

Man too is a product of God's creative, salvific act.

> It was I who made the earth
> and created mankind upon it (45:12).

Here in Deutero-Isaia we have an example of *causae ad
invicem causae*: Two basic religious ideas, Yahweh's great
redemptive acts in history and His mighty act in creating the
world, coalesce to strengthen one another. Deutero-Isaia sees
the great redemptive act of the new exodus as though it
were taking place before his very eyes. With ecstatic rap-
ture he finds himself witnessing God's power to create a
new Jewish commonwealth out of the chaos of the Babylonian exile.

The act of creation at the beginning of all things will

naturally appear as a pledge of the rebuilding of the Israelite state. Such is the line of argument in 40:12ff. In both
cases, Yahweh is accomplishing a work which far exceeds
the ability of man and gods. In Deutero-Isaia *bara'* clearly
indicates, therefore, an action proper to Yahweh alone, an
action which transforms chaos and confusion into order and
beauty for God's glory and man's happiness.

Creative Power of the Word

Deutero-Isaia's second major contribution to the creation-
theology of the Old Testament was his respect for the power
of the word of God. To Deutero-Isaia it was sovereign, irresistible. We shall soon consider how the prophet's attention to the Word resulted in a revival of that characteristic
most proper to biblical religion: the worship of a *personal*
God, knowing, loving and choosing, yet always remaining
supremely transcendent, since "no man sees me and still
lives" (Ex 33:20).

What an intimate friend of God must Deutero-Isaia have
been! He was the prophet anointed by the spirit to announce
what is most deep, intimate and personal to Almighty God,
His secret thoughts or words. God's words are never weak-
ened by an "if" or "maybe." On the contrary, the life of
God pulses within their syllables with power to *create* exactly and immediately what is said.

Deutero-Isaia proclaims God's word with a rich vocabulary, a masterful style, and an intuitive grasp which surpass
those of any previous prophet. God's words are hurled from
the mountain tops by "heralds of good news" (40:9) or
whispered in "the heart of Jerusalem" to "comfort my people" (40:2). God speaks and at the touch of His words the
desert wilderness is covered with the luxuriant shade of
cedars, oleasters and cypresses (41:17-20). The "voice" of

Ps 28 sounds again, and lo! the way of the Lord levels off uneven ground and turns rugged heights into delightful valleys (40:4). Stars are summoned into existence at the word of God who "calls them all by name" (40:26). When the poor and needy seek water, God answers their prayer by the gift of His word (41:17).

> Heed me, and you shall eat well,
>   you shall delight in rich fare.
> Come to me heedfully,
>   listen, that you may have life (55:2-3).

When God is silent, sorrow and gloom spread over the lives of the Israelites (42:14), but at the sound of His word, all the world breaks into a melody of song (42:10). His own people are being redeemed as they hear Yahweh calling them by name. "You are mine" (43:1)—these words create, form and make Israel "for my glory" (43:7). This word is the great *"I am"*—"I, the Lord, am the first, and with the last I will also be" (41:4). Its sound fills all space and time (45:18-19), not as a vain display of power but that . . .

> To me every knee shall bend;
>   by me every tongue shall swear,
> Saying, "Only in the Lord
>   are just deeds and power" (45:23-24).

This "word of our God endures forever" (40:8), not passively like a statue in a niche but charged with vital, creative power.

What Deutero-Isaia adds to the theology of the word is the notion of *creative power*. He was the first to emphasize that creation was effected by the *God who speaks*. By creation we here mean especially the origin of the material universe, but we do not exclude the re-creation of the exile nation in their Promised Land.

The creative power of the Word can be deduced from these silent thoughts constantly overlapping: the creation of the universe; the re-creation of the Hebrew nation; and the omnipotent power of the Word. Deutero-Isaia so quickly passes from one of these ideas to the other, so that all three become different ways of expressing the same reality. This compenetration of ideas is achieved, not merely by juxtaposing clauses or lines, but even more effectively by the use of the present participle. The participle so coalesces with the principal verb, that God *speaks by, through and simultaneously with* the act of creating.

We find that parallel with the emphatic: "Take note: Who *created these?*" stands the explanatory clause: 'He *calls* all of them by name leading out their host and numbering them" (40:26). The participle "leading out their host" continues the thought of the verb "He calls all of them." He thus answers the question, "Who created these?" Still other examples reveal the skill of Deutero-Isaia to use participles for extending the idea of God's word.

> Thus says God, the Lord,
> > *creating* the heavens and *stretching* them out,
> > *spreading* out the earth with its crops,
> > *Giving* breath to its people
> > and spirit to those *walking* on it (42:5).

> But now, thus says the Lord,
> > *creating* you, O Jacob, and *forming* you, O Israel;
> > Fear not, for I have redeemed you;
> > I have called you by name: you are mine (43:1).

> Listen to me, Jacob,
> > Israel, I am *naming* you!
> > I, it is I who am the first,
> > and also the last am I.
> > Yes, my hand laid the foundations of the earth;
> > my right hand spread out the heavens,

> As I am *calling* them,
>   they stand forth at once (48:12-13).
>
> Therefore, on that day my people shall know my name,
>   that it is I, *the one speaking*. Yes, I myself (52:6).

In these passages Deutero-Isaia speaks of creating, leading out the stars, forming a new people, extending the earth and laying its foundations. In each instance the act of *creating* is not only simultaneous with the act of *speaking* but is indeed identified with it.

Deutero-Isaia was certainly not blind to all the implications contained in this teaching. *Creation-by-the-word* emphasizes certain features of the divine act which at first seem contradictory: for example, God's exalted transcendence and His condescending love. The prophet marvels at the tremendous, omnipotent greatness of God. Over and over again he stresses the contrast between the divine "I" and the created "you." In many ways he points to that stretch of infinity between the Creator and His creature. Notice the juxtaposition of: the weakness of flesh and God's glory (40:5); withering grass and the enduring word (40:8); the suckling lamb and the shepherd (46:11); the watery abyss, a drop in God's hands (40:12). God challenges the universe with:

> I am the first and I am the last;
>   there is no God but me.
> Who is like me? Let him stand up and speak. . . .
> You are my witnesses! Is there a God
>   or any Rock besides me? (44:6-8).

At the same time there is something very personal in a word. A word expresses what is most secret, precious and intimate; it shares its treasures with the recipient of the word. "I have called you friends," says Our Lord, "because all things that I have heard from my Father I have made known to you" (John 15:15). And again: "I have made known to them thy name, and will make it known, in order that the love with which thou hast loved me may be in them, and I in them" (John 17:26). The word is like a mirror held up to God's heart, a letter written by divine hands. Yet, God's heart and hands are fully alive, not passive like a mirror or a letter; therefore, His words pulse with dynamic activity that is always tender and kind. Deutero-Isaia calls men: worms, insects and grasshoppers (40:22; 41:14); "lambs he carries in his bosom" (40:11); faint, weary and prostrate people (40:28-30); poor and needy ones (41:17); blind men in the dark (42:7). God speaks thus, yet not with disdain, but rather as signs of endearment. For we read:

> Fear not, O worm Jacob,
>   O maggot Israel;
> I will help you, says the Lord (41:14).

Thinking about the created power of the Word, Deutero-Isaia realized that nothing is so transcendent about God as His condescending love! The *deepest* mystery of God's infinite life is the mystery of His goodness and love.

> Can a mother forget her infant,
>   be without tenderness for the child of her womb?
> Even should she forget,
>   I will never forget you.
> See, upon the palms of my hands
>   I have written your name (49:15-16).

Thus we see how Deutero-Isaia restores the most characteristic feature of the biblical theology of God: God as a *person*, living, acting and helping. His is not a ruthless throwing about of power. His voice does not roar and crack like thunder; it falls gently like rain and snow

(55:10-11). His almighty word reaches even to the minutiae of daily life. God hides Himself beneath the poverty, sorrow and littleness of His exiled children.

> Truly with you God is hidden,
>   the God of Israel, the savior! (45:15).

Mysteriously by the utterance of a word, He accomplishes His mighty acts of salvation.

Consequently, when Deutero-Isaia joins the notion of creation with the power of the Word, he invests creation with transcendent dignity and loving condescension, with mighty power and well-planned purpose. The might of God's word reaches from beginning to end of Hebrew history and controls every moment in between.

At the Beginning of Time

The third contribution of Deutero-Isaia to the theology of creation is the notion of *eternity*. He is the first to connect creation with the eternity of God. He calls upon Israel to sing:

> God everlasting is Yahweh,
>   creating the ends of the earth (40:28).

Yet, what did he mean when he called the Creator a "God everlasting"? Closely linked with this question is another: what are we to derive from the many places where Deutero-Isaia speaks of God as *the First?*

The answer lies in an apparent contradiction, which the Hebrew notion of a living, personal God will unravel. Yahweh stands above all time, not with the static unchangeableness of an eternal truth, but with a personal involvement in every moment of time which He controls as its Master and Lord. To be vitally in touch with every moment demands that God not be chained down to any particular point of time. Yahweh, who calls Himself: "I, Yahweh, . . .the first, and with the last," also asserts in the same verse that He is the one "calling generations from the beginning" (41:4). Since He is the first, He is always ahead of future events, controlling them with steady strength and even accomplishing them by the sound of His word.

> *Things of the past* I foretold long ago,
>> they went forth from my mouth, I let you hear of them;
>> then *suddenly* I took action and they came to be (48:3).

From this verse, as well as from others already considered, we realize that God announced the future, not primarily to forewarn, but in order to accomplish it. The divine word creates! If the *principal* purpose were to share knowledge with man, fulfillment would not come "suddenly" and unexpectedly. The *beginning* of the future lay in the initial *creative word* of God. God creates by His word pronounced *at the beginning.*

Deutero-Isaia is here revealing how the teaching of his master was sealed up in his heart (Is 8:16). The eighth century prophet had eyes keen enough to pierce through the confusion, fear and weakness which swept fog and whirlwind over the kingdom of Juda during the Assyrian period. The prophet Isaia detected purpose and orderliness in every event from beginning to end; he saw the mighty hand of God directing all things. The silent waters of Siloe, he wrote, possessed a stronger current to carry history forward than "the water of the River [Euphrates], great and mighty" (8:6-8). God was present among His people, and therefore:

> The Lord of hosts has sworn:
> As I have resolved,
>> so shall it be;

> As I have proposed,
> so shall it stand (14:24).

Yahweh is directing events by plans formed *from the beginning!* This truth which the prophet of the royal period presented with staunch faith, his disciple of the exile experienced as a living reality and, thereby, was able to understand more clearly. With ecstatic wonder Deutero-Isaia was seeing the fulfillment of the great prophecies. If the impossible had happened when Jerusalem and her glorious temple were reduced to rubble—for Jeremia met a wall of unbelief when he predicted this catastrophe—God was again turning the impossible into a reality. Yahweh was bringing Cyrus, His "friend," to "do his will against Babylon" (48:14). Like the quick ringing of many bells, the prophet's words pour out:

> Go out from Babylon—flee from Chaldeans!
> With voice of singing proclaim—make it known;
> Send it forth—to the ends of the earth.
> Say: Yahweh redeems—Jacob his servant (48:20).

From the concatenation of various texts we hear the message of Deutero-Isaia, proclaiming that *from the beginning* Yahweh is creating these new things. The trumpets are sounding, the people are marching. Ahead of them stretches the Arabian desert, but this new exodus from bondage will follow *the way of the Lord* upon which "the glory of the Lord will be revealed ... for the word of our God endures forever" (40:3-8). During this long trek:

> The afflicted and the needy seek water in vain,
> their tongues are parched with thirst.
> I, the Lord, will *answer* them... (41:17).

After a description of the many marvels produced by the answering word of God, the poet-singer concludes:

> That all may see and know,
>   observe and understand,
> That the hand of the Lord has done this,
>   the Holy One of Isreal has created it (41:20).

After another joyful account describing the victorious re-
habilitation of the Promised Land, God asks and then
answers:

> Who has performed these deeds?
>   He who has called forth the generations
>   since the beginning.
> I, the Lord, am the first,
>   and with the last I will also be (41:4).

We see how naturally Deutero-Isaia passes from first to
last, from *Urzeit* to *Endzeit,* from creation to eschatology.
He could make this transfer or leap because of his faith in
a living God who stands above time, even though always
personally involved in time. Previously, we saw how the
exilic prophet deepened and popularized the meaning of
bara', extending the word of cosmic creation, yet keeping it
always within a redemptive framework of salvation-history.
The same transformation is now seen to affect the notion
"from the beginning."

Very clearly and forcefully Deutero-Isaia declares that before the beginning of all things stands Yahweh, the one and
only God, uttering the word of creation. We cannot distinguish the cosmic from the historical, since the creation of
the material universe is an historical act of salvation and the
creation of historical events involves the elements of nature.
Deutero-Isaia explicitly places the creative word of Yahweh
at the start of everything:

> Do you not know? Have you not heard?
>   Was it not foretold you from the beginning?
>   Have you not understood? Since the earth was founded
> He sits enthroned above the vault of the earth (40:21-22).

Semitic creation myths could go no further back into pre-historic origins than chaos. Chapter one of Genesis pictures a chaotic whirl of raging water, which the spirit of God quiets and gradually changes into a well-ordered universe. In Deutero-Isaia, however, even this chaos is God's creature, made to serve His redemptive purposes:

> I am the Lord, there is no other;
>   forming the light and creating the *darkness,*
> Making well-being and creating *woe,*
>   I, the Lord, doing all these things (45:6-7).

Yet, chaos was never intended as a permanent situation but only as a condition leading to order and happiness.

Implied in these many expressions is the profound truth: *in the beginning* even before chaos, God alone *is,* the creature *will be.* God speaks the creative word, the creatures await the sound of this word before leaping obediently into existence. Absent from Deutero-Isaia and certainly nowhere in the Bible, is the story of how God came into existence. Alone among all Semitic creator-gods, Yahweh underwent no birth nor metamorphasis.

> I, the Lord, am the first,
>   and with the last I will also be (41:4).

Yahweh, the great "I am," is always there at the beginning of each creative work.

Eschatological Meaning of Creation

We come now to Deutero-Isaia's fourth and final contribution to the theology of creation, eschatology, the theology of the last things. In his thought the eschatological nature of creation unites the two furthest limits of the past and of the future, combining the first moment with the last; seeing an act of creation in the wonders of the final day;

recognizing the initial stage of the final glory in the first moment of cosmic existence; investing creation with the honor of a salvation-event. Such a quick transfer from the first moment of creation to the final moment of God's eschatological kingdom was not as difficult a leap for Deutero-Isaia and his audience as it is for us today. God stands above time. Yet, He is also personally involved in each moment of time. He is present at the start of every series of redemptive acts, speaking the word which sets each series in motion along a pre-ordained and well-defined route. In this *way of the Lord* every obstacle is marvelously removed, and each turn in the road reveals the *glory of the Lord,* "for the mouth of the Lord has spoken" (40:3-5). The living God holds with a firm yet tender hand the beginning and the end, and Deutero-Isaia delights in joining these two ideas together.

> I am God, there is none like me.
> At the beginning I foretell the outcome;
>   in advance, things not yet done.
> I say that my plan shall stand,
>   I accomplish my every purpose (46:9-10).

What is meant, we ask, by calling creation a salvation-event and linking it with a series of divine acts culminating in the eschatological day of the Lord? Such a statement places the doctrine of creation within a *biblical-historical* framework of thought. Creation is considered the first of many divine attempts to surround man with happiness and with the fullness of life. Like the call of Abraham and the choice of the Hebrew people, creation was a *free* act of God, dominiated by love. The founding of the universe, like the establishment of the Israelite nation, can be traced to no other reason than this: "it was because the Lord loved you" (Deut 7:8). Gerhard von Rad remarks that the story of creation was placed at the beginning of our Bible, not because the Hebrews were concerned about a material universe and how it originated, but rather because the priestly redactor was careful to include creation as the first of many acts of salvation.

To call creation a salvation-event at once imparts an eschatological quality to this first act of God; at the same time eschatology becomes the completion, the fulfillment or the goal of creation! Eschatology is the final everlasting *amen,* ratifying for all time the dependence of everything upon God. It is the eternal finale, the unending paean, proclaiming the reign of God over creation. On this day of the Lord, the law of creation—that all things were created by God and therefore for God—will receive public recognition. This glorious song of praise to God the Creator will be sung in full chorus and with universal orchestration only on the final day of the Lord. However, its dominant theme was written across the peaks of the mountains and the waves of the sea and upon the tablet of the human heart, when God created the universe and put man in charge.

Man finds salvation only when he humbly recognizes this law of creation. The *one,* omnipotent God declares: "My glory I surrender to no other" (48:11). Only when man acknowledges the luminous splendor of God's loving presence in all things can he be happy (40:5). Yet, how often man willfully sins. By the touch of sin, the world is polluted and the darkness of chaos descends. Creation is partially undone! In the beginning creation gave the earth a very perilous existence. Above and below the earth roared the breakers of death. Just as the earth emerged out of chaos through the power of God's word, the waters of the depth can again engulf the universe if man sins and separates himself from the word of God. The struggle of creation in all its physical and moral magnitude continues till the end of days. Creation is an ever-present act. At each moment of time, darkness must be dispelled and the raging waters of the abyss kept in their place by the creative word of God. In the chaotic deluge of the exile, which was let loose by sin, the nation prays:

> Awake, awake, put on strength,
>   O arm of the Lord!
> Awake as in the days of old,
>   in ages long ago!
> Was it not you who crushed Rahab,
>   you who pierced the dragon?
> Was it not you who dried up the sea,
>   the waters of the great deep? (51:9-10).

God answers this prayer. By the word of His mouth and by the power of His spirit, Yahweh recreates the new kingdom of Israel. If this salvation-event of the new exodus is an act of creation, then the first dawn of existence was itself a redemptive act of God. The song of glory, sung by the returning Israelites, echoes the song of first creation. It is a *"new* song" only in this respect that its notes had been smothered by the heavy chaos of the Babylonian "deluge."

> Sing to the Lord a new song,
>   his praise from the end of the earth;
> Let the sea roar, . . .
> Let the steppe and its cities cry out, . . .
> Let the inhabitants of Sela exult, . . .
> Let them give glory to the Lord (42:10-12).

In this eschatological song, all the universe turns with obedience and love to its Creator and Lord. But in each moment of time this law of creaturehood should echo in the hearts of God's children, inspiring a staunch faith and a humble trust.

God everlasting is Yahweh
  creating the ends of the earth.
He does not faint nor grow weary, . . .
They who wait on the Lord renew their strength (40:28-31).

For Deutero-Isaia, then, the world is not a systematized
and controlled mechanism, but a tremendous wonder which
stirs devoted faith in its Maker and unwavering confidence
in its Creator who has only to speak and His purpose is
achieved.

Something of eschatology's final trumph, therefore, exists
in each moment of time, because God, the Creator, put it
there. Consequently, Deutero-Isaia felt justified, when he
invested first creation with the glory of the final day. The
total God-mindedness of the final day grows out of the
seed, planted in the universe at creation. The King who will
be revealed in the last age is the Creator of the first age:

I, it is I who am the first,
  and also the last am I.
Yes, my hand laid the foundations of the earth (48:12-13).

Conclusion

By way of conclusion to this chapter we can say that the
contribution of Deutero-Isaia to the Old Testament theology
of creation consisted principally, not in the revelation of any
new ideas, but rather in a *development* of the traditional
teaching of Israel.

By his frequent use of *bara'* Deutero-Isaia goes far in
making this word a technical term for the creation of the
material universe. *Bara'* always implies an act which only
God can perform. The historical wonder of re-creating
Israel out of the chaos of the Babylonian exile revealed a
series of redemptive acts, stretching back to the beginning.
Deutero-Isaia clearly attaches *bara'* to the *first* of these

redemptive acts, the creation of all things at the beginning. The most important feature, however, of this act of "first creation" was God's loving kindness towards Israel; He was preparing a home for His chosen family.

Creation is achieved by the power of the *word of God.* This fact makes creation a personal, responsible act of God; His word is neither magic sound nor caprice. "It shall not return to me fruitless, without accomplishing the effect for which I sent it" (55:11).

The purpose of Creation is to provide a promised land of happy life with God, first of all for Israel, and through Israel for all mankind. The élan of all things towards God is a firm law, divinely inspired in the heart of creatures by first creation and divinely fulfilled by second creation on the eschatological day of the Lord. Creation, therefore, is an act of salvation, an indissoluble part of salvation history.

We see clearly in chapters 40-55 that God is existing "from the beginning," making all things. At the start of every great work God is present, speaking a word which will accomplish His purpose. At the beginning God is already accomplishing the final act, since His creative word "cannot return to me fruitless."

Who has performed these deeds?
  He who has called forth generations since the beginning.
I, the Lord, am the first,
  and with the last I will also be (41:4).

The magnificent songs of Deutero-Isaia may have prepared for the composition of chapter one of Genesis as we have it now in the Bible. Yet, these lyrics performed an even more valuable service to Israel. They provided the organ accompaniment and choral chant for the recitation of Israel's *credo*: the *Torah* of the Bible. After the liturgical services were finished, the echo of these songs continued to ring in the soul of every true Israelite, as he worked in the fields, pastured his flock in the wilderness, or trimmed the citrus trees along the coastland. These songs made him reflect that all this was made—no, *is being* created right now —by my God and my Lord, who loves me more than a mother loves her suckling infant. Right now it is being transformed into the peace and the joy of the first day, for the final day of the Lord is at hand. "I, the Lord, the first, and with the last."

The contribution of Deutero-Isaia to the theology of creation is not just one of words and ideas. Like the word of God which His songs are, He has given life—a full life of *peace* or *shalom*—so that all hearts "sing for joy . . . shout from the mountain tops . . . give glory to the Lord . . . your Maker . . . your husband" (42:10-12; 54:5).

CHAPTER 7 THE POSTEXILIC
PROPHETS AND
THEIR MESSAGE

THE LAST of Israel's prophets are almost faceless, so absorbed are they into the religious institutions of their age. One of them, in fact, was probably no real person at all but only the subject of a make-believe story. The name of at least one other has been lost, and still another has given us the shortest book in the Old Testament. Compared to the earlier prophets, these men not only lack distinctive features, they do not always qualify as prophets at all. They often strike the pose of assistants to temple-priests; seldom do they step forward as fierce reformers, discarding the official backing of civil and religious leaders and taking their stand simply on the strength of truth and on the impelling will of God. At least, so it seems at first reading of the postexilic prophetic books.

To understand the preaching of the last of all the prophets, therefore, one must know the stretch of years in which they lived. These years, too, possess a vague monotony; they are called "the age of silent retreat," when tiny Juda withdrew into itself and tried to ignore the rest of the world. Another name for these years is "the postexilic age," the age following the Babylonian Exile.

These prophets must not be sloughed aside as nonentities. Because they were so much a part of their times, they were able to save this time of silent retreat from being swallowed up by the jaws of bleak despair.

In the postexilic age—the years after 538 B.C.—history had run full cycle. Like Abraham, who had lived in the shadowy days of the second millenium B.C., these Jews had been led by God out of Mesopotamia (modern Iraq) and into the Promised Land of Palestine. They too had to find their strength in faith, for their existence was overshadowed by small beginning and large obstacles.

While reading the account of the postexilic days in the books of Ezra and Nehemia, one would think that great moments of Israelite history were repeating themselves.

Once again God seems to appear in glory on Mount Sinai, giving to another Moses the pattern of the temple and its worship, promulgating the law on tables of stone. For these latter days were marked by the construction of a new Tabernacle to replace the temple of Solomon and by a stern loyalty to the least jot of the Law. Moses had staggered at times into pits of discouragement, not only because of the deadly stretch of the vast and fearful desert surrounding him, but also because of the cowardly murmuring of his faithless people. The people of the postexilic age saw around them *their* desert of crop failures and drought; they had their quota of selfish, small-minded people. They were content, as the prophet Aggai bluntly told them, to dwell in their own paneled houses, while the house of God lay in ruin (Ag 1:4).

When the first caravans returned to the deserted, ghost-town area of southern Palestine in 537 B.C., there was even an attempt to restore the line of David. The first governors to be appointed by the Persian emperor, Sassabasar and Zorobabel, were born of royal blood. People were asking one another if the promises of an eternal dynasty and of a Savior-King were now to be fulfilled (cf. 2 Sam 7). When the pre-exilic kings, the successors of David, had failed, prophets like Isaia and Jeremia sustained the people's faith in the divine promise that someday a new Son of David would emerge from the hidden, almost dead root of the Davidic family (Is 11:1). The first postexilic prophets now encouraged the royal pretensions of Zorobabel. They announced that God "will overthrow the thrones of kingdoms." He will make Zorobabel "my servant . . . a signet ring . . . a chosen one" (Ag 2:22-23). God even orders the prophet Zacharia to take "silver and gold . . . and make a crown; place it on the head of Zorobabel. . . . He shall build the temple of the Lord, and take up the royal insignia, he shall sit as a ruler upon his throne. The priest shall be at his right hand" (Zach 6:11-13). The past was repeating itself, not only in the Davidic restoration but also, tragically enough, in its collapse. The Persians suspected revolt, and Zorobabel quickly and silently disappeared.

In so many ways the past was coming to life again! Those most responsible for the carry-over of ancient traditions were Ezechiel and Deutero-Isaia. Living during the exile itself, they spanned the pre-exilic and the postexilic days. The golden, exquisite poetry of Deutero-Isaia (Is 40-55) not only kept the people humble and penitent (Is 53) but also lifted their purified hearts into the "dream world" of the new creation (Is 43). The other prophet, Ezechiel, proved to be more practical and, therefore, more influential. He staked out the future Promised Land in such a way that all life pivoted around the Temple and was controlled by the Temple's priesthood (Ez 40-48). That he was successful is immediately evident in the total dedication of the post-exilic prophets to his priestly ideals. They copied his language; they put his ideas into action. Zacharia placed the high priest Josue on the right of Zorobabel, and when that royal pretender was whisked into oblivion, the high priest emerged as supreme ruler of the Jews.

History does repeat itself, but never quite in the same way. It was soon evident to the Jews, especially after the collapse of Zorobabel, that a new kind of existence lay before them. The glorious days of David and Solomon could never be recaptured; they were gone forever. The people settled down to insignificance. What else could they do in a country only twenty miles long and twenty-five miles wide? Their state, called Yehud (the aramaic form for Juda) was no more than a plot of land supporting Jerusalem's temple. It fell within the administrative district of Samaria and in the fifth Persian satrapy, *Abar Nahara* ("Beyond the River," the Euphrates). The population of Yehud numbered no more than 20,000, hardly one-fifth of what it was before the fall of Jerusalem in 587 B.C.

In 538 B.C. the first Zionists were commissioned by the Persian emperor Cyrus II the Great to "build the house of the Lord . . . in Jerusalem" (Ezra 1:3). Once in Palestine, however, they were so depressed by the ghost towns of their former kingdom, so discouraged by drought and beggarliness, so worried about naked survival, that they had little energy left for building the house of the Lord. In 520 B.C. the preaching of *Aggai* and *Zacharia* shook them loose from their stagnant listlessness, and five years later the Temple was consecrated. This Temple was so small, however, that "many of the priests, the Levites, the heads of families and the elderly men who had seen the first house ... wept with a loud voice" (Ezra 3:12).

After 515 B.C. Palestine was wrapped in silence, but this was not true of the rest of the world. The clash of war thundered throughout the empire. Persian armies lost the battle of Marathon to the Greeks in 490 and ten years later were defeated again in the sea battle of Salamis. The roar of all this thunder, however, hardly echoed against the mountains of Yehud.

The silence of Palestine was broken toward 460 B.C. by the prophets *Malachia* and *Jona*. We can almost wish that they had never spoken, because in their words we glimpse a dismal picture of the Jews: unworthy sacrifices, broken marriages, social injustices, proud isolationism. The religious leaders and landed aristocracy certainly took advantage of being big fish in the tiny pond of Yehud. Thanks be to God these prophets had the courage to speak out; they preserved the nation until the arrival of Nehemia in 445 B.C. and of Ezra in 427 B.C.

Ezra and Nehemia were strong, clear-headed, competent men, perhaps a little irascible, but just the kind of leaders the people needed. They, and especially Ezra, overhauled Judaism from top to bottom. The temple liturgy was reformed; the ancient laws were codified; synagogal schools were instituted; the sacred writings were edited; the Sanhedrin or governing body of priests, scribes and elders was instituted. When *Abdia* and *Joel* appeared, perhaps around 400 B.C., there was a sense of satisfaction in the air. Everything was in good hands, in the good hands of the priests and elders.

In 333 B.C. Yehud was swept into the swirl of world events. The victorious army of Alexander the Great marched south along the Mediteranean coast and entered Jerusalem without a struggle. The Jews, perhaps, were content at first to be rid of Persian domination, but very soon they soured on the Greeks.

The last of the prophets now spoke. For want of a name we call him Deutero-Zacharia. He is the author of the last six chapters in the book of Zacharia. The cataclysm of world events resounds in his preaching—hopes built high only to be smashed, quick changes, great sorrows. He remained loyal to the priestly ideals of Ezechiel throughout, for this meant loyality to Moses, the great founder of the Jewish religion.

The age of the prophets was now ended. They had finished their work and were satisfied simply to be absorbed into this work. They were too high-minded to limit their thoughts to the tiny world of self; they did not want monuments in their name. They cared little that their prophecy was added to someone else's book or that a pseudonym was attached to their writing. They labored only that God be loved and man be happy. Their goal was finally achieved with the manifestation of Jesus, and so it can be said that they prepared for His coming. Everyone who prays "Come, Lord Jesus!" must listen to these last of the prophets.

THE PROPHET AGGAI

A decree of Cyrus II the Great in 538 B.C. officially ended the Babylonian Exile of the Israelite people. One year earlier, Cyrus' Persian armies had marched through the gates of Babylon, swung open to them at night by fifth-column traitors. Since Cyrus pursued a policy of benevolent despotism, he was particularly anxious that the ancient shrines of the empire be restored and the native populations be returned to their homelands. He wanted the gods of each place dutifully worshiped. Ezra 1:2-4 records the decree allowing the Israelite to re-establish in Palestine a sacred state for the worship of Yahweh.

The prophet Aggai enlisted in the first caravan. His eyes sparkled as they looked forward to a future of unparalleled glory. The golden messianic era predicted by the prophets of the Exile, Ezechiel and Deutero-Isaia, was here! This was the "time of favor" and the "day of salvation," when God said to the prisoners "Come out" and "to those in darkness: Show yourselves!" To the mountains of the earth God gave the order: "Break forth into song,

> For the Lord comforts his people
> and shows mercy to his afflicted" (Is 49:13).

Such was the song of promise singing in the hearts of the first Zionists. What a dismal reality faced them in Palestine—streets overrun with weeds; homes haunted by the atrocities of pagan soldiers; the Temple area, a pile of rubble! The people mustered enough strength to clear the hill of Sion where Solomon had built the Temple and to lay the foundations for a new structure. But opposition and then terror-tactics from local inhabitants and jealous neighbors forced them to give up. Crop failures brought poverty and unemployment. People began to lie and to steal, while landowners enslaved their poorer brethern. Tired, disappointed and discouraged, the people allowed their interests to shrivel to the incidental needs of daily life. They were facing a spiritual crisis.

Another kind of crisis suddenly gripped the kingdom of the Medes and Persians, and the international embroilment was partly responsible for new hopes and vigorous activity in Israel. Cambyses II, son of the great Cyrus, committed suicide in 522 B.C. Revolts at once erupted throughout the sprawling empire. Darius, son of the satrap Hystaspes, was proclaimed king by the army, but it took him two years to secure a firm hold upon the empire. Darius looked favorably upon a request from the Jews to complete the Temple; he wanted to secure the loyalty of this difficult people (Ezra 5, 6-15).

The Prophet Appears

At this crisis, the Jewish people needed a leader with a strong faith in God and a down-to-earth sense of reality. He must speak the people's language, direct, simple, and straight-from-the-shoulder. The golden oratory of an Isaia would have sounded pompous and ridiculous to these men with empty stomachs, dull wits and trivial concerns. God chose well when He called Aggai.

Aggai (his name means "solemn feast") concentrated upon the one, practical task of rebuilding the Temple. His was the essential, pioneering work of a missionary bishop today: to establish a home and to build a church where people can assemble for prayer and instruction.

Aggai waved aside the prophetic practice of speaking in lyrical poetry. Perhaps he was not even capable of it. Among all the prophetical books of the Bible, his is the most colorless in literary style. He made a direct appeal to start work; he bluntly answered a few questions; He spoke four times in four months, and then he disappeared. His task was finished; the Temple would be rebuilt!

The Sermons of Aggai

In 520 B.C., eighteen years after the return of the first caravan, God first inspired Aggai to speak. It was the feast of the New Moon during the month of Elul (Aug-Sept). Aggai was certainly imitating the style of his master Ezechiel when he provides elaborate details of year, month and day before each of his prophecies. His prosaic book opens with the announcement: "On the first day of the sixth month in the second year of King Darius. . . ."

The contrast of the unfinished Temple with the completed homes of the people made Aggai speak his mind, but not with the cutting edge of the pre-exilic prophets. But neither were these earlier men of God very anxious about the Temple; in their judgment there was already too much sacrifice and too little moral living. At once we notice a shift from prophetism to priestly legalism, from vitality to form. Aggai is only at the beginning of this change; Our Lord and St. Paul attack this attitude when it has hardened into an obnoxious type of "Pharisaic" holiness.

Aggai put the worshipers to shame:

> Consider your ways!
>   Go up into the hill country;
>   Fetch lumber, and build the house
> That I may take pleasure on it
>   and receive my glory, says the Lord.
> You expected much, but it came to little;
>   but what you brought home, I blew away.
> For what cause? says the Lord of hosts.
>   Because my house lies in ruins,
>   while each of you hurries to his own house (1:7-9).

Though his sermon was blunt and awkward, nevertheless, it was effective, "and the people feared because of the Lord" (1:12).

Within twenty-four days, plans were drafted, and men were at work on the house of the Lord. About a month later, within the octave of the feast of Tabernacles, the Israelites gathered again at the Temple for worship (Lev 23:33-43). Some felt despondent at the tiny size of the new Temple, but Aggai's heart beat fast. This Temple, he prophesized in his second recorded sermon (Ag 2:1-9), is a pledge that one day all nations will submit to the kingdom of God, joyfully consecrating themselves and their treasures to the promised Messia.

> One moment yet, a little while,
>   and I will shake the heavens and the earth,
>   the sea and the dry land. . . .
> And I will fill this house with glory,
>   says the Lord of hosts. . . .
> Greater will be the future glory of this house
>   than the former, says the Lord of hosts (2:6-9).

What God first promised to Moses at Mount Sinai and partially fulfilled in the imposing temple of Solomon will one day from this place spread out into world-wide glory. This new Temple may seem small and cramped compared to Solomon's, but it was a pledge of the presence of God. Rightly then do the epistle to the Hebrews (Heb 12:26) and the Advent liturgy find this passage fulfilled in Jesus, a temple of divine presence, not made by hands. All peoples are united in Him, not so much as blocks of marble to a material edifice but as members of one body, animated by one spirit.

Unfortuantely, uncleanness spreads more quickly than holiness! In his third sermon (Ag 2:10-19), Aggai rejected the offer of the Samaritans to help reconstruct the Temple. Half pagan and half Jew, these people, he was convinced, would corrupt authentic Judaism (Ezra 4:1-2). From this point onward, Jew and Samaritan hated one another with a growing insolence and sometimes a raging bitterness. Only in and through Jesus would this wall of separation be removed.

The fourth and last sermon of Aggai (Ag 2:20-23) was delivered on the same day as the preceding one, the twenty-fourth day of the ninth month (Nov.-Dec.). Aggai showered messianic titles upon Zorobabel, who was of the royal, Davidic line: "servant," "chosen one," "signet ring," "chosen by God." Thus Aggai kept alive an ancient tradition that the Messia of Israel would be David's son.

THE PROPHET ZACHARIA

Scripture links the names of Zacharia and Aggai (Ezra 5:1; 6:14). They were partners in securing the reconstruction of the Temple. Yet even a quick reading of Zacharia's prophecy makes one realize that its author was not just an assistant behind the scenes. He was a vigorous person with definite ideas. One can make his acquaintance only from the first eight chapters of the book carrying his name; chapters nine to fourteen, as shall be explained later, are a later addition to the original prophecy.

What really makes Zacharia different is his mysterious style of preaching. St. Jerome called it "most obscure." Even after the reader hears an angel explaining the meaning of the visions, he is still left guessing! Not all the blame for this obscurity can be leveled against the Hebrew text, although it was damaged in transmission, or against the early Greek translation of it, which has readings all its own.

The awe and mystery surrounding Zacharia's message reflect the visions of Ezechiel, which saw the future caught up in a burst of splendor and reeling under the impact of God's transforming power (cf. Ez 1-2; 40-48). This style of writing is called *apocalyptic,* and Zacharia is an important figure in its literary development.

It is extraordinary that Zacharia should ever have used the apocalyptic style in preaching to an impoverished people worrying about food and clothing. What is even more surprising is that such a prophet should possess a keen sense of the people's ordinary problems. Zacharia was one of those rare persons who is able to combine high hopes with practical solutions.

Once we have pieced together this much of his character, there is little more to say. Quite likely he belonged to the priestly caste, to the tribe of Levi and the family of Aaron (Neh 12:16). He appears before us, however, less the priest officiating at worship than the prophet preaching to his people. His ministry overlapped Aggai's by two months, but Zacharia continued preaching for another two years after that. The book's last date is in the month of Casleu (Nov.-Dec.), 518 B.C. (Zach 7:1).

Introductory Discourse

Zacharia's inaugural discourse was spoken in the eighth month (Oct.-Nov.), 520 B.C. We notice at once his loyalty to the great prophets of the past, men who strove to avert the tragic Babylonian exile by urging justice and charity, but who were struck down, like Jeremia was, as blasphemers against the Jerusalem Temple (cf. Jer 7:1-15; 26). Zacharia the prophet knew that God was not satisfied with a temple of wood and stone. He would again destroy such a temple, if that was necessary to save the interior temple of holiness.

> Be not like your fathers whom the former prophets warned: ... Turn from your evil ways and from your wicked deeds.... Your fathers, where are they? And the prophets, can they live forever?

Then they repented and admitted: "The Lord of hosts has treated us according to our ways and deeds" (1:4-6).

By a prophetic paradox, Zacharia's doctrine of threat and doom proposes the consoling doctrine of hope. God destroys only to save.

Eight Visions

In the month of Sabat (Jan.-Feb.), 519 B.C., Zacharia again preaches, this time casting his sermon in the apocalyptic form of a vision. Four horsemen have patrolled "the whole earth" and have reported back that all is "tranquil and at rest" (1:11). Throughout the empire, Darius had just finished suppressing the revolts which had erupted when Cambyses II had committed suicide and Darius had seized the throne. If the Jews had been expecting a violent overthrow of Persian power and the establishment of God's glorious kingdom at Jerusalem, then we can sympathize with their cry: "O Lord of hosts, how long will you be without mercy for Jerusalem and the cities of Juda that have felt your anger these seventy years?" (1:12). "Seventy years" was a term first used by Jeremia for the long, dismal period of exile (Jer 25:11; 29:10). The Jews were questioning if the exile had really come to an end! God then promised that the Temple would be rebuilt and would stand as a symbol of the prosperity awaiting Jerusalem in the messianic age.

In explaining this vision and the others to follow, it is not easy, and sometimes not even possible, to identify all the symbolism used.

In a second vision (2:1-4), Zacharia reported that "I raised my eyes and looked: there were four horns," and later "the Lord showed me four blacksmiths" (2:1:3). Horns symbolize power (Deut 33:17; Jer 48:25), and in this vision they stand for the powerful enemies of God's people. The number *four* expresses all God's enemies, who come from the four corners of the earth. The four blacksmiths signify the full strength of divine power—or possibly angels —poised to destroy the horns. Even though God's people watch their country crumble and feel themselves cast into the dirt, they still impress the onlooker with their mighty spirit of hope. God, through them, will be victorious. Faith demands this sustaining hope, and charity is its pledge.

A third vision (2:5-17) predicts the world-wide expanse of God's kingdom. The new Jerusalem of the messianic age is not to be measured by human yardsticks. There will be no necessity of walls to protect the city, for who fears danger when God is present with His people. The prophet calls upon everyone to return with singing and rejoicing. Babylon, city of evil and oppression, will be plundered and humiliated. God will then transform Juda into "the holy land"—here is the first time this name occurs in the Bible—and Jerusalem will be chosen as messianic capital. Juda and Jerusalem, therefore, which at present are gloomy places full of disappointment, will eventually be the center of God's glorious kingdom on earth. The vision ends with a call for "Silence, all mankind, in the presence of the Lord!" (2:17). What God has in mind for His people will overpower them with its grandeur. "What eye has not seen nor ear heard. . . ." (Is 64:3; 1 Cor 2:9).

The details of a fourth vision (3:1-10; 4:4-10) are at once more certain and more confusing. Zacharia identifies the high priest and the civil governor as Josue and Zorobabel, but he leaves us guessing about the rest. Moreover, the Hebrew text has been scrambled in transmission and each commentator upon it makes some rearrangement of the text to unscramble it.

The high priest carries the guilt of his fellow priests and of the people to the throne of God. He is accused by Satan, who is portrayed hostile to men but not necessarily an enemy of God. Here, as in he prologue to the Book of Job, Satan stands in the throne room before the divine presence. The biblical writer is struggling with the mysterious fact that Satan, though abetting evil and inspiring sin, cannot frustrate the will of God and in some way acts as a servant of God.

The angel of the Lord—Zacharia's indirect way of referring to God—removes the guilt, and in doing so He washes away the sins of all the people. Like another Moses, the high priest now enjoys free access to the presence of God. In this chapter we watch the high priest rise to the height of power over the Temple and the destiny of the chosen people. Before this time, in the pre-exilic days, the king exercised great authority even in religious matters. From now on it will be different.

Whoever worships at the earthly Temple, must accompany the high priest and with him be mystically swept up into a heavenly sanctuary. Here, no doubt, is the inspiration for some of our Lord's words in John 2:13-22.

Zacharia accords messianic honors to Josue the high priest: "man of good omen," "shoot," "my servant"—the same phrases used by Aggai. Likely enough, Zacharia like Aggai addressed these titles to Zorobabel, the civil governor of the Davidic line. Later, when priests were supreme in Israel, the scribes adapted this text as well as another, in Zach 6:11, to the new condition. But already in Zacharia's day the priesthood had eclipsed the Davidic heir and represented the hopes of the nation.

In a fifth vision (4:1-3, 11-14) Zacharia sees the lamp-stand, that is, the Temple of the messianic age, receiving oil for its glorious light from the two anointed ones of Israel, the king and the high priest. This text reveals the Jewish expectation of two Messias, a tradition very evident in the Dead Sea Scrolls. It is fulfilled in Jesus, who was both priest and king (Heb 5:5-6; John 18:37).

A sixth and seventh vision have much in common. Zacharia watches the land swept clean of sin by an enormous scroll upon which the curses and the filth of the country were inscribed. Wickedness is deposited in a large bushel and flown away to Senaar, an ancient name for Babylon (cf. Gen 11:2). There people worshiped their own sins and made gods from their basest passions.

A terrifying vision, the eighth, now ensues. God's anger roars in all directions like madly driven chariots, like an explosion in blinding colors. Before He devastates the north (Babylon), however, God will rescue His chosen ones. His anger is not irresponsible; rather it is prompted by a love unwilling to tolerate hate and sorrow. These same four horsemen will reappear in the book of Apocalypse of the New Testament; they will be summoned by the Lamb as He opens, one by one, the seals of the great scroll and unravels the final age of the world (Apoc 6:1-8).

A Coronation

The book of Zacharia now describes the coronation of Zorobabel (6:9-15). In placing a golden crown upon the descendant of King David, Zacharia was not organizing a revolt against Persia. His action was not intended for the present but for some future, messianic day when God would fulfill His promises to David. At that time king and priest would work together for God's glory. By faith and hope the audience immediately before Zacharia participated in the future glory. The Persians, however, may have interpreted this action in another way and immediately whisked Zorobabel away. At least from this moment onward, we no longer hear any more of the Davidic family. It vanishes into oblivion. The high priest emerges as the supreme power in the tiny state of Yehud.

At some later date, the name of "Josue, son of Josedec, the high priest" was substituted in this passage for Zorobabel. Such tampering with the text surprises, even scandalizes us, but for the Jews it meant an "actualization" or an adaptation of the past and even of the future of each present *now.*

True Fasting

Two questions are now presented to the prophet, each about fasting (ch. 7-8). In answering them differently, the prophet is not inconsistent. Two points of views are necessary because of the different spiritual needs of each audience. The first question is put to the prophet by a delegation from Jews still living away from Palestine in exile (7:1-3; 8:18-19).

These men, who bear Babylonian names, arrived in the ninth month (Nov.-Dec.) and asked if it is still necessary to fast. The Temple is now being rebuilt. Why must they continue mourning over its calamitous destruction? Four great fast days, one of them soon coming up, were being rigorously observed: in the tenth month (Dec.-Jan.), when the siege of Jerusalem had begun; in the fourth month (June-July), when the Babylonians had breached the walls of Jerusalem; in the fifth month (July-Aug), when the Temple had been burned; and in the seventh month (Sept.-Oct.), when renegade Jews had assassinated the governor Godolia.

Zacharia does not directly answer the delegates (8:18-19). "Be encouraged," he seems to say, "fasting is good, for it brings joy and gladness. But value faithfulness and peace still more!" These various days of fasting gradually disappeared and in their place the Jews substituted the *one* great Day of Atonement, *Yom Kippur* (Lev 16).

With the Palestinian Jews, Zacharia is more severe (7:4-14). He saw the outrage present when "religious" people profess concern for God's family even when they plot evil against the children of that family! The Palestinian Jews fasted and mourned over the anguish once suffered by the people of God; they ate and drank at sacrificial banquets to show a common family spirit before God. All the while, they were destroying that family with the hard blows of injustice! God wanted not mere fasting from them but faithfulness and peace.

Zacharia now introduces seven promises with the formula: "Thus says the Lord of host" (8:1-17). Here the heart of a loving father speaks with simple charm about old men with staff in hand, boys and girls playing in the streets, remnant of this people, and honesty. The Jews loved their children and venerated their aged, but both of these groups were missing in the new Zion. Many of the Zionists were young couples, still awaiting children.

In a final section Zacharia sees peoples of many nations who "take hold of every Jew by the edge of his garment" and go up with him to the holy city (8:20-23). Charity for *all* must be the spirit behind fasting, for in the messianic City of God all men will be brothers. Little did Zacharia foresee how beautifully his prophecy would be fulfilled, when the cross of Jesus would unite the world in the pierced heart of the Savior.

THE PROPHECY OF MALACHIA

That the humble man acts courageously and thinks clearly is proven by the prophet Malachia. Fearless in denouncing evil, loyal to the point of blood, consistent in what is right and wrong, straightforward in speaking his mind, such was Malachia. And all the while he humbly hides from us not only the data of his life but even his real name! The ancient editors of the book called him Malachia, giving us the only instance in the Bible of a man bearing that name. But in so doing, the editors were simply borrowing a word from chapter three, which is there correctly translated as "my messenger." With no other name at hand, we must follow them in calling the prophet *Malachia.*

A name can be suppressed, but not courage! This prophet could not refrain from speaking openly in behalf of God and God's people, and from his plain speech we can reconstruct his time and his character.

There are indications that he lived during the Persian period (539-333 B.C.), such as his use of the Persian word *peah* for governor (Mal 1:8). The Temple has been rebuilt, so it seems that the prophet speaks after 515 B.C. Again, he attacks the same social evils and the same religious abuses which Nehemia and Ezra would later take in hand and remedy promptly, and so we conclude that Malachia precedes these reformers. We can place Malachia, then, toward the close of those silent, languid years between 515-445 B.C.

Weary years they were: blighted by crop failures, locust plagues and withered grape vines. How different all this was from the golden, messianic panorama described in the lyric poetry of Second Isaia! What a letdown, even after the prosaic utterances of Aggai!

The "pious" people wanted to know why *they* must put on pentitential dress. Were not even the proud being blessed? Malachia answered by bluntly challenging the piety of those "good" people. And yet, should these people be blamed, when the priests themselves merited such stern judgment that God is reported as saying, "I will strew dung in your faces!"

Without religious leadership, the whole social structure of the tiny nation was cracking badly. There were frequent, easy divorces; older men discarded their good Jewish wives to marry pretty, foreign girls. Cheating in business and forcible selling into slavery broke the backs of the poor.

Someone must speak out for God, so Malachia stepped forward! In such times a prophet could no longer get a hearing with the simple statement: "Thus says the Lord. . . ." He had to line up reasons for what he said and argue the matter out. Malachia, therefore, adopted a catechetical method. First, he gives a statement: "I have loved you, says the Lord"; then, the people's question: "How have you loved us?" Finally, the prophet answers. His answers were as clear, simple and forceful as the prophet himself. They made little demand upon the imagination but did expect humble good will. Proud people would reject the warning of Malachia, but they could never escape the terrifying knowledge that in so doing they were rejecting God!

Israel Preferred

Malachia's first words ring with loyalty towards his own nation (1:2-5). God has loved Israel more than any one else. This love is shown to be all the greater—and Israel's questioning of it, all the more shameful—because it was not deserved, though freely given.

Maddened by the people's response, a questioning shrug of the shoulder, Malachia proved his point. Edom, the craggy land to the south of the Dead Sea, is proof enough. Edom and Israel hate one another, and this hatred stretches back to their forefathers, Esau and Jacob. When they were twins as yet unborn, so Genesis reports, the boys "jostled each other" in their mother's womb (Gen 25:21-26). God chose Jacob as His favorite, and even into the time of Malachia this favoritism continued. Yahweh allowed Edom to be invaded by a desert people, the Nabateans, who gradually pushed the Edomites out of their mountain kingdom. In biblical language, God "hated Edom." Yet Israel, whom Yahweh loved, was re-established in its homeland after the exile.

St. Paul will further develop this doctrine of God's generous love, as he adds that God can just as easily transfer His special affection from the Jews to the other nations (Rom 9:25-33).

Sins of Priests and Levites

The sins of the Levitical priests are now exposed (1:6-2:9). These men are too bored with their sacred office to insist upon worthy sacrifices. They allow the people to offer in sacrifice what the law forbids, maimed and sick animals (Deut 17:1). This sickening irreverence in the temple scene itself forces Malachia to shut his eyes and to dream of messianic days ahead. What God then reveals to Malachia does not shatter the tablets of the Mosaic Covenant nor does it stray outside a genuine prophetic tradition. Isaia had dreamed of *all* nations streaming towards Jerusalem and climbing the mount of the Lord (2:1-5).

Malachia predicts a *liturgical* sacrifice, as the Hebrew text makes clear. The nations, he declares, will "bring sacrifice ... a pure offering." The Hebrew words are those used consistently and exclusively of ritual undertakings. This sacrifice, he says, is to be offered "from the rising of the sun, even to its setting." This last phrase does not refer to sacrifice every moment of the day but rather to participants from every part of the world. Still, it will be in accord with the

Mosaic Covenant, for it will be offered to Yahweh, God who revealed Himself to Moses. The Levitical priests, as Malachia will later make clear, will continue to have a prominent part in this sacrifice: Malachia remains within the hopes and teaching of Moses.

Vaguely, from a distance, Malachia heralded the Mass, the only liturgical sacrifice of the messianic age. The Sacrifice of the Mass continues the paschal sacrifice of the Mosaic Law, as this act of worship has been renewed and transformed by the most pure and pleasing sacrifice of Jesus upon the Cross.

Malachia now turns upon the Levitical priests. They "will be carried off" to destruction. The worst corruption is that which befalls the best, and Malachia's respect for the priesthood sharpens his recognition of the shameful disgrace before him. He actually curses them in the name of God:

> I will send a curse upon you
>   and of your blessing I will make a curse. . . .
> I will strew dung in your faces . . . (2:2-3).

Immediately, however, he must have lowered his head into his arms to conceal his grief, as with poignancy he spoke of their high estate:

> . . . I have a covenant with Levi. . . .
> My covenant with him was one of life and peace;
>   fear I put in him, and he feared me,
>   and stood in awe of my name (2:4-5).

He tries to forget about their debased condition by thinking of the ideal priest—the mediator of life and peace, the messenger or angel of the Lord, the source of truth, the keeper of knowledge, the steward of uprightness (2:6-7; 3:1). Quite clearly, then, Malachia's terrible indictment of the priesthood reflects, not a sour disposition, but rather the sad, disappointed words of a saint!

Sins of the People

He proceeds to denounce the people's sins: not sarcastically, but sorrowfully; not in any soft, sickly way, but with vigor and manliness (2:10-17). Malachia's strength and kindly sympathy come to him from God and help him to see everything in God. His vision is all embracing, passing from God to marriage, from temple liturgy back again to God.

God is a father to all. Breaking faith with his brother, man does violence to the family circle of God. God is a creator, who unites man and woman in marriage, making them "one being, with flesh and spirit" (2:15). Each man who sheds the wife of his youth now that she is elderly, to marry some attractive, foreign girl "has profaned the Temple" (2:11) and has covered "the altar of the Lord . . . with tears, weeping and groaning" (2:13). He makes God cry out, "I hate divorce!" (2:16). And yet this same insolent man carelessly asks, "Where is the just God?" (2:17).

The Final Reckoning

Chapter three of the prophecy gives God's answer to the cynic's question. Unfortunately, His answer is intelligible only to the man of faith, who can take God at His word. The cynic laughs it off, but "the day is coming, blazing like an oven, when all the proud and all evil doers will be stubble" (3:19). It is the day of the Lord of hosts, when judgment will be pronounced against adulterers and perjurers, against those who defraud widows and orphans. In one last chance, God will send His messenger before that great and terrible day, to turn the hearts of the fathers to their children, "lest I come and strike the land with doom" (3:24).

"Doom!"—the word seems a dreaded ending to the book,

which itself ends the collection of the Twelve Minor Prophets, when these are given in their usual order. To avoid such an ending, therefore, Jewish practice required the repetition of a part of verse twenty-three. Soon, editors added the words to the manuscripts, with the result that the Book of the Twelve concluded with the mention of Elia, who was such a prominent figure in rabbinic speculation at the time of Our Lord. Jesus saw Malachia's word fulfilled in John the Baptist (Matt 11:10). Indeed, when John the Baptist said of Jesus, "He must increase, but I must decrease," he proved to be a worthy follower of Malachia, the anonymous prophet whose identity is covered by the Hebrew phrase "my messenger."

THE BOOK OF JONA

There was once a prophet Jona, a son of Amathi. In the days of Jeroboam II (783-743 B.C.), he announced the territorial expansion of the king's domain (4 Kgs 14:25). Some 400 years later, he came forth from the belly of a great fish, this time to prophesy the expansion of the *spiritual* kingdom of *God.* An incredible story? Not if the reader accepts this second event *as a story.* Then he will discover its true historical setting. Otherwise, he will be like a reader of *Gulliver's Travels* who takes the story so seriously as to be insensitive to its barbed satire. Much of recent biblical interpretation denies that the Jona who was spewed up on the shore of Palestine by the fish was a real person. It says that what we read about him in the Bible is not history, but only a parable, a story! This interpretation is soundly based, however, and the present author subscribes to it.

History in Parable Form

If Jona is not allowed to live in the belly of the fish for three days and three nights, it is not because God is unable to work such miracles. To deny miracles in the Bible would be to rewrite it wholly! In the book of Jona, however, miracles come in such quick succession—they are so sparse in all the other prophetic books—that we soon begin to suspect that these wondrous happenings are no more than simple literary flourishes.

Literary reasons exclude this book from the category of eighth-century prophecy. For one thing, Aramaic words and expressions are so lavishly strewn throughout its four chapters that this fact alone would date the book to the postexilic age. Aramaic came into common Jewish usage only after the Exile, much later than the time of Jeroboam II. Moreover, the postexilic age produced many edifying stories. Some, like Tobia and Judith, are in the Bible; others were collected by the rabbis and are preserved in the midrashic literature. These stories always center about ancient personages or events, and so they have their roots in history. But from these roots, there springs something new, a story which is at once interesting, instructive and practical. A final literary argument for the non-historical interpretation of Jona lies in the variation of style between this book and every other work of the later prophets. The works of the later prophets consist of prophetic judgments; Jona is a story. Compared with the other prophets, Jona is seen to be uniquely concerned with himself; yet it is characteristic of many of the postexilic prophets that they are lost in anonymity.

Archaeological discoveries belie the details of Jona. When the Assyrian capital, Nineve, was rediscovered, it was noted from the city's walls that this metropolis—tremendous for the times—could hold about 300,000 people. This is far short of the 1,000,000 inhabitants which would be required by the presence of the 120,000 infants indicated in Jona 4:11.

Nor is there the tiniest cuneiform inscription, the slightest biblical evidence that an Assyrian king and his people ever underwent such a conversion upon the word of an Israelite prophet as this book records.

Jona is a type, a foreshadowing of our Lord; the New Testament makes this clear (cf. Matt 12:38-41; Luke 11:29-32). Typology is satisfied if the type has a literary existence in the biblical narrative; it need not have real existence as well. The *Canticle of Canticles* is another type of Christ which no one hesitates to interpret symbolically. Consequently, when Jesus refers to Jona's three days in the belly of the fish, He is not thereby guaranteeing the historicity of that prophet.

Why, then, it may be asked, was Jona put among the prophets? Because the author of Jona drew heavily upon the prophecies of Jeremia and Ezechiel and gave their teaching its clearest and most forceful expression. The book of Jona taught the author's contemporaries that God was not their exclusive property, that racial and liturgical privileges were not the greatest of glories, that God loved everyone—even the despicable Assyrians!

The symbolism of the Jona story reveals an immense amount of historical data about the postexilic age. Many Jews of this age walked with stubborn rigidity down a narrow path trodden by generations of men. There were innumerable signposts along the way—laws, prescriptions, and interpretations of laws and prescriptions—so that these people could not fail to be "very holy." They naturally looked with disdain and hatred upon the rest of the world who not only broke the law, but who did not even know about it. Not all Jews, however, were so haughty and secure; one of these crusaded for tolerance, humility and compassion.

He was the anonymous "prophet" who wrote this book. He too was a real, historical figure.

The First Mission

The author attracts the sympathy of his listeners at once. His opening words cater to the fierce nationalism burning in their veins. If they follow their natural tendencies, they applaud Jona for fleeing from a mission of mercy to the wicked Ninivites. Very soon, however, the author shows his own point of view. Like Deutero-Isaia (Is 40-55) and the inspired writer of Ruth, his was a spirit of worldwide sympathy, a vision embracing all men. Grimly, he sets himself to unmasking the hypocrisy of his readership.

Aboard the boat, the foreign sailors—pagans though they are—upbraid Jona for not praying. Soon they discover that Jona, the worshiper of Yahweh, "the God of heaven, who made the sea and the dry land," dares to flee from the Lord! They are understandably frightened. What will be their punishment from Yahweh for having had a hand in this flight? Jona, however, offers them a way out. "Pick me up and throw me into the sea, that it may quiet down for you." It is as though he says, "Do whatever you want; God will take care of *me*. Even storms at sea depend upon *me*!" With reluctance and only after carefully telling the Lord that theirs is not the guilt, the sailors follow Jona's direction. The wondrous results leads them to worship Yahweh.

The Real Jona

Within the belly of the fish, Jona chants a song of thanksgiving (ch 2). Some scholars feel that the psalm—like Jona—is in the wrong place. They prefer to put it after verse eleven, where Jona is once more on land and safe. Such transferral misses the point of the psalm completely.

Jona is never safer than in the fish's belly, because he is being saved from his own determined self-will.

This episode became a type of Jesus' death and of our baptism. Jona in the depths of the sea, Jesus in the silence of the tomb, we beneath the waters of baptism—all are plunged into darkness and submit completely to God's will. We come forth infused with new life.

The conversion of Nineve (ch 3) shows that God's mercy is as far removed from man's as the heavens are above the earth. Nineve, the capital city of Assyria, stood in Jewish memory as a monstrous evil. No nation in the course of Israel's sacred history had ever been so oppressive in government, so vicious in warfare as Assyria. Yet there is God forgiving the Assyrians completely! The author of Jona does not forget the Jewish Temple and its sacred liturgy, for all his universalism. Like Joel, he preaches the necessity of fasting and sackcloth.

In chapter four we see that at the slightest touch Jona's mood swivels round like a chair. He is hot in anger, then happy, then angry again in turn. The pivotal point is his comfort or self-will. He pouts because the gourd plant dies and its shade is taken away. Jona the Jew needs conversion to Yahweh's will more than the Ninivites! God's lesson, that He has concern for the non-Jew, is so clearly taught that none can miss it.

The greatest mystery in the book is not the survival of Jona in the fish's belly, but the choice of this reluctant prophet as the instrument of the Gentile's salvation. The mystery vanishes when we go behind the story to its composer. The *real* Jona, the author of the book, is just the opposite of his literary hero. What a humble, saintly Jew he must have been. He knew of God's love for all mankind and taught his contemporaries this lesson of tolerance to save them from themselves and to force them to humility, compassion and penance.

THE PROPHET ABDIA

The book of Abdia—"Obadiah" in Jewish and Protestant editions of the Bible—is the shortest in the Old Testament. Its twenty-one verses must supply all we know about the prophet. Little as it is, even this must be pared down, because Abdia wrote less than half of the "book." He borrowed heavily from another source. Much of this prophecy parallels what the prophet Jeremia says in chapter 49, verses 7-22.

"Edom" is the key to understanding Abdia and his prophecy. Edom and Israel were kinsmen; they descended from Esau and Jacob, the twin sons of Isaac. Genesis tells how the two boys jostled one another in their mother's womb; their posterity continued the quarrel (Gen 25:19-26). Difference and distrust grew into hostility, and hostility turned into intense hatred. David and Amasia, kings of Juda, ruthlessly massacred the Edomites (2 Sam 8:13-14; 4 Kings 14:7). The Edomites in turn gloated when Jerusalem was destroyed in 587 B.C. At that time, they ambushed fugitive Judeans and handed them over to the Babylonians (cf. Ez 25:12-14; 35). They also occupied the Negeb district of southern Juda. Helpless, Juda felt like a drowning man whom Edom was not attempting to rescue but to shove down beneath the waters of despair.

All the prophets shouted vengeance against Edom. How else could God's people go on believing in His justice and mercy? Abdia, like Jeremia, snatched the angry, impatient cry of an earlier prophet, and hurled it against the craggy mountains of Edom: "Up! Let us go to war!" (Abd 1).

The mountains of Edom bred a proud, insular people who

were always looking down from their high perch upon a midget world. These mountains of prophyry, red granite and black basalt ranged southward for the hundred miles between the Dead Sea and the Gulf of 'Aqaba. Falling off into steep crevices in the west, leveling to grain covered plateaus to the east, these mountains carefully guarded their inhabitants. The Edomites grew into a nation which was not only proud and secure, but also wealthy, for they "protected" the caravan routes moving northward out of Arabia and Egypt.

Around 550 B.C., the Nabateans came from the desert to the east and began to push the Edomites from their mountain fortress. The Nabatean conquest was not complete till 312 B.C., but Israel's savage temper was relieved to see Edom receive its deserts. Sometime after 550 B.C. Abdia wrote this book in his quick, impassioned style, exclaiming his "Amen!" to each new defeat suffered by Edom.

His book is fiercely nationalistic, intensely narrow in its vision. If this troubles the reader, let him remember that Abdia is only one part of the Old Testament, and that the smallest part. Its message, however, had to be told. Persecuted people of every age find sustenance for their hungry faith in Abdia. Evil *shall* be crushed; goodness *shall* triumph!

The first part of the prophecy is addressed to the Edomites (2-9). Edom, we hear the prophet saying, you will be sought out in the clefts of the rocks and your country stripped to its rocky bones. Your wise men, like those who came to comfort Job (cf Job 4:1), will disappear; your warriors will be overpowered; your land, destroyed! You have provoked this vengeance by your inhumanity to Juda (10:14).

The perspective now widens and Abdia speaks to his fellow Judeans (15-21). On "the day of the Lord," Yahweh

will judge all nations. He will then restore the ideal boundaries of the Promised Land (cf. Num 34). Jerusalem, with
its Temple on Mount Sion, will become the capital city of the
world, the center and source of universal salvation. This and
similar prophecies will find fulfillment, when Jesus comes
from the *heavenly* Jerusalem to rule a universe of peace and
joy (cf. Apoc 21-22).

THE PROPHET JOEL

Several Old Testament figures bore the name Joel, which
means "Yahweh is God," but none of them can qualify as
the prophet. The prophet Joel, therefore, is a mysterious
figure, whose only personal reminiscence is the name of his
father, Phatuel. Despite his sublime self-forgetfulness, the
prophet pours much of his character and disposition into his
book. Not afraid of other people's judgment, he speaks with
the utmost confidence, almost with abandon.

The Prophet and His Book

Joel has fine thoughts about everyone; he is one of Scripture's great optimists. To some, such a statement may sound
unbelievable, because Joel summons priests and people to
sackcloth and ashes. With heavy speech and leaden tones he
mourns the plague of the black, rattling locusts. Yet,
despite his tone of sorrowful lamentation, Joel is kind in his
thoughts, encouraging in his words.

He never puts the blame of the plague upon anyone.
Dried up vines, withered fig trees, stripped pomegranates
and date palm, trees with their bark sheared off, their
branches made white—all these mute testimonials to the
ravenous locusts are not viewed as so many tombstones marking the presence of wicked people and dead souls. Joel

never "theologizes" on the cause of the sorrow. How different he is from the other prophets!

It is enough for Joel to know that God is "gracious and merciful, slow to anger, rich in kindness" (2:13; Ex 34:6-7). The overpowering sense of God's goodness keeps the prophet from seeing evil anywhere among his co-religionists. He speaks freely, and no one feels offended. Not only that, his audience is fascinated by his melodious rhythm, his musical sound. At times his lines spring up as quickly as the locusts which "leap on the mountain tops," or again, his words drag heavily in monotonous sing-song which tells how the casks rot away, the barns are broken down, the beasts groan and cry out.

A cry to God—such is the book of Joel. Some scholars consider it to be a ritual for temple worship and put the prophet himself among the Temple's personnel. They point out Joel's constant call to prayer and fasting, his continual turning to God for mercy, his many allusions to earlier prophets, his abundant use of liturgical language. Most scholars, however, reject this view. Locusts, they point out, are not featured in the rituals of the ancient Near East. More likely, the prophet proclaimed his message at some temple service held during a national disaster. Quite naturally, he borrowed many ideas from the liturgy.

Was Joel describing a real plague of locusts? St. Jerome and some others felt that the locusts were simply a literary device of the prophet's to aid him in presenting vividly the darkness and struggle which attended the day of the Lord's judgment. But this view is certainly in the minority. The language is too graphic, the reactions are too personal, the impressions too powerful for anyone but an eyewitness. Chapters one and two describe a real event.

All four chapters are from the same prophet. To be sure,

there are differences which exist between the two major parts of Joel, but there is also a chain of continuity, even in the differences. The first part of Joel, chapter 1-2, was composed after the passing of a plague of locusts. The second part, chapters 3-4, never mentions the locusts, but it does carry forward the theme, already begun, of the "day of the Lord." In each part this "day" is a terrible and a frightening thing, but the "Lord is a refuge to his people" (4:16). The second and final "day" whirls around the earth like a cyclone, turning the sun into darkness and the moon into blood, summoning the whole human race to the Valley of Josaphat for judgment. While the Gentiles on this final "day" do not implore pardon, the Jews on the earlier "day" of the locust plague did humble themselves and did do penance. Each part of Joel climaxes in abundant blessings; the first, in rain and grain, wine and oil; the second, in the outpouring of the Spirit of God.

The center of this joy, the place where the Lord dwells, is Sion. This fact, which is mentioned in the last line of the prophecy, when put together with other details of the book, helps us to place Joel in his proper setting. The Temple has been rebuilt on Sion, and the entire community can be assembled within its courtyard. Priests and elders are the leaders; there is no trace of royalty, nor even of a governor. We think at once of the tiny state of Yehud. Further pinpointing reduces the date to a point around 400 B.C.—after the re-editing of the earlier sacred books— because Joel borrows frequently from other prophets, even from Abdia. (Compare Abdia 17 and Joel 3:5.) Because the allusion to the Greeks in Joel 4:6 is much more moderate in tone than that in Zacharia 9:13, Joel's prophecy is usually dated at sometime before 333 B.C. and the conquests of Alexander the Great.

All to Penance

Joel stands before the assembly and calls for attention (1:1-12). He must have rehearsed his sermon repeatedly in the silent sorrow of his heart during the dreadful plague. The reader can guess at the fearful size of the plague from the fact that within the last century a single swarm of locusts over the Red Sea was estimated as having 24,420,000 insects.

Weighted with sorrow, Joel's words fall with a heavy thump, not slowly but in quick succession, like the fast beating of a bass drum. Swiftly he shifts from one depressive scene to another: mourning among newlyweds; the suspension of temple sacrifice; the appalling sight of a devastated countryside.

The priests are begged to proclaim a fast and to summon an assembly of prayer, "for near is the day of the Lord" (1:13-20). This phrase, "the day of the Lord," was first used by the prophet Amos (Am 5:18). That plain-spoken, shepherd prophet warned the Israelites of his time, who lazily awaited the glorious fulfillment of God's promises, that God's "day" would be *for them* a day of darkness! Blessings did not automatically come to everyone: bad, good and indifferent! For Joel, the "day of the Lord" is overcast with sorrow, but it does not explode into panic. God controls the massive power of the locusts, and so Joel prays, "to you, O Lord, I cry!"

This "day" falls like a shroud of mourning over a blackened earth (2:1-17). Joel describes this "day" in the doleful language of Sophonia, Michea and Lamentations. Joel asks, "Who can bear it?" Yet such sorrow has a purpose. When man is pushed to the brink of frustration, he finds God closer than ever before. At the black pit of despair, the mighty voice of God booms forth: "Return to me with your whole heart." Sorrow makes man rend his heart, in order to surrender his deepest self to God. Only then can God trust man with the gift of happiness.

Blessings and Judgment

Blessings transform the world into another paradise (2:18-3:5). This paradise is to begin with the presence of the Messia. Rightly, then, does this section of Joel find echo in the annunciation of St. Luke's Gospel: "Fear not . . . exult . . . the Lord has done great things" (Luke 1:18, 30, 46-49).

Joel borrows not only "day of the Lord," but also "spirit" from ancient traditions. It was the spirit who mastered chaos at the moment of creation (Gen 1:2) and who girded the judges and the prophets with extraordinary power (Jdg 6:34; Is 42:1). The same spirit was to rest upon the Messia (Is 11:2), and now Joel promises it to everyone. St. Peter quotes these words of Joel on the first Pentecost (Acts 2:17-21), when the Spirit of Jesus inaugurates the messianic work, transforming "the remnant" of the apostles into a kingdom of God's chosen ones. Pentecost gradually becomes an eternal "day of the Lord," when all the elect are at home with God and the whole earth is a "heavenly Jerusalem."

Everyone is summoned to the Valley of Josaphat, where, as the name indicates, "Yahweh judges" between good and evil (ch. 4). God's enemies are turned into "a desert waste," but Juda becomes a land flowing with milk and dripping new wine. Symbolism? Yes, but behind the symbolism is the stark reality of present suffering and the wondrous reality of the promised Paradise.

THE PROPHECY OF DEUTERO-ZACHARIA

Passing from the first to the second part of Zacharia is like leaving a room full of furniture from an older period and entering another decorated after modern tastes.

Search for the Prophet

No more dates, months, or years; no concern for Zoro-babel the governor or Josue the high priest; nothing about the reconstruction of the Temple; not a single mention of the prophet's name—these striking differences from chapters 1-8 of Zacharia argue strongly for another author who is responsible for chapters 9-14. The differences go beyond subject matter to stylistic features. The thoughts of chapters 9-14 move in a more regular poetic rhythm. The earlier Zacharia described his visions *as visions*, extraordinary bursts of the divine, which an angel must explain; Deutero-Zacharia makes visions seem to be a normal feature of real life. The world of earthy substance splits apart catastrophically. The "apocalyptic style" of the first Zacharia now comes to full maturity.

Most scholars find no difficulty in distinguishing First from Deutero-Zacharia, but these same experts are baffled in their effort to identify the inspired author (or authors) of chapters 9-14. We are reminded of John the Baptist's words about Christ: "He must increase, but I must decrease" (John 3:30). The closer the Old Testament prophets approach in time to John the Baptist and Jesus Himself, so much more anonymous do they appear. It is their message, not themselves, which they put forward. It will come as no surprise, then, that this prophet, so frequently quoted in the New Testament, is never mentioned by name.

There is another reason why the authorship of Zacharia 9-14 remains obscure. Between 330 and 200 B.C., the history of Palestine is enfolded in silence. Scholars usually date Deutero-Zacharia to the period following the death of Alexander the Great in 323 B.C. Although this conclusion is far from certain, it is the best, for want of a better explanation. Alexander's victorious march down the Mediterranean coast seems to be the divine judgment mentioned in Zacharia 9:1-8. Yet the reference to the Sons of Yavan" (Greeks) in Zacharia 9:13 is probably a late intrustion into the text. The highly apocalyptic style of writing leaves us guessing about minor details and complicates the dating of the book.

The First "Burden"—ch. 9-11

The first section of Deutero-Zacharia (9:1-8) is introduced by the single word, "a burden." The same word occurs before chapters 12-14 and once again at the opening of Malachia's prophecy (in Hebrew). Does this inscription introduce *three* separate units, each by a different, inspired author? Many scholars think so, and proceed to split chapters 9-11 from chapters 12-14.

The "burden" or "judgment with weighty consequences" of Zacharia 9:1-8 is God's decision to smash all opposition and set up His promised kingdom. The geography of these verses cuts a path from Damascus, in the interior of Syria, westward to the Mediterranean coast, then south from one seaport to another. The swift march of Alexander's conquering army provides a picture for Deutero-Zacharia as it topples the colossal Persian empire and establishes the Hellenistic world state. We see the swiftness with which God fulfills His promises. God's army, however, is not ruthless. Even the Philistines become part of the "remnant" of His people. The center of the new community is "my house," the Temple.

A herald joyfully proclaims the messianic restoration (9:9-17). "Rejoice heartily" is repeated again, when the angel Gabriel announces to Mary that the Messia is to dwell beneath her immaculate heart (Luke 1:28).

The style of this passage is heraldic, resembling the formal acclamation of the king's arrival. *This* king is a "just savior," that is, he is the "just" fulfillment of all God's promises. "Humble and meek," he saves the poor by becoming one of them. His riding on an ass shows his peaceful intentions. The ass symbolizes royalty and peace (cf. Gen 49:11). On Palm Sunday, Jesus fulfills this prophecy to the letter, but even if He had not entered Jerusalem "riding on an ass," this prophecy would have been accomplished in Him, since Jesus was a humble, peaceful king.

Deutero-Zacharia now describes the future in the language of the past (10:1-11:3). The mind of the prophet has so absorbed the word of God that the prophetic message pours out in the phrases of Osee, Isaia, Jeremia and Ezechiel.

God has launched a power in this world which cannot be resisted. Mighty cedars, symbolic of the great political forces like Assyria and Egypt, will be devoured by fire and then forgotten.

When Zacharia writes the allegory of the shepherds, his language is most obscure (11:4-17). Perhaps the prophet could not write any differently about a subject so full of mystery. Like the prophet Ezechiel, he too becomes a man of signs, not speaking but acting out the message. God, out of pity for sheep who are neglected and maltreated, tells the prophet to shepherd them. Yet, the people do not want God's help. Their sins unleash the cruelty of wicked shepherds, who are in turn destroyed by their own recklessness. God orders the good shepherd to smash the staff "Favor" and later, the other staff "Bonds." Thus God withdraws what the people rejected, His loving favor and the bond of His covenant.

To the people, the good shepherd is worth no more than the price of a slave (Ex 21:32). The prophet hurls their money into the Temple's treasury. God cannot look with "favor" upon their worship. When another false shepherd rejects the Good Shepherd centuries later, he too breaks the "bond" of God's "favor" and destroys himself (Matt 26: 16; 27:3-10). The New Testament incident of Judas is well known and understood, but the Old Testament account in Deutero-Zacharia still baffles the scholars. There is a long list of evil men among the postexilic priests, but which of them were the shepherds of the allegory?

The Second "Burden"—ch. 12-14

A final section (chapters 12-14) begins with the ominous word "a burden"—a divine oracle, a stern judgment. Again the prophet throws an aura of mystery around his message by the abundant use of prophetic symbolism. He speaks of an intoxicating bowl of madness; the war of the nations against Jerusalem; a weighty stone; the pouring out of the spirit; a day of mourning. He constantly repeats the phrase, "on that day." The hopes, the fears, the sorrows, the joys, the madness, the fright, the wars, the victories of all ages are heaped together and thrust upon *that day!*

The prophet announces a victory of God for that day. A fire roars forth from Jerusalem to devour every hostile group. The faithful Jews of the countryside, the poor and weak become as strong as David.

On that day the bells of victory ring out tumultuously, but suddenly they stop and begin to toll. God's people must not forget the innocent one "whom they have thrust through"; his grief was the price of victory (12:10). Many questions arise at this point, because the Hebrew text is damaged and its references are obscure, particularly the reference to Adadremmon (12:11). All classes of people will mourn the one pierced through; kings of the family of David, priests of the family of Levi, men and women.

This prophecy was lived out on Calvary (John 19:37), but it reaches its final "day" of fulfillment when Jesus the supreme judge "comes with the clouds and every eye shall see him, and they also who pierced him" (Apoc 1:7). In heaven the scars of Christ's wounds will be a precious reminder of the cost He paid for our happiness.

Deceit will end on that "day" (13:1-6). All filth will be washed away by the fountain of purification. Its waters will also bring life, since water always vivifies the dry soil of tropical Palestine. This life-giving water flows from the Temple of Jerusalem (Ez 47:1-12).

Prophets who slash their bodies in frantic orgies and then attempt to conceal their immorality under the honored "hairy mantle" of Elia (4 Kgs 1:8) will be evecuted by their own parents. Goodness cannot live with wickedness.

The final section of Deutero-Zacharia presents the fight for Jerusalem, a war waged with fierceness and finality (ch. 14). Jerusalem symbolizes the supreme goodness, the divine promises, the messianic hopes. Here at Jerusalem, the holy city wherein God dwells with His people, the heavenly city of eternal joy—here the deadly battle between good and evil is fought.

All that is said here of Jerusalem is true of Jesus Christ, against whom the Prince of Darkness rose to wage a mortal struggle.

The prophet, therefore, writes about unbelievable sorrows resulting in wondrous joys. His language is highly symbolic, extremely impressionistic. But behind the symbolism lies the real and terrible picture of vanquished evil.

Though "God is love" (1 John 4:8), His love is strong and pure and will never tolerate the least sin or unhappiness to tarnish the eternal life of His chosen ones.

PART III

*The Prophets who foretold the grace
    that was to come
    made earnest inquiry and search
    concerning this salvation* (1 Pet 1:10).

CHAPTER 8

THE OLD
TESTAMENT
ADVENT

In Old Testament times the advent or coming of God into
the lives of His people was concealed beneath the mask of
human lowliness.

The Word of God Become Flesh

The Bible is the word of God, but this divine word is
spoken by human lips. Within its pages heavenly thoughts
are revealed not as blinding streaks of lightning nor yet as
shattering clashes of thunder, but in the measured speech
of the human tongue. In the Scripture we find God's ideas,
vaster than the universe, cramped within the limited space of
a human writer's mind. Out of regard for us God conceals
the luminous splendor of his divine majesty and becomes
such a familiar part of our earthly existence that we call him
Father and Spouse. God wants to be recognized, not as the

unmoved Mover of Aristotle, nor yet as the Perfect Exemplar
of Plato and much less as the Eternal Fire of the Stoics; our
God comes as a *living Person,* knowing us most intimately,
loving us most tenderly. He says in the book of Isaia: "See,
upon the palms of my hands I have written your name"
(Is 49:16).

True, there are rare moments in the biblical story when
the touch of God's presence so overwhelms man that God is
said to be shaking the earth with fright and turning the sky
into a fiery blaze. Ordinarily, however, God comes—as he
revealed to His prophet Elias—not "in a great and mighty
wind, rending the mountain and splitting the rocks" but
"in the sound of gentle stillness" (3 Kgs 19:11-13). Without a delicate sense of faith, man can never detect the quiet
advent of God. Man *seems* to hear merely a human voice,
to see merely a human face and to touch a completely earthy
substance. This humble condescension of God hiding His
majesty and coming to us beneath a drab human exterior can
be called the *dominant advent theme of the Bible.*

Every sentence of the Old Testament was preparing man
for that supreme moment of divine condescension when God
would actually sit down to break bread with men; when
God would allow the cynical or the ignorant to disagree and
even to argue with Him; when the face of God would be
smeared with human spittle and the heart of God ripped
open. Christ had warned: "Blessed is he who is not scandalized in me" (Matt 11:6). Caiphas was more than scandalized at this advent of God in *such* human appearance; in
outrage he shouted: "Blasphemy!" Poor Caiphas, knowing
his Scriptures by heart, had failed to recognize the advent
theme of the Bible. For centuries God was conditioning His
earthly family for the advent of the Savior, for that supreme
moment when "the Word became flesh and dwelt among us"

(John 1:14). There was once a time when Abraham dined with Almighty God; when Jeremia called God "a treacherous brook, whose waters do not abide" (Jer 15:18); when the temple of God's presence was profaned with the lewd immorality of the Israelites and the destructive force of pagan fury. Caiphas, however, shrieked "Blasphemy!" because without faith he was blind to the Old Testament theme of God's humble condescension.

Today the part of Caiphas is played by people who are scandalized by the humanness of the Bible. Some impulsively shut the sacred book and look for God in a better enviroment. Others are tempted to rewrite the Bible. It would be much easier, they think, if the advent themes of the Old Testament were formulated in a series of theological conclusions, clear and precise, admitting no doubts and hesitation. The Bible would then state in unmistakable terms the nature and the attributes of God, would furnish exact details on the person and the work of the Messia, and would remove all necessity of investigation and thought on man's part.

God comes to us, however, not as a list of cold statistics, nor as pronouncements of static, imperishable truth; He comes as a *living Person,* who wants nothing so much as the adoration of our friendly acquaintance and the worship of our intimate love. Somehow He will contrive to remain God, but at the same time—as He confesses in the book of Osee— he will take us up in his arms and he will lead us with human cords (Os 11:3-4).

The advent of God in Old Testament times announces the coming of his divine majesty in and through the most routine matters of daily life. The prophet Deutero-Isaia put it very beautifully: "Truly with you God hides himself" (Is 45:15). God is hidden in everything. The psalmist exclaims: "Where can I go from your spirit? If I go to the heavens, you are there; . . . to the nether world, you are present there; . . . at the farthest limits of the sea, your hand shall guide me" (Ps 138). Man has only to reach out his hand and immediately his finger touches God! But this finger is the finger of *faith* which draws aside the veil of the human and the natural, to reveal the presence of God. Without faith there is only earth or sea or another human being. But with the faith of an Isaia, a man can sing of divine redemption rushing in from every corner of the universe:

> Let justice descend, O heavens, like dew from above.
> like gentle rain let the skies drop it down.
> Let the earth open and salvation but forth;
> let justice also spring up! (45:8).

These words of Isaia, repeated in the hymn *Rorate Caeli,* proclaim the advent of God through all the creatures of the universe. It is not that God is reduced to something earthly; not that religion degenrates into poetic exaltation, but that God hides his glorious person beneath an earthly exterior. This awareness of God's personal presence, as the psalmist exclaimed, turns "darkness into light" and "is too wonderful for me." Faith introduces us to the living Person of Almighty God.

The dominant theme of the Old Testament is the coming of God, not as a theoretical statement spelled out in words but as a living Person known and loved in everyday life. The divine word of the Old Testament is intricately involved in the geography and the history of daily events. In this way, the Bible prepared for the Word to become flesh and dwell among us, so that—as Saint John was to write— "we have heard, . . . we have seen with our eyes, . . . we have looked upon and our hands have handled: of the Word of Life" (1 John 1:1).

Advent through Struggle

The first advent theme of the Old Testament is that salvation is not like a meteor suddenly dropping down from the heavens but comes from and through the lowliness of this earth. God's advent in our midst is ordinarily through human mediators, through kings, prophets and priests; through parents and acquaintances; through strangers and enemies. Enemies? Yes! God can and does make use of everything for his purpose. Brutal Assyria is called "my rod in anger, my staff in wrath" (Is 10:5). Adad Nirari, Emperor of Assyria, is the promised savior in the Fourth Book of Kings (13:5). Cyrus is addressed "the Lord's friend (who) shall do his will" (Is 48:14). For his work of salvation God summons all forces, evil at times though they may be.

In fact, is not every human instrument tainted with sin? The earth bears the curse of sin, causing St. Paul to declare it "subject to vanity," in "slavery to corruption." "All creation," he writes, "groans and travails in pain until now" (Rom 8:20-22). As the advent of God is through earthly means, then struggle must ensue. Forces of evil are on their guard, ready to prevent, or at least to hinder, the meeting of God and man. Isaia warned us that before "the glory of the Lord shall be revealed," there must be the sweating labor of raising up valleys of weakness, and the courageous work of lowering mountains of pride (Is 40:5). These words of Isaia, repeated by John the Baptist as he announced the coming of Christ, enunciate the second advent theme of the Old Testament—man achieves the *victory of God's presence only through struggle.*

Victory through struggle is the leitmotiv occurring over and over again in the pages of the Bible. At times it is sounded in the single notes of a soloist, as in the soliloquies of Jeremia; again, in a duet of conflicting parties, as in the encounter between Eve and the serpent, between Jacob and Esau, between David and Saul; or, recognized in the full orchestration of world powers, as in the struggles between Israel and Babylon, or in the universal cataclysm of apocalyptic literature in books like Zacharia or Daniel. Never is there a victory of goodness without a struggle against evil. This theme is expressed in the first chapters of Genesis, which are a prologue to the entire Bible. The Lord God said to the serpent, the monster-progenitor of all evil:

> I will put enmity between you and the woman,
>   between your seed and her seed;
> He shall crush your head,
>   and you shall lie in wait for his heel (Gen 3:15).

The intricacies of this difficult text cannot be adequately treated here, but this much is certain. At the dawn of human life, God foresaw a continual struggle between good and evil. But there is hope, because the head of the evil one eventually will be crushed. This victory will entail much sorrow and endurance, because the evil one is poised, ever ready to snap at the heel of his conqueror. The seed of the woman, that is, human beings on the side of God, shall certainly triumph. Their salvation, however, does not drop suddenly from the sky but emerges slowly and painfully from the earth. *God* is at work through frail *human* mediators.

The advent of God into the lives of Old Testament saints took place upon the battlefield of earth. These saints found God by struggling to cut themselves off from evil entanglements. When "the Lord said to Abram: 'Leave your country, your kinfolk and your father's house, for the land which I will show you'" (Gen 12:1), Abraham was not merely to travel from one geographical spot to another. Through God's help he was to make the interior sacrifice of every human attachment. The departure of Abraham's descendents from Egypt was more than a tramp through the Sinai desert. Under the leadership of Moses, God was leading them by wondrous deeds from the land of Egypt where pleasure meant carnal delights, out into the desert where they might follow the Lord unreservedly and make a covenant of love with him.

When God solemnly made the covenant of Mt. Sinai, He said to the Israelites: "You shall be my special possession, dearer to me than all other people" (Ex 19:5). The unbelievable extent of such love provoked a question which tortured their mind. Men like the prophet Habacuc could not help asking God:

> Too pure are your eyes to look upon evil,
>   and the sight of misery you cannot endure.
> Why, then, do you gaze on the faithless in silence
>   while the wicked man devours
>   one more just than himself? (1:13).

God's immediate answer to Habacuc was very simple. He was to write it—it amounted to only three words in Hebrew—in letters so large "that one can read it on the run." "The just man lives by faith" (2:2, 4). Only by faith can anyone detect the advent of God in such human events as innocent suffering.

About a century later God revealed still more clearly the power of suffering to unite man with Himself. The recipient of this revelation was the great unknown prophet of the Babylonian exile. He was continuing the mission of Isaia of Jerusalem and his words were added to the latter's preaching to form one book. He was summoned by God as a divine call resounded in the heavenly assembly: "Comfort, give comfort to my people ... Speak tenderly to Jerusalem" (Is 40:1). To these people, often innocent victims of circumstances, scattered at times throughout slave-labor camps in the land of exile, this Great Unknown declared that the innocent suffer for the guilty. He wrote about the "Servant of the Lord," saying in melancholy plaint:

> He was spurned and avoided by men,
>   a man of suffering, accustomed to infirmity,
> One of those from whom men hide their faces,
>   spurned, and we held him in no esteem.
> Yet it was our infirmities that he bore,
>   our sufferings that he endured, . . .
> He was pierced for our offences,
>   crushed for our sins;
> Upon him was the chastisement that makes us whole,
>   by his stripes we were healed (Is 53:3-5).

This message is penned in a style—broken, sobbing and recurrent—with Hebrew words sounding such notes of sorrow as in the following phrase: *lo' to'ar lô welo' hadar* (53:2b).

This sound of sorrow is but an echo of the lamentation choking the hearts of the desolate exiles. Deutero-Isaia's words are a messianic prophecy, not picked at random from a cloudless sky but drawn from the lives of men and women. These words evoke a spirit of faith, enabling the exiles to remove the veil of mystery from suffering and to watch the advent of God into their midst. They reassure them that salvation is always that way; now and in the future, suffering ushers in the day of the Lord. This day is a victory through struggle. God is present *upon* this earth, removing the curse of sin *from* this earth, in order that He may reign over the world in the lives of His people. Faith transforms suffering from a decaying process of death into an invigorating productive force of life. It is the advent of God into human life.

God Alone

The first advent theme considered in this chapter is the humble condescension of God who makes use of every bit of earthly reality to achieve his purpose. God calls upon everything, from stones and food to saints and angels, to announce his glorious presence. The next theme recognized the fact that the victory of God's presence upon this earth demands struggle. This struggle against sin sharpens men's wits to recognize what we call the third theme in the Old Testament: *only God can save.*

It is practically the unanimous consent of Old Testament scholars that nowhere does the Old Testament contain a clear announcement that the Messia will be divine. In an indirect way, however, the Old Testament prepared for the human birth of the Second Person of the Holy Trinity. The Bible shows how every human means failed and disappointed the hopes of man. More and more the people experienced the truth: only GOD can save.

Every one of the human instruments utilized by God failed repeatedly and disastrously. Their failures were never chance occurrences. God had a purpose in allowing each sin. When the blundering, irreligious policy of King Achaz opened the flood-gates of sorrow and allowed the Assyrian army to sweep across the land, the prophet Isaia still repeated "Emmanuel," which means "God with us" (Is 8:8). God *must* be with His people. Otherwise, they would perish. He alone could send the Spirit, to dry up the waters of suffering and to re-create a paradise of happiness, washed clean of defilement.

Isaia's insistence upon "Emmanuel—God with us" enunciated a truth deep in biblical tradition. During the days of Moses when the people were almost annihilated by the Egyptians, God saved them by leading them through the waters of the Red Sea. The people afterwards sang in chorus:

> My strength and my courage is the Lord,
> He has been my savior (Ex 15:2).

Seven hundred years later sin cast the people out of the Promised Land into the jaws of another destruction, the Babylonian exile. In desperation the people cried to the Lord:

> Awake, awake, put on strength,
>   O arm of the Lord!
> Awake as in the days of old,
>   in ages long ago (Is 51:9).

Again in the dreary, insignificant days of postexilic Israel, still another disciple of the Isaian school prayed in anguish:

> Oh, that you would rend the heavens and come down,
>   with the mountains quaking before you, . . .
> While you wrought awesome deeds we could not hope for,
>   such as they had not heard of from of old.
> No ear has ever heard, no eye ever seen,
>   any God but you
>   doing such deeds for those who wait for him (Is 63:19-64:3).

How the Israelites waited and longed for the advent of God who alone can save! They were faced with what seemed to them an agonizing contradiction; God alone can save, but He demands that human instruments be used. So they prayed: "Oh, that you would rend the heavens and come down!" It was a prayer of desperation, asking for what seemed impossible.

Faith, however, is strong enough to remove mountains of impossibilities. Faith can rend the heavens that God may come down. No saint of the Bible possessed a faith so strong as that which fibered the soul of the Maid of Nazareth. Her immaculate heart was an Ark of the Covenant, preserving most purely the heritage of Old Testament teaching. The advent themes of the Bible inspired her prayers, her begging God to come and to help His people. No one felt so intensely the aching need for God as this poorest and most humble of God's handmaids.

Conclusion

How can these three advent themes of the Old Testament be summed up? First of all, God does not come as a streak of lightning disrupting our ordinary existence. With humble condescension God clothes Himself with the earthly details of human existence—"born of a woman, born under the law" (Gal 4:4).

The Old Testament, therefore, must not be studied as a series of formal statements, nor must its messianic prophecies be laid out as a list of cold statistics. The Bible is the record of human hopes and desires. It shows that God is present as a part of the living fabric of daily existence. His revelation through prophets or priests is a response to the needs of His people.

Jesus did not so much fulfill statistics and formulas as he answered the accumulated hopes of the human race. The struggle against evil, which these hopes endured throughout history, raged most bitterly of all in the flesh of Jesus. As He crushed the serpent's head, Christ Himself suffered the sorrows of crucifixion. Here then is the second advent theme—victory through struggle.

As we witness the condescension of God, coming to us in the lowly attire of an infant, or in the humiliating status of a crucified criminal, only by faith can we hold back the charge of blasphemy and in its stead whisper, "My Lord and my God!" The third advent theme is fulfilled: God is personally present in our midst.

CHAPTER 9 THE PROPHETS'
PORTRAIT OF
THE MESSIA

"HE CAME unto His own and His own received Him
not" (John 1:11). In these few words St. John sums up
the reaction of the Jewish nation to their long-awaited
Messia. Beginning with cynicism, the attitudes of the Jewish
teachers and leaders finally ended on Good Friday with
the violent cry, "Crucify Him!"

The Scriptures in the Year 30

Here is a mystery of baffling dimensions, a mystery which
tortured the minds of St. Paul, St. John, St. Stephen and
many others in the early Church. How could the Scribes
and Pharisees, the world's most dedicated Scripture students
at the time of Our Lord, many of whom had their whole
Bible memorized—how could they have missed one of the
most basic teachings of Old Testament faith? Did not

259

Jesus Himself solemnly declare: "You search the Scriptures . . . and they bear witness to me" (John 5:39).

We can understand this mystery only if we go back and try to read the Old Testament anew, only if we forget for a moment that the Messia has already come, only if we try to ignore the bright light of Christian revelation and read the Bible with the darkened minds and the limited vision of the Jews before the time of Christ. And this will be more than just an idle task for us.

Reading the Scriptures as they were interpreted in the year A.D. 30 will bring sympathy for our Jewish brethren and for all men without Christian faith. No longer will we immediately question their sincerity, as they reject Jesus as their Messia. Such a reading will help us identify ourselves with the doubts of the contemporary world and then enable us gradually to work out of the problems of unbelief. It will also show us just far human wisdom, applied to the Bible, can take a man in recognizing and accepting Jesus as Savior of the world. The ecumenical spirit demands this effort from us.

But such a reading of the Old Testament will do more than just bring sympathy into our hearts for those who do not understand it as we do. It will also deepen our own understanding of Scripture. It will help us to grasp what Pope Pius XII called "the supreme rule of interpretation," which is "to discover and to define what the [ancient] writer intended to express." The Pope urged Catholics to look at the *human* side of the divine Scriptures, at "the peculiar character and circumstances of the sacred writer," because he is "the living and reasonable instrument of the Holy Spirit."

Before all else, then, it must be determined how the Old Testament writer understood his own words and what meaning he intended to communicate. Later Christian development must always rest upon this foundation, and a clear formulation of Old Testament belief will reinforce this substructure of Christian faith.

What ideas, then, formed in the minds of those Jews who sat beside the boy Jesus and His foster father, Joseph, in the Nazareth synagogue on the Sabbath day? As the rabbi explained the scroll, unrolled on the table before him, what kind of a Messia did they picture to themselves? Surely they never dreamed of a Messia born in a poor laborer's family in their own country village of Nazareth.

Later, when Jesus had grown to manhood, He preached before His neighbors and friends in this same synagogue, and "all . . . were filled with wrath. Driving Him out of the town, they led Him to a steep cliff, intending to hurl Him down headlong" (Luke 4:28-29). It is little wonder that someone else asked ironically, "Can any good come out of Nazareth?" (John 1:46).

We need no guesswork in determining how pious Jews of the year A.D. 30 understood the "messianic prophecies" of the Old Testament. The recently discovered Dead Sea Scrolls reflect the hopes and the faith of a select group of saintly Jews. These men kept constant vigil, rotating not only during the day but even through the night, reading and expounding the Sacred Scriptures. We learn from their writings that they expected at least two Messias. They felt that one man alone could never bring to pass all God's promises.

A Portrait from Human Hopes

We now attempt a portrait of the promised Messia. As the background of our picture we have the bold, crossing strokes of Hebrew life through the centuries: the camel-caravan days of Abraham, the slave-labor camps of Egypt, the scorching sands of the Sinai desert, the victorious conquest of the Promised Land, the wondrous days of David and Solomon, the smashing devastation of the Babylonian conquest, the lonely exile, and then the silent retreat back to the homeland.

Set against this background of Israelite history is the figure of the promised Messia. The entire picture is painted by artists, divinely inspired, who draw their colors and shading from the hopes and triumphs, the sorrows and defeats of God's chosen people.

This portrait of the Messiah contains such a wealth of startling details that, as our attention is engaged by any part of it, we tend to forget the rest of it. This hand, raised aloft with a sword of victory in its grasp, makes us overlook the people gathered at the feet of the Messia. In their eyes there is no look of tense fear but a sparkle of radiant love. As we admire his royal diadem, glistening with the world's richest gems, we forget that he wears workmen's clothes, soiled and torn.

The fact is that the picture of the Messia is never given all at once in the Bible. Fragments of it are scattered throughout the Old Testament. How all the pieces fitted together was a secret which God kept to Himself, until "the Word became flesh" (John 1:14).

Messianism without a Messia

The first sketches of the picture's background were attempted around 1850 B.C., in the days of Abraham; color was not applied until the time of Moses, some 600 years later.

God took the initiative by sketching a hope of world-wide blessing in His first words to Abraham. From the start, therefore, God imparted a forward vision to biblical faith. Unlike their neighbors who longed for a renaissance of a past golden age, Abraham and his children longed for a new glorious age of the future.

In the beginning this hope contained no idea of a personal Messia, no idea of an individual sent by God to save His people. The whole nation was pictured in the role of a Messia, mediating blessings to all the world. God promised Abraham: "I will make a great nation of you. I will bless you, and make your name great, so that you shall be a blessing. . . . In you shall all the nations of the earth be blessed" (Gen 12:2-3).

Several centuries later, when Abraham's children were being led out of Egypt by their great leader Moses, God addressed them as "my special possession, dearer to me than all other peoples. . . a kingdom of priests" (Ex 19:5-6). Even though God loved them as His favorites, He still looked kindly upon all the rest of the world. He therefore gave His people a priestly office to perform. They were commissioned to bring all nations to the knowledge and the worship of the one, true God. Theirs was a vision of a whole people on a universal mission of salvation.

When foreigners reacted with hatred and hostility, Israel's faith summoned the people to military action. They had to fight if their faith was to survive. At the sight of Israel's conquering army, Gentile nations would be forced to glorify the God of Abraham and Moses. The Bible also shows the Hebrews peacefully absorbing large groups of Gentiles: nomadic desert wanderers like the Cinites of the Sinai peninsula (Jdg 1:16); cultured Canaanites of Sichem in central Palestine (Jos 24:1).

At this early date we cannot find a portrait of an individual, personal Messia. Instead, we see a picture of a nation, strong, determined, *hopeful*. God was at work in their midst, saving the world and partially fulfilling what we today call the messianic promises. This unfinished picture can be entitled "Messianism without a Messia!"

It will be noticed that although the eyes of God's people looked hopefully to the future, they were *not* staring at a *distant* horizon. In fact, the book of Josue gives the impression that the joyous unfolding of a glorious era was no further off than a "tomorrow." In his farewell address, Josue called upon the nation to "acknowledge with your whole heart and soul that not one of the promises which the Lord, your God, made to you has remained unfulfilled" (Jos 23:14).

The Royal Messia

Time and history would be the best of teachers, helping the inspired artists to add more specific details to the portrait of the Messia. The background must include something more than the walls of fortified cities, the golden expanse of wheat fields and the purple streches of grapevines. Now to be added are heavy strokes of black, breaking through the walls of cities and cutting across the gold and the purple of the landscape. We have come to the dark days of the Judges (1170-1030 B.C.).

During this century of "storm and pressure," prosperity led to moral laxity; softness of life invited invasion from plundering desert nomads. The agonizing cries of the people moved God to send deliverers or "Judges," but no sooner did a judge die than the people "would relapse and do worse" (Jdg 2:19).

To remedy this desperate, even hopeless, situation God raised up kings—first Saul, then David. There begins to form upon the canvas of messianic hopes the figure of a kingly Messia or a "Son of David." God entrusted the destiny of the nation to David and to his royal descendants. The prophet Nathan gave David this pledge from God: "I will raise up your heir after you . . . I will be his father, And he shall be my son. . . . Your house and your kingdom will be confirmed before me forever" (2 Sam 7:12-16).

For a long time thereafter the messianic picture did not single out any king in particular. The figure of a "Son of David" was more of a symbol than a portrait. At each new coronation the people couldn't help hoping that maybe *this* king would herald the fulfillment of God's promises. The congregation chanted over the new king God's solemn promise to David: "I will proclaim the decree of the Lord: . . . You are my son; this day I have begotten you" (Ps 2).

Enthusiastic hopes vested the new king with majestic power: "O God, with your judgment endow the king. . . . May he endure as long as the sun. . . . May he rule from sea to sea" (Ps 71).

Dying in order to Live

The picture of the Messia was far from completion. Time with its sorrows must add more colors and lines. Once again God turned the misfortunes of sin into an occasion of deeper religious understanding. The sins of Israel's kings would destroy the monarchy, but in so doing change the symbol of a "Son of David" into a portrait of an individual royal Messia. This transformation, however, came slowly.

David's successors, for the most part, were a line of weak, indifferent, undisciplined monarchs: Solomon the extravagant; Joas the betrayer; Sedecias the undecided; Achaz the apostate; Manasseh the persecutor; Joakim the idolater.

To prevent the kings from distorting out of recognition

the picture of Israel's messianic hopes, God inspired a succession of courageous religious leaders. These men, called "prophets," would be more responsible than anyone else for the complete portrait of the Awaited One. Their labor was to extend over a period of more than 300 years!

God commissioned them "to root up and pull down, to wreck and to ruin, to build and to plant" (Jer 1:10).

The prophet Amos used a coarse, thick brush upon the canvas. He daubed it with heavy black smears, lest there be any false impression that Israel's messianic triumph was "Glory! Alleluia!" for everyone indiscriminately. For messianic promises belonged only to the "remnant," to the faithful few who were able to sustain the demands of God's love. Love? Yes, because God wrecks and ruins, precisely that He might build and plant.

A Personal Messia

The colors of the picture begin to fade; dust gathers upon the canvas of Israel's messianic hopes. Prophets like Isaia, Sophonia and Jeremia tell us what was happening to God's chosen people. Heavy clouds of unbelief had enveloped the land. A storm was gathering. Finally, it struck with a blast of fury. Foreign armies marched across the land, devastating the fields and vineyards, chopping down the trees, smashing the city walls, humiliating the women, looting the homes, killing the people. What seemed to be the end of Israel was actually a new beginning.

The last of the Davidic kings was blinded and carted off into exile, his memory haunted by his final view of this earth, the execution of his children.

The gathering of this storm extended over 150 years. The prophets who preached during these years finally lost all confidence in the Davidic kings. Slowly but surely they came to the conclusion that not just *any* king but a *definite, individual* king to be born in the distant future, was the Awaited One. Because the present poverty, sorrow and destruction were intended by God precisely to save His people, the prophets concluded that the same law of "salvation through suffering" would inaugurate the messianic era. The Messia must be portrayed poor and unknown, in order that He might lift the poor and the lowly to the glory of God's kingdom.

A New Creation

The harrowing experience of the Babylonian exile, strangely enough, added bright, pleasing colors to the messianic picture. The "artist" was an unknown prophet, whose words are found in the book of Isaia, chapters 40 to 55. He taught the lesson of suffering in the most beautiful of lyrical poetry.

He did not predict a divine Messia, but his picture of the messianic kingdom was so glorious as to burst the limited boundaries of this earth. Henceforth, although messianic salvation would spring from this earth, it would lead to a glory far beyond this world.

> I the Lord will answer them; . . .
> I will open rivers on the bare heights,
>   and wells in the midst of the valleys; . . .
> I will plant in the desert the cedar, . . .
> I will set in the wasteland the cypress, . . .
> That all may see and know, . . .
>   That the Holy One of Israel is creating this
>   (Is 41:17-20).

This new creation, which the prophet expected "sometime" after the exile, would bring salvation to the "lame," the "blind," the "imprisoned," the "poor" (cf. Is 43). Sorrow, he realized, destroyed only the proud; the humble were purified and strengthened by it. But no sorrow was more purifying and more strengthening than that patiently endured by innocent people. On this occasion God revealed to the prophet that the most redemptive suffering of all times would be that undergone by the most innocent of all God's servants, the promised Messia. Because of this inspiration, the prophet was able to portray the "Suffering Servant of the Lord."

> It was our infirmities that he bore,
>   our sufferings that he endured, . . .
> The chastisement of our peace was upon him,
>   by his stripes we were healed" (Is 53:4-6).

A Picture of Many Parts

When the edict of Cyrus the Great ended the Babylonian exile in 538 B.C., the picture of the awaited Messia had become large, complicated and perplexing, like the centuries from which it had been drawn. There is, indeed, a continuity of history; but there is also the confusion and chaos of human history, combining as it does defeat and glory, sorrow and happiness, lowliness and kingliness. The picture of the Messia had absorbed Israel's hopes, achievements and failures, but all lines and colors converged to form a design of divine salvation.

God was still unsatisfied with the picture; there were still more details to be added.

Israel's messianic hopes were now given a pronounced liturgical or priestly shading. The portrait of a Messia-priest was begun before the close of the Babylonian exile by the prophet Ezechiel. It was continued by Aggai, Zacharia, Malachia and Joel. It would be truer to assert, however, that they thought of a messianic *priesthood,* not of an individual

Messia-priest. Again, we meet "Messianism without a Messia."

This change from a royal Messia to a priestly one is easily explained. The high priest was now in supreme command. Jewish life revolved around the Temple. It was natural that the Jews should project priestly ideas into the messianic picture.

Not to be overlooked in this later period is the esteem and honor shown wise men. We can detect a messianic coloring in Proverbs' praise of wisdom in chapters one to nine.

The Son of Man

It was the author of the Book of Daniel who added the last, bold lines to the Messia's portrait. Writing during a blackout of terrible persecution (167-164 B.C.), the author saw a vision of the persecuted saints. As they rose from their graves to receive an everlasting kingdom, there appeared in their midst a mysterious personage:

> One like a son of man coming,
>   on the clouds of heaven; ...
> He received dominion, glory, and kingship
>   (Dan 7:13-14).

The language of Daniel is very much like a burst of light, so brilliant that we see nothing distinctly. We blink in bewilderment as one facet upon another of Israel's messianic traditions shine before our eyes: prophet, king, priest, wise man; purifying suffering; exalted glory.

When Daniel, however, asked the angel of vision: "O my Lord, what shall be the latter end of these things?" he was told: "Go your way, O Daniel! for the words are bound up and sealed till the time of the end" (Dan 12:8-9).

Till the End of Time

Time sped forward from the year 164 B.C., when "in the fullness of time . . . God sent his son, born of a woman, born under the law" (Gal 4:4).

In the year that Christ was born, how were the people to recognize Him? What was the messianic portrait which they found in their sacred traditions?

First of all, the Old Testament had charged the land with explosive, messianic hopes. In the Dead Sea Scrolls we see a group of pious Jews who had withdrawn into the desert, precisely to prepare for the final, deadly struggle between good and evil. They were in spiritual training for the great moment.

False Messias were appearing. Men like Theodas and Judas the Galilean were rallying people with the rebellious proclamation of the day of the Lord's vengeance upon Rome (Acts 5:36-37).

Aged and saintly Simeon had been assured by the Holy Spirit that he would not die without seeing the Messia (Luke 2:26).

Along with this certainty there existed great uncertainty about the character of the Messia. The people along the Dead Sea expected at least two Messias: a royal Messia of the family of David and a more important priestly Messia. These people were ready to endure persecution and suffering before the final victory, but that the Messias would live as "Suffering Servants" was unbelievable!

The uniqueness and the splendor of Jesus' messianic role was to unite in Himself alone *all* of the people's sufferings and expectations. No single part of the Old Testament ever gave a complete picture of the Awaited One. The key explaining how all the designs and colors unite in one huge portrait was a secret which God kept to Himself until His Son was born of the Virgin Mary.

The sacred traditions of Israel formed a portrait, clear enough to a person of humble faith. Mary and Joseph, Zachary and Simeon recognized Jesus as the Lord's Anointed. The prophecies, however, were also vague enough for the proud to reject Jesus. What the Old Testament demanded most of all was faith, a spirit of unconditional obedience and of patient waiting.

PART IV

For the word of God is living and efficient
and keener than any two-edged sword,
And extending even to the division of soul and spirit ...
a discerner of the thoughts and intentions of the heart
(Heb 4:12).

CHAPTER 10

THE INFLUENCE
OF ORAL
TRADITION

THE PAST fifty years have witnessed a revolutionary change
in biblical studies. The previous concern over written documents has been replaced by an overwhelming interest in
literary forms and oral tradition. Although many discoveries
of the documentary theory still retain their value, the modern
exegete no longer pinpoints his attention to the date of
written composition. He is now engaged in the larger task
of pursuing his subject back into the earlier centuries of
oral transmission. The *Religionsgeschichtliche Schule* has
demonstrated how the religious thought of the Semitic
people as well as their public acts of worship were sustained
and controlled by oral tradition. This chapter attempts to
summarize the effects of oral tradition upon the interpretation of the Old Testament and particularly of the prophetical
books of the Old Testament. The conclusion will make some

applications to the various senses of Scripture, including the highly controversial *sensus plenior.*

Most Jewish, Catholic and Protestant exegetes recognize the fact of an oral transmission supplementing the written Scriptures. A review of the reasons for this acknowledgment will enable us to understand better the nature and salient characteristics of oral tradition. We will then have a key to the second and more important section of this chapter: the effects of oral tradition upon modern scripture interpretation.

THE REASONS FOR ORAL TRADITION

Before advancing further, it will be helpful to anticipate certain conclusions and to point out several qualifications or distinctions. The oral tradition about which this chapter is concerned must not be confused with Christian tradition dealt with in dogmatic theology. This Christian tradition is found in the official pronouncements of the Popes and Councils, in the prayers and rites of the liturgy, in the preaching of the Fathers and Doctors, in the writings of theologians, in the consensus of belief among the faithful throughout the world. It is evident that although Christian tradition deals with supernatural truths it directs little or no attention to the literary expression of these ideas. Except for certain technical phrases or official pronouncements, there is no fixed literary form; very few of these phrases can be traced back in their exact wording to apostolic orgin.

Oral tradition in Old Testament times embodied more than religious truths. It also included a definite, literary form in which these ideas were transmitted. It was concerned with the earlier stages of what we now call the Bible. The early inspired accounts of the Bible were inscribed upon the memories of the Hebrew people. Granted the extraordinary retentive power of the Semitic memory, it mattered little whether the inspired message was inscribed upon paper or upon human memories. When these sacred accounts were orally passed down from one generation to another, there would be a general inclination to adapt, modify or clarify, according to the needs of changing circumstances. Yet, oral tradition was different from Christian tradition, for the former was working not with ideas alone but also with the literary form in which those ideas were cast. Such oral transmission and adaption of inspired accounts do not exist today, because our Sacred Scriptures are fixed and unchangeable. In Old Testament days the divine message or inspired account was continually being recast in the vocabulary and style of each succeeding era and also made to reflect the spiritual problems of every new period. Oral tradition, then, can be defined as the recital under religious auspices of God's redemptive acts towards Israel, according to a divinely influenced (or inspired) literary form.

Even though oral tradition is to be distinguished from the method and form of Christian tradition, yet we do not deny that something similar to Christian tradition also existed in Old Testament times. Its Old Testament counterpart, living tradition, included: customs, especially in the matter of law and worship; oral development of popular stories, more or less issuing from the Bible or rooted in it; beliefs already received but not yet inscribed in the sacred readings. Such a living tradition included everything that is part of the patrimony of the people of God. At times both oral tradition and this living tradition will seem to merge together, since the roots of both are sunk in the national, religious and cultic life of Israel. The sacred accounts of oral tradition will be recited during the performance of the liturgy, and the demands of the cult will introduce modifica-

tions and additions into the oral tradition. B. Couroyer, for
instance, remarks that in the Book of Exodus the Mosaic
teaching is gathered from three different traditions, commonly called the Yahwist, the Elohist and the Priestly. Each
reveals its own proper style, vocabulary and tendencies. Each
in its own way enshrined the memory of the great deeds of
the past. These reminiscences from the life of the people
and the echo which they found in the liturgical rites have
given to the Exodus account the color of an epic narrative
and sometimes of a liturgy. These developments, it must be
remembered are the expression of living tradition which
certainly goes back to the origin of the people and to its first
leader, Moses.

While emphasizing the importance of oral tradition for
the transmission of the sacred message, we do not deny the
existence of written documents in early Israel. At the present moment, it is extremely difficult, if not impossible, to
determine the precise relation between these two media of
communication in Old Testament times. Writing appeared
in the early, semi-nomadic and uncultured days of the Mosaic period; oral tradition, on the other hand, held a prominent
place along with the written text in the late, postexilic and
intertestamental period. Granted the two facts of oral tradition and written documents—oral tradition that adapted
the sacred message as it passed down to succeeding generations, and written documents that embodied the sacred message in the form current in its own day—we are still faced
with many unsolved problems. Was there a constant rewrit-
ing of the sacred texts in accord with the changing life of
each new era, or was such literary activity confined to certain
critical periods of war or religious reform? Were all the
modifications introduced into oral tradition inspired in the
technical sense of this word, so that we can rightly speak of

an inspired tradition? Or can we claim inspiration only for certain redactors who gave a quasi-definitive form to the traditions or who revised the written text in the light of a long, oral transmission?

Questions such as these cannot be satisfactorily answered at the present moment, although the investigation of the Dead Sea Scrolls and rabbinical traditions will undoubtedly be of great assistance. Nonetheless, this chapter seeks to show that the books of the Bible have been adapted and modified through the various periods of Old Testament times; that these changes can often be best explained by oral tradition; that the sense or meaning of any particular verse cannot be determined without first establishing the age and milieu of its origin and transmission.

Oral Recital

In any period of history when very few persons can read and write, both religious beliefs and profane folklore are kept alive principally through oral recitation. The memories of such people show a phenomenal power of retention. There is little of our Western dependence upon books and newspapers. Modern man must be reminded that illiteracy does not necessarily mean primitive and uncivilized conditions. This fact is true of Medieval Europe, when the spiritual and cultural treasures of the ages were preserved, developed and handed down by the sacred liturgy, sculptural or pictorial representations, mystery plays and singing troubadours. In a similar manner in the Old Testament world when the great body of the people were illiterate, oral recital naturally emerged as the normal and more popular way of teaching, praying and entertaining. Is it merely coincidental that the Bible seldom speaks of writing in the preexilic period; or that scanty, epigraphic material has turned up in Palestine? We recall at once the statement in Deut 31:24-30:

> When Moses had finished writing out on a scroll the words of the Law in their entirety, he gave the Levites . . . . this order: "Take this scroll of the law and put it beside the Ark of the Covenant of the Lord, your God. . . . Therefore, assemble all your tribal elders and your officials before me, that I may speak these words for them to hear. . . . Then Moses recited the words of this song from beginning to end, for the whole assembly of Israel to hear.

Some two hundred years after the Deuteronomic reform, Nehemia manifests the continual existence of illiteracy and the consequent stress upon oral transmission. Again we have an example of that unwritten tradition, in part interpreting and applying the written Torah, in part supplementing it. We read:

> Then Esdras the priest brought the law before the assembly. . . . And he read from it in the square before the Water Gate. . . . The Levites instructed the people in the law, while the people remained standing. So they read from the book of the law of God, translating and giving the sense, so that they understood the reading (Neh 8:2-8).

Practical Slant of Semitic Mentality

The Hebrews shared in a common Semitic pattern of thinking and acting, which centered around the present, the concrete and the practical. Such a mentality presents an even more demanding reason for oral transmission than the mere inability to read or write. The written text sets down a static record of the past; pen and ink are like hammer and nail, fixing an event to a definite point in time. Oral communication, on the contrary, is free of this restraint. In immediate contact with a living audience it feels the need of revitalizing the historical past. The written record pinions an idea firmly beneath the thought-patterns, vocabulary, circumstances and needs of a previous era, but the spoken word breathes the atmosphere, experiences and tension of its own current day. It was the present moment which preoccupied the Hebrew mind. Surrounded by pressing hardships and urgent problems that left little or no leisure for cultural endeavors, the Israelites wanted to know the relevance of the past to their own day. Like other inhabitants of the ancient Near East, the Israelites felt little or no interest in a lifeless account of the past. We suspect that the biblical narrator was constantly asking himself: what does this passage really mean *to me and to my fellow-countrymen right here and now?*

Oral tradition rescued past events from the dusty book of history. It kept such written texts as existed from hardening into a mummified body, jealously guarded in its richly decorated tomb. The written word was thus constantly brought up to date by current religious thought, vocabulary and problems. The sacred message was integrated into the contemporary life of the worshipper and in the words of G. Ernest Wright became "a challenge to commitment." The devout Israelite felt in his own life the impact of the great deeds of the past. These became a present reality and were lived over again. Cultic recitation and liturgical drama seemed to remove all barriers of time; faith in the past and hope for the future sustained the present life of the chosen people. Oral tradition was thus meeting the inherent, practical demands of the Jewish mentality.

Reliving the Past

This preoccupation of the Semite with immediate needs and current problems never severed his contact with the past. On the contrary, this practical mentality made a special demand upon him always to keep his life firmly attached to deep, ancestral ties. It was particularly this dependence upon the past that gave a sense of stability to the Semite, as he found himself a wandering nomad in the desert, a small nation surrounded by hostile neighbors, an exile uprooted from his homeland. The rights of a family or clan to such things as land, springs of water, caravan routes, and vested privileges were secured not by bank accounts but by oral contracts and ancient covenants. A sense of solidarity with the past made not only the future descendant already alive in the loins of his forebear but also gave the ancient patriarchs a continued existence in the person of their offspring. It was therefore necessary that the past endure as an active, sustaining power. Otherwise, the world, as the Semite knew it in his own day, would fall apart and return to primitive chaos.

Such a tendency of reliving the past existed among all Semites. If we compare the Hebrews with the other Near Eastern people, we will observe many points of similarity but we will also notice differences. This disposition to actualize the past will emerge along parallel lines, Hebrew and non-Hebrew, for the lines are not identical. Running side by side, they have separate points of departure and different terms of arrival. By indicating how this is true in the realm of religious ideas we shall see not only the advantage of oral tradition over the written medium but we shall also be prepared to recognize in what way the Israelite differed from his neighbor.

The non-Hebrew, Semitic religion was a divinization of natural phenomena and elemental forces. This resulted in a continual reliving of the past, because nature was thought to exist in the present in the same way that it once began. The lives of the gods and goddesses represented a continual act of creation. Winter, summer and the cycle of fertility, violent clashes between thunderbolts and devastated earth, constant tension between roaring ocean waves and defenseless shores—all these gigantic and mysterious forces were an extension into the present of that primeval struggle which originally produced the cosmos. So overawed was the Semite by these struggling, cosmic powers that of necessity he worshipped and served them. He transformed them into a brood of gods and goddesses who loved and hated, who were dominated by sensual and cruel human passions, who died and who came back to life again. The names and powers of these nature gods varied among different Semitic people, and even possessed an extraordinary fluidity of personality and function in a particular nation or city. The sacred stories which enshrined their divine exploits developed into what we now call myths (to use a very controverted term): complex, highly symbolical explanations of the cosmos as it was thought to have originated in the past and was continued in the present.

Nothing so obsessed the Semitic mind as the power of sex. The primeval sex-union of gods and goddesses produced the cosmos in the very beginning and sustained it at each succeeding moment. The continual existence of the world was guaranteed by cultic recital and liturgical performance of the myths, which naturally resulted at times in the staging of wild and revolting scenes of sex orgies. These scenes were as sensuous as the story related in the Ugaritic texts about El, who seduced two women, then had them "driven into the desert after the birth of two children, 'Dawn' (Shahru) and 'Sunset' (Shalmu)." Little wonder that Osee changed the name of Bethel (House of God) to Beth-Aven (House of Guilt) or that the Bible often substitutes *Bosheth* (shame) for Baal (Lord).

But we should always remember that basically these fertility rites were an attempt to relive the past and identify the worshipper with these former acts and latent powers of the gods in order to preserve the present intact.

Hebrew faith, however, looked to no divinized powers of nature. Yahweh was never immersed in cosmic forces, but rather was accompanied and served by them. "Peals of thunder and lighting" announced his presence (Ex 19:16). "The heavens declare the glory of God" (Ps 18:2). "The voice of the Lord" was heard in the mighty storm, breaking the cedars, twisting the oaks and shaking the wilderness of Cades, so that the whole world was transformed into a majestic temple where all nature shouted "glory" to God (Ps 28).

The Hebrew religion was not based upon an awesome fear of nature. It was centered upon certain historical facts when God intervened in their national life to make the Hebrews, as he declared, "my special possession, dearer to me than all other people, . . . a kingdom of priests, a holy nation" (Ex 19:5-6). Their entire existence depended upon God's free choice: "It was not because you are the largest of all nations that the Lord set his heart on you and chose you, for you are really the smallest of all nations. It was because the Lord loved you and because of his fidelity to the oath he had sworn to your Fathers . . ." (Deut 7:7-8). He was a mighty God, more powerful than nature, but like nature he could manifest Himself to them at will. The Old Testament confessions of faith enumerate the incidents when Yahweh revealed His glory by being present in a luminous way among His people. The Bible dwells upon five great redemptive acts of God in Israel's history: the promise made to Abraham, the election of the Hebrew nation, the solemn convenant on Sinai, the conquest of Palestine and the pledge of an eternal dynasty made to David. They are strands of gold, as Père de Vaux has written, which cross and recross upon the woof of the Pentateuch, and continue to thread their way through the entire Old Testament.

As a consequence of this belief, the problem of life for the Israelite was not regarded as an integration with the powers of nature, but as an adjustment to the will of God who had chosen them. Biblical religion was not rutted in a *status quo,* accepting as inevitable the regular cycle of nature. It was, instead, a continual fidelity to the demands of God in ever-changing circumstances.

The Hebrew and non-Hebrew lines of religious thought, therefore, run parallel, but never merge together into one. The fearful powers of nature were the point of departure for the other Semites; God's redemptive acts formed the basis of Israel's faith. However, they had this in common: each sought by means of cultic recitation and liturgical re-enactment to relive the past and once again to experience its dynamic influence. Hebrew national existence would fall apart, once Israel ceased to be God's covenanted people. Her great feasts not only commemorated past events but also acted as solemn renewals of the covenant with each generation. Harvest festivals were later associated with these feasts, but the holy days still preserved their historical motif.

The liturgical celebration of these feasts was intended to associate the worshipper in the effects of these great redemptive acts. Oral recitation was much better adapted to the accomplishment of this purpose of reliving the past than the written document. Cultic recital gave the participant an active role to play. It brought the moral demands of God to bear upon changing circumstances. In this way Egypt, for instance, became no longer a place, but a state, of bondage—the inevitable result of sin (cf. Deut 26:88). Conquering sin and removing idolatry brought shouts of joy and claps of hands; Jericho's walls were falling once again (Jos 6). While the written document was a static record confined to the past, oral tradition though rooted in the past was living in the present. It best expressed that solidarity with the great men of old; they were living again in each succeeding generation.

The Living God

A final reason can be touched upon to emphasize the importance of oral transmission over the written medium. This was the Hebrew understanding of Yahweh as the "Living God," dynamically active here and now. Even though Hebrew faith in Yahweh was founded upon the five great redemptive acts of God, still they recognized that His power was not confined to these events. Yahweh transcended history as He did nature. His strength was not exhausted when He brought the Israelites out of Egypt with an outstretched arm; His goodness was not spent by His loving care for the wandering tribes in the desert; neither was His mercy overtaxed as ours would be by repeated acts of forgiveness. "For I am God and not man," He declared through Osee, "the holy one in your midst" (11:9). Yahweh was no Baal, Asherah or Tammutz, who died each May and June and feebly awaited the autumn rains to be resuscitated. The earlier teaching became clear and distinct in these words of Deutro-Isaia: "I, I am the Lord who am the first, and I will be with the last, always I" (Is 41:4). Yahweh is the Living God, forever the same.

Yahweh, who lives in the midst of His people, is the one and same God who appeared to Abraham and brought His people to the Promised Land. "I am he who is always there" —such is the meaning of the sacred name of Yahweh. I am

Yahweh, calling you in Abraham, forgiving your sins in a continual exodus out of Egypt, carrying you on my shoulders through the desert of this world's sorrow. The name of Yahweh was itself a promise and an assurance that God was always there, living in their midst, forever the same, forever repeating His great redemptive acts of the past.

Oral tradition enabled the divine message to participate more fully in Yahweh's property of being a "living God," by giving a continuous existence to the past in each present and future. For every point of time is simultaneous with this fullness of life. Since the divine word came from God and shared in God's life, it too must possess a certain simultaneity. While the written medium tended to confine the redemptive acts to the past, oral transmission transcended any fixed moment of time. By means of a confessional or ritual recital of God's saving acts, the people felt themselves drawn into this divine activity. As the past event was adapted to current needs and problems, it was endowed with the same undiminished power and sustaining life of Yahweh. Oral transmission was thus a partial fulfillment of the divine promise, "I am he who is always there," the living God in your midst.

Nature of Oral Tradition

The reasons upholding the importance of oral tradition: the general illiteracy of the people, the practical character of the Semitic mentality, and the biblical notion of Yahweh as the "living God," present us with the elements necessary not only for establishing the nature of oral tradition but also for understanding its effect upon biblical interpretation. Oral tradition, then, can be defined as the recital under religious auspices of God's redemptive acts towards Israel, according to a divinely influenced literary form.

The words *religious auspices* stress the place of the sanctuaries or temple in the transmission of the sacred traditions. It was at the sanctuaries that Israel assembled in order to exalt the powerful deeds of God and to recall his benevolent care for the people He had chosen; there they recounted the great accomplishments of their ancestors. God first manifested His mighty acts in the assembly of His people and there He preserved the living record of them. This record was transmitted according to a definite literary form, which was divinely inspired. Its style, vocabulary and general attitudes were sensitive to the cultic needs and religious problems of succeeding ages. Yet, the literary form was not lightly changed; Israel, on the contrary, often preferred to maintain the archaic phraseology and even the opposing ideas of older periods along with newer modifications.

The phrase *redemptive acts* underlines that strong, unbroken fidelity to the past, so characteristic of Jewish faith.

> Look to Abraham, your father,
>   and to Sara, who gave you birth;
> When he was but one I called him,
>   I blessed him and made him many.
> Yes, the Lord shall comfort Sion
>   and have pity on all her ruins (Is 51:2-3).

Yet, this devotion to the past never stiffened nor ossified into a static antiquarianism. History, for the Israelites, was not an inert matter, a past thing. It was always totally present. It was a patrimony by which they lived, a mystery in which they were actually involved. This theme of *today* explains how a prophet is able to envisage future generations in a discourse directed to a contemporary audience. It is seen in the liturgical festivities which restore actuality to past events. It is inscribed in the stories of their forefathers who were considered to epitomize the lives of their descendants. This theme is a constant refrain in the book of Deuteronomy. "Here, O Israel, the statutes and decrees which I proclaim *in your hearing this day,* that you may learn them and take care to observe them. The Lord, our God, made a covenant *with us* at Horeb; not with our fathers did he make this covenant, but *with us, all of us who are alive here this day*" (5:1-3). This progressive march of Hebrew faith was carried further by Israel's hope for the future. Each redemptive act of God not only had dynamic power in the present moment, it was also a pledge of *the* great redemption of the future.

THE EFFECTS OF ORAL TRADITIONS

Let us look more closely at the Sacred Text, the Bible, as it now exists, and examine the influence of oral tradition upon its formation and interpretation. We will divide the Old Testament into: 1. Laws; 2. Historical Narratives; 3. Prophetical Books; and 4. Songs.

Laws

Laws are confined for the most part to the first five books, called the Pentateuch or the Torah. Unfortunately, the ancient Greek translation, the Septuagint, accented the historical feature of these books, and most modern Christian editions of the Old Testament follow the Septuagint division. Actually, the Pentateuch is a melange of literary genres, but more than anything else it is the foundation *law book* of the Jewish religion. In this aspect we can compare it to the gospels. It is false to look upon the Torah either as a merely historical narrative, or as a mere verbal repetition of divine commands without conscious application to changing circumstances.

If we ask how oral tradition influenced the transmission

of the Law, we can answer first of all that it insured a constant contact with the changing world of men. Law must live on the life of those it governs, direct and moderate this life, and itself be influenced and adapted by this life. Otherwise, it becomes a "dead law," which has lost its power and right to govern. True change never means radical departure, but the preservation of the identical spirit in new circumstances, a normal defense of the ancient heritage against false innovations. Oral tradition lends itself to this constant adaptation.

All Hebrew law was incorporated into *the* law book, the Torah, and thus covered itself with the mantle of Moses. The Pentateuch reflects a gradual, organic growth from the semi-nomadic days of Moses into the later settled life of Palestine. Prophets left the mark of their mind and style upon this body of legislation. The hard years of the exile formed the psychological background for the Priestly Law Code. Therefore, if contradictory laws exist in the Pentateuch, oral tradition points the finger of explanation to different historical periods.

Furthermore, the Torah like any written law was never intended to be an independent, self-sufficing authority. G. F. Moore writes:

> Thus in every sphere there always existed beside the written law a much more extensive and comprehensive body of unwritten law more or less exactly and permanently formulated. From our point of view the authority of this consuetudinary law was common consent or the prescription of long established usage. To the Jews, on the contrary, inasmuch as the written law took into its province all spheres of life, the unwritten law, dealing with the same subjects and often defining how the former should be carried out or enforced, was equally of religious obligation. And since religion with all its duties and observances

was revealed by God, the revelation necessarily included the unwritten as well as the written law.

The immutability of all revelation . . . . is particularly alleged only of a few laws. [As the Torah was searched] for a principle, an implied provision, or a precedent, . . . the result, if approved by the authorities as deduced by valid exegetical procedure from the Scripture in which it was implicitly contained, was itself revealed, and became part of the Mosaic tradition.[1]

It seems valid to conclude that before the fixation of the Pentateuch in the postexilic period oral tradition was constantly inserting new modifications into the sacred law. But these adaptations, like the original Mosaic legislation, were fragmentary and relied upon a continuous unwritten law for their actual application. As examples, Moore cites Deut 24:1-4 on the remarriage of a divorced woman and again the prohibition of labor on the Sabbath.

Priests were the official interpreters of the Law. In the postexilic period priests and scribes took the place of the earlier prophets as mouthpieces of God's will. Since these laws were preserved, applied and transmitted under religious auspices, we are not surpriesd to find in the Torah: liturgical hymns like Gen 1 and 49, Deut 33; doxologies to God's holiness, "Be holy for I am holy" or "I, the Lord"; prayers of thanksgiving and praise in Ex 20:5-6; 34:6-7; the priestly blessing of Num 6:22-27; lyric refrains in Num 10:35-36; Deuteronomic homilies. In deciding the literal sense of these passages, attention must be given to the literary genre and to the historical period of the author. What may be a mysterious, unknown meaning of Jacob, Moses or Balaam was actually the literal, conscious intention of an inspired redactor of the time of Ezechia, Jeremia or Esdra, who was reworking the earlier texts of Jacob, Moses or Balaam.

---

1 George Foot Moore, *Judaism in the First Centuries of the Christian Era* 1 (Cambridge, 1927) 251.

The Historical Narratives

The Jews appropriately call the historical books of Josue-Judges-Samuel-Kings by the title, the earlier prophets. For this reason it is much more accurate to speak of an Israelite historical genre rather than of historical books. Here, as in the Pentateuch, history is told in the form of stories that center around individuals: Josue, the Judges, Samuel, Saul, David, Solomon, Elia, Eliseus, Jehu, Ezechia and Josia. These narratives manifest the historical roots of the Israelite religion. However, they are primarily the application of the Deuteronomic theme of threat and promise to each succeeding generation. The Israelite people are forcibly reminded that the ancient, historical fact of being God's chosen people must not degenerate into a superstitious or formalistic cult of the past but must continue as a presently existing factor in their life.

This same tendency will emerge somewhat differently in the historical literature of the postexilic period, in those books now designated as *midrashim.* The great heroes of the past are introduced to a new era with its own particular problems. The prophet Jona, who predicted the extension of Jeroboam II's domain, comes forth from the belly of the whale to announce the extension of God's spiritual kingdom over the Gentiles. In the book of Jona, the author's principal purpose is to correct the chauvinistic, narrow limits of Jewish thought and charity in the period following the exile. The books of Chronicles are an example of commenting upon older texts by later traditions. This commentary was inserted into the very fabric of the older texts. In these last two books of the Jewish Bible, Moses lives again in the reorganizing achievements of David. But David is portrayed, not according to a historical tableau of the past but according to the author's wishes for the future Davidic

King of the messianic era. The story of David is prophecy more than history, and should be interpreted accordingly when we are seeking the literal sense.

In all the historical genres of the Bible—from the earlier form with its accurate presentation of details, even the sins of Moses and David, to the postexilic midrashim of Chronicles—biblical history was a means, not an end. It never forgot its religious purpose to instruct and edify. The word of God became an irresistible power, productive of future events, a dynamism which carries history forward, conformable to God's demands and holiness. Priests and prophets did not speak of the past unless to invite hearts to accept the moral purpose of the divine conduct, to do penance, and to await with confidence the coming of God's kingdom. Therefore, even if some of these historical narratives were put into writing before the exile, oral tradition still would seem to remain the principal means of their transmission and adaptation. Oral tradition continued to give to Israelite faith its characteristic note of fidelity to the past in an ever-changing present.

The Prophetical Books

The prophecies of Isaia, Jeremia and Ezechiel as well as the works of the minor prophets, are a combination of history, theological teaching, future predictions and liturgical hymns, but most of all they are a record of pastoral preaching and religious reform. Prophetic preaching is the oral presentation of God's word. It is a very difficult and delicate task to determine when these words were first put into writing. Osee's long years of preaching extended from the luxurious reign of Jeroboam II into the chaotic years that followed. Yet, only a fragment of his sermons have been preserved. The preaching of Isaia seems to have been gathered at first into separate, independent sections. Before these individual sections were reduced to writing, each underwent successive redactions which can best be explained by the theory of oral tradition.

We might study the effect of oral tradition upon the prophetical books by examining in detail one small but typical section of Isaia, the Book of Emmanuel, chapters seven to twelve. Since this was the initial Isaian collection, the inaugural vision was prefixed to it (ch. 6). The Book of Emmanuel originated at the time of the Syro-Ephraimite league when the combined armies of Israel and Damascus marched into Juda to dethrone its king, Achaz. God's message to Achaz was formed by divine fire in the heart of Isaia. This fire was struck by the Seraph at the same time that the prophet's lips were cauterized. Something of God's resplendent and transcendent majesty burst into flame in the heart of Isaia, casting a shadow upon everything human, human pleasures and human plans. This message of Emmanuel— the Hebrew word for "God with us"—seemed national suicide to Achaz. To do nothing but trust in God hardly appealed to this irreligious king, reared in the materialistic culture of Ozias and Joathan. Such a message could be accepted only by a man of stalwart faith. "Unless your faith be firm, you shall not be firm" (7:9). The theme of "God with us" pervades the Book of Emmanuel. God is present in the silent waters of Siloe, in the Child born to us with the government upon His shoulders, in the tender shoot sprouting from the hidden root of Jesse, in all the seemingly weak and foolish things of this world.

The original nucleus of the Emmanuel prophecy was adapted during the sad days of the Babylonian exile by an unknown disciple of the prophet Isaia who had the teaching of his master sealed up in his heart (cf. 8:16). With an anticipation so staunch and sure that it was almost vision of a present reality, he described the future exodus. The Mosaic past came back to life in the teaching of this great saint of the exile. We sense his influence in chapter 11 where we read that plagues will spread over Babylon, which he calls the land of the Nile. "There shall be a highway for the remnant of his people that is left from Assyria, as there was for Israel when he came up from the land of Egypt" (11:16).

The Book of Emmanuel was subjected to another modification in the postexilic period. Two hymns of praise were added to form a melodious conclusion (c. 12). These are liturgical adaptations by which the entire sacred assembly could publicly ratify and confirm in their own lives the Isaian teaching of salvation through God alone, Emmanuel.

The final changes came from the hand of the Septuagint translator. He altered some of the historical allusions; he replaced the mention of the Arameans and Philistines of the Isaian epoch with the current enemies of his own day, the Syrians and Hellenists. He frequently imparted a pastoral application to the original words. Where the Hebrew reads, "Gird yourselves; you shall be overcome. Devise a plan; it shall come to nothing," the Septuagint adapted it, "If you should again become strong, you will again be broken. And were you again to devise a plan, the Lord will scatter it" (8:9-10). And a little later the original words, "And he will be a holy place ... to both the houses of Israel," became "And if you have put your trust in him, he will be to you a holy place." Are we entitled to claim inspiration for the Septuagint translator(s), as Gelin, Benoit and Auvray are inclined to do? This question is still debated. Even if we grant that these Septuagint variations are written rather than oral modifications, nevertheless, the freedom to adapt the sacred text of a prophet so highly esteemed as Isaia was a right previously vindicated by oral tradition. Furthermore, these written adaptations are a revision according to theological advance. They are an attempt to have a previously formed text adapted, modified or clarified in the light of later theological and historical developments.

Oral tradition was thus keeping the inspired word always alive, firmly rooted in the early existence of Israel, yet maturing and bearing fruit in each new era of Israelite life. The Scriptures thus echoed a community on the march, as they received and assimilated the word under the motivating influence of the same Spirit which controled sacred history.

If the Book of Emmanuel shows the influence of oral tradition upon the literal sense, chapter eleven of Osee can be cited as an example relating to the typical sense. Osee was certainly conscious of what we call the exodus typology. Sin was a return to the land of Egypt. "The Lord," wrote the Deuteronomist, "will send you back in galleys to Egypt" (26:68). Redemption from sin, for which Osee sighed, was a deliverance from the oppression of Egypt, a striking-off of sin's shackles, an abandonment of unlawful pleasures, a continuous march through a desert of purifiying suffering. The first exodus was a pledge and pattern of every future one; it was infused with a divine power to accomplish repeatedly what it signified about the first redemptive act of God.

Chapter eleven of Osee is acclaimed the supreme expression of divine love in the Old Covenant. Through its words we hear God speaking with Himself, as though to provide an outlet for His mighty love "My heart is overwhelmed; my pity is stirred" (11:8)

> When Israel was a child I loved him,
>> out of Egypt I called my son.
> The more I called them,
>> the farther they went from me,
> Sacrificing to the Baals
>> and burning incense to idols (11:1-2).

The stiff-necked, hard-hearted attitude of the Hebrews in the desert persisted in the Baal worship of Osee's day. But God's love also persisted, for "I am God and not man" (11:9). He is still carrying His chosen people in His arms, leading them with loving cords. Yet, it is a holy love that will not tolerate sin and moral corruption; therefore,

> He shall return to the land of Egypt,
>> and Assyria shall be his king; . . .
> because they refused to repent (11:5-6).

Assyria is the punishment for sin and so merits to be called Egypt. But eventually,

> They shall follow the Lord, . . .
> Out of Egypt they shall come trembling,
>> like sparrows, . . .
> And I will resettle them in their homes,
>> says the Lord (11:10-11).

Once again, God will call His son out of Egypt; the remnant of Israel will return.

When St. Matthew's Gospel cites this text in reference to the child Jesus' return from Egypt with Mary and Joseph, is he not making a new application of this typical sense, adapting it to his time and to the needs of his hearers? The war between sin and goodness began its final mortal struggle when Christ was conceived. In her Magnificat, Mary sees God already scattering the proud, putting down the mighty, sending away the rich, fulfilling the promises of salvation made to Abraham and the prophets. This struggle against sin would rage in Christ's own body, for he came "in the likeness of sinful flesh as a sin offering" (Rom 8-3). It began with His conception and was completed in the Passion-Resurrection. In Christ, therefore, all humanity was journeying out of an Egypt of sin to the Promised Land of peace with God. Christ's geographical journey from Egypt to Palestine, in the thought of the first gospel, was to Matthew this spiritual journey of the exodus. The evangelist recognized that this typical sense, present in Osee, was definitely fulfilled in Christ. "That there might be fulfilled what was spoken by the Lord through the prophet, saying: 'Out of Egypt I called my son' " (Mt 2,15).

The Songs

The songs or lyric sections of the Old Testament are the parts most easily committed to memory and passed on by oral tradition. True, at a very early age some of these songs were put into writing, *i.e.,* The Book of the Just, the Book of the Wars of Yahweh, the Song of Debora; but oral transmission remained the rule. This is presumed by the modern Catholic and non-Catholic tendency to divide the Book of Psalms according to the *Gattungen* of Gunkel. These categories reach into almost every situation in the life of the individual Hebrew or of the entire community. In these sacred songs the Hebrews liturgically relive the past, rooting their faith in the former redemptive acts of God and adapting this past to present conditions. This naturally resulted in a continuous redaction of many older texts, bringing these up to date with theological growth and changing historical circumstances.

Many examples can be cited. The exodus theme has many liturgical variations: a hymn of praise honoring God's fidelity in Ps 104 (105), "He remembers forever his covenant

... which he entered into with Abraham"; a collective supplication or confession of guilt in Ps 105 (106), "We have sinned, we and our fathers, ... Our fathers in Egypt considered not your wonders"; a didactic psalm in Ps 77 (78), "Hearken, my people, to my teaching. ... I will utter mysteries from of old"; a processional hymn of thanksgiving in Ps 67 (68), "In your choirs bless God; bless the Lord, you of Israel's wellspring"; a processional hymn of praise to God the Creator of the world and of the chosen nation in Ps 94 (95), "Come, let us bow down in worship; let us kneel before the Lord who made us. ... Oh, that today you would hear his voice!" This last psalm reduces all history to an eternal today, which the author of the Epistle to the Hebrews will further adapt to the everlasting today of rest in Christ (Heb 3-4). These are the royal psalms, celebrating the kingship of Yahweh or of His anointed Son of David.

Here we will confine ourselves to Ps 21 (22), the gem of the Psalter consecrated by the blood of the dying Christ. From a study of its various historical phases we will draw some important conclusions for the interpretation of the Bible. Albert Gelin recognized four successive readings of this psalm. Each rereading was a major step in its development and adaptation. The changes inserted into the psalm at each step can best be explained by oral transmission, for the modifications result from its liturgical use or from the impact of later theological advance. The psalm may have been rewritten at different times, but such literary revisions would have been dictated by previous oral adaptations. The first stage was an individual plaint or expression of sorrow. "Be not far from me, for I am in distress; be near, for I have no one to help me" (21:12). Most scholars detect in the earliest stage of this psalm a description of personal suffering. The second phase was liturgical when the psalm forced its way, so to speak, into the temple ritual by its extraordinary beauty and power. "He has not spurned nor disdained the wretched man in his mercy, nor did he turn his face away from him. . . . So by your gift I will utter praise in the vast assembly" (21:25-26). Shining through every detail of suffering is a beauty of character, untouched by any bitter complaint, remorseful excuses or personal concern. It is a magnificent portrait of a lonely soul, hounded by suffering yet deeply at peace in its abandonment to God's holy will. "To you I was committed at birth, from my mother's womb you are my God" (21:11). This naturally prepared for the third phase, its messianic use by the community of the anawim. "The lowly shall eat their fill; they who seek the Lord shall praise him" (21:27). These poor and lowly were given a central place in the messianic kingdom by Sophonia, Jeremia, Deutero-Isaia and Zacharia. The Messia will be one of the anawim. The psalm now becomes a prophecy of the future. The fourth psalm according to Gelin is its New Testament use. Even though the New Testament writers associate the psalm with certain external details of the Passion, their primary intention was to link the *interior* spirit of Christ with the teaching of the psalm.

Certainly, the application of the external details to Christ's passion demands much further study. The warning of Father Roland Murphy against accepting too easily such precise messianic predictions is particularly true here. Verses 8-9, "All who see me scoff at me," are similar to Wis 2:17-20. The evangelist could be borrowing their words from both this psalm and the Book of Wisdom to describe the mockery of Christ by Jewish leaders. Verse 17, "They have pierced my hands and my feet," is involved in hopeless textual difficulties, and furthermore the evangelists never utilize it. Verse 19, "They divide my garments among them, and for my vesture they cast lots," becomes less forceful as a prediction of a Passion-detail when the poetic laws of parallelism are applied to it .

Even though the third phase of the psalm is an inspired prophecy of the suffering Messia, is it not possible to admit that what it predicts is the essential, theological teaching of a meek, innocent sufferer, rather than any individual, external details of this suffering? If the evangelists use the words of this psalm to refer to any physical suffering of Our Lord, it is only to provide a point of contact for the larger and more important theological ideas. This explanation may remain hypothetical, but at least it points out the need of first investigating thoroughly a solution by way of oral tradition, before concluding to a *sensus plenior*. If God intended to predict certain incidents of Christ's passion, we have a *sensus plenior* beyond the scope and purpose of the sacred human authors. If God is restricting the messianic prediction to some general notions of an innocent sufferer, then He is not exceeding the conscious intent of the human author-redactor, and we have a literal sense.

Conclusion

In the life of the Hebrew, it can be said in conclusion, oral tradition is seen as the normal means of transmitting religious thought, not only because of the general illiteracy of the people, but in a stronger sense because of the practical bent of the Semitic mentality and the Hebrew faith in a living God. The explanation of oral tradition, as the recital under religious auspices of God's redemptive acts, sinks the roots of biblical religion into the saving events of the past, but at the same time keeps the past alive in an every-changing present. Oral transmission left its mark upon the sacred message in much the same way that the use of a word in any language influences the meaning of that word.

The first conclusion regards the typical sense. Israelite faith constantly looking back to God's past redemptive acts by which He called Abraham, redeemed Israel from the slavery of Egypt, sealed his love in the Sinaitic Covenant, conquered the Promised Land and entrusted the fulfillment of the covenant to the Davidic dynasty. It was especially these five redemptive acts which became a pattern or type for all future ages. Their cultic recital and liturgical dramatization were a divine strategy to actualize these past events in each new era of Jewish life. Such an understanding of the typical sense will insert many Old Testament and New Testament passages into a conscious, Scriptural stream of thought and remove the necessity of appealing to an unconscious or mysterious *sensus plenior*

The second conclusion pertains to the literal sense which will benefit even more from an appreciation of oral tradition. One of the most characteristic qualities of oral transmission was its propensity to actualize older texts and bring them up to date by means of a continuous redaction. This tendency will have a double impact upon the literal sense—if we define literal sense as that meaning flowing immediately from the words and intended directly and clearly, or at least formally implicitly, by the Holy Spirit and the hagiographer. First of all, what may be a deeper, unknown meaning to an earlier author (i.e., first author of Ps 21) is actually known and intended by the later redactor (the anawim who gave the psalm its messianic application). The dogmatic question of the inspiration of the entire Sacred Scripture remains intact, but the historical and literary problems of dating the various segments of a section present a challenge. Second, when a later, inspired author cites a pre-existing sacred text, he does not confine himself to the original meaning of the earlier author. He will be inclined to adapt the text to the theological development of his own day. He will manifest his devotion to God's word, by expressing his own thoughts, which are also God's, in the sacrosanct language of the past. He will use the sacred words to express his own, consciously intended sense; therefore, it seems in better accord with Scriptural usage to speak of a literal sense of the later redactor than of a fuller sense of the earlier author. God certainly intends "the fuller sense" at the later period; whether He wanted to communicate it in the earlier age remains debatable.

In the realm of hermeneutics oral tradition does not destroy the possibility of a *sensus plenior.* The denial of such a sense of Scripture woul be heavy-handed *a priorism,* imposing man-made rules upon the sacred text instead of deducing these rules from the divinely composed Scriptures. Oral transmission, however, cautions us to use care in the application of the *sensus plenior.* Closer to a biblical way of thought is to seek a solution by way of a literal sense. Only when this attempt fails should the fuller sense be invoked.

Because of its intimate association with the sanctuary, priesthood and liturgical rites, oral tradition shared in the divine authority of these sacred institutions. It can be looked upon as a mold that preserved, developed and passed on the sacred message of God's saving acts. Yet, this mold was itself under the same supernatural control that produced the original event and its initial literary expression. Scripture, therefore, underwent an organic growth, leading with steady sureness to the fullness of time when God sent the Word, born of a woman. This mold was really the image of Christ, the lengthening shadow cast by His Body upon the ages which preceded Him (cf. Col 2:17).

The various Old Testament traditions perfected and enriched one another, while each received additional modifications as new problems and needs confronted Israel. The faith and hope, for instance, pulsating in the Yahwist tradition acquired more precision from the Elohist tradition, which provided a more stable foundation for Israel's hopes than the protection of the monarchy. The Deuteronomist account showed that God never abandoned His people; they had first to abandon Him. The Priestly source reminded the people that the presence of God in their midst transformed them into a liturgical community and sacred temple. Yet God was hidden by the priestly redactor behind clouds of smoke in Holy of Holies. None of the traditions were complete in themselves; all manifested an inherent dependency and weakness. The synthesis of all these traditions came not by way of philosophy, nor by rabbinic casuistry, nor by an apocalyptic struggle of political powers in which the sons of light overcame the sons of darkness. Neither did the greatness of the revelation as the Dead Sea Scrolls infer, demand many Messias, one priestly and another secular. "All the promises of God find their yes in him," who is the Word made flesh (2 Cor 1:20). All the hopes and longings of the ages were fulfilled when God came to dwell among His people in and through Christ.

We, "upon whom the final age of the world has come," receive "enlightenment concerning the knowledge of the glory of God [as we see it] shining on the face of Christ Jesus" (1 Cor 10:11; 2 Cor 4:6). Since "all the promises of God find their yes in him," Our Lord rightly claimed the power of transmitting and explaining the sacred traditions. "The only-begotten Son, who is in the bosom of the Father, he has revealed him" (John 1:18). Christ could freely declare: "You have heard that it was said to the ancients, . . . but I say to you. . ." (Matt 5:21-22). He was not thereby destroying the Law and the Prophets but fulfilling them in a way far exceeding the prophets' fondest hopes. This prerogative of orally adapting and passing on the sacred deposit was continued in the preaching of the Apostles. The New Testament writers witness to this apostolic power of presenting Christ's words according to their original meaning, yet at the same time modifying them to meet the needs of the primitive Church. Since Christians were the true sons of Abraham and the new Israel, the sacred Scriptures and divine traditions belonged to them, and especially to their apostolic leaders. Today, the Scriptures remain fixed and unchangeable, but they still demand a divine authority to interpret and apply them to modern problems; we still stand in need of a preaching, an oral transmission, of the word of God that is powerful and effective through the assistance of the Holy Spirit living in both the sacred word and in the soul of the preacher. Of such apostolic preaching St. Paul wrote: "But how are they to believe him whom they have not heard? And how are they to hear, if no one preaches? And how are men to preach unless they be sent? . . . Faith then depends on hearing, and hearing on the word of Christ" (Rom 10:14-15, 17).

PROPHETIC
BACKGROUND
FOR GENESIS

GENESIS, the first book of the Bible, is a solemn, masterful introduction to Israel's sacred literature. Giving as it does the setting and background of the Bible story, it poses life's most searching and most serious questions. Who is God and what is man? What has happened to man, and how is God remedying man's tragic situation? The answers found in Genesis interest everyman today, simply because those questions are still being asked.

Everyman's Story

A masterpiece like Genesis is quickly understood superficially, but fully appreciated only very slowly. Many of its modern readers, therefore, at first find its stories very delightful, but upon second reading they are baffled by the puzzling, complicated narratives. We must admit that a book which probes man's deepest problems will be as puzzling and as complicated as human life can be. In fact, there are problems in life which no book can answer. Each person must find the solution for himself. A book is valuable if it forces the individual to face up to searching questions. Genesis is a questioning book for everyman.

Genesis ranges the wide expanse of the human heart. It soars high and it tumbles low; it heroically marches forward and it listlessly drags on. It opens with jubilant praise over God's act of creation; then abruptly the mournful sound of sorrow moves like a black thunder cloud across the world. The melancholy account of man's first sin is presented not only with the naiveté of a fanciful, make-believe story but also with the keenest psycholanalysis of "man" and "woman." Admiration mingles with tears in the tragic recountal of Abraham's intended sacrifice of his only child Isaac (ch. 22), but the tension relaxes almost immediately in the joyful serenity of the Isaac-Rebecca marriage scene (ch. 24). The divine soliloquy of 18:17, "Can I keep from Abraham what I am about to do?" and the childlike mannerisms of Abraham's reasoning with God (18:23-33) occur in a section besmeared with homosexuality and incest. Bitter sarcasm and playful satire, idyllic family life and violent crime—all intermingle as closely in Genesis as they do in society anywhere today.

In Genesis the sacred author has delicately caught the varied emotions of the human heart so that everyman of every age hears an echo of his every thought. This echo is the hard sound of reality as man struggles with fellowman for gain and plunder or wrestles with himself in the moment of temptation. This echo hums with joy or shouts with triumph, as each reader finds his own peace or exultation in those words of Genesis. These words are so real that all of life's reality is possessed within their syllables, and yet these same words reach beyond the limited reality of space and time and symbolize in their echo man of every age and every place.

The inspired author of Genesis is truly an artist, making use of the most common scenes of family and national existence to communicate his own delicate perceptions of human life, its problems, its joys, its failures, its triumphs. He mixes his pigments from the tears of pain and happiness; for background he uses the panorama of world history or desert wandering; for inspiration, he received help from God to know the basic religious truths which hold all together in the one large design of world redemption. Throughout his work God was present, guiding the artist's hand, so that Genesis is a divine as well as a human masterpiece.

God, it seems, used many human artists to "paint" this masterpiece of Genesis. Its stories represent an inspired tradition of many centuries, each contributor as much inspired as his predecessor. The prophets concurred in the composition of Genesis, sometimes giving words or phrases, at other times imparting a spirit or attitude which helped to transform the whole message of Genesis. The prophets asked the questions which made the answers of Genesis deep and searching.

Is Genesis First?

These questions reach back to the beginning when God invited man to take the first step in the way of salvation. But with so much later history packed into its lines, how can it be said that Genesis is first in any way?

The book placed first in the Bible is admittedly not the first biblical book to have been written. Genesis, as already stated, acts as an introduction to the sacred literature of the Israelites. Like the preface of most great works, Genesis was among the last parts of the Bible to be put into its final, definitive form.

Even granted that the opening words of chapter one state very clearly, "In the *beginning* God created the heavens and the earth," still, chapter one represents the religious thinking of an age, roughly 800 years after Moses. Other parts of Genesis, like the patriarchal stories of chapters twenty-five to fifty, were transformed from ancient folklore into inspired, sacred traditions by the religious genius of Moses. But these sagas of the patriarchs were already 400 to 600 years old when Moses integrated them into the religion of God's people. From the viewpoint of literary composition, Genesis is hardly the first step in the story of redemption. This last statement is loaded with startling implications.

Genesis may stand from one to five billion years away from the beginning of time and the creation of all things. And to pass from the first eleven chapters to chapter twelve, we must leap a gaping chasm of hundreds of thousands of years. The first eleven chapters span the stretch of nameless years called prehistoric. The prehistoric age has left little record on the earth of what had transpired, but even that little is passed over by the Bible.

Digging into the earth, paleontologists encounter such wonders as primeval forests buried beneath tons of rock and now converted into coal. Primitive man with all his human problems, with all his trials and sorrows, with all his joys and achievements, has been swept away by the roaring winds of world cataclysms. Nothing is left of him but some shriveled bones, lying buried at the bottom of many feet of ice age debris. But does the Bible tell us even that much about him? Scripture silently passes over the Neanderthal man who sketched rough drawings of animals inside a cave of northwestern Spain, a man known to every high school boy. Again we have to ask: why call Genesis the first step in redemption?

Furthermore, when the Bible enters the era of recorded history with the mention of Thare, the father of Abraham (Gen 11:27), it is some 1200 years behind the rest of the world, for at the earliest, Abraham lived around 1850 B.C. By that time the golden age of Egypt which had lifted over five million tons of granite into the pyramids had come and gone. In Mesopotamia the great Sumerian culture had been absorbed by her conquerors, while the Sumerians themselves had been killed or enslaved. Hoards of Elamites had already devastated Abraham's home town of Ur near the Persian Gulf. God was certainly interested in the salvation of all these generations of energetic and gifted people, but the Bible says nothing about them. How can Genesis be considered the first step?

Not only was the scriptural story of *Beginnings* written by no eye witness and not only did it ignore aeons of time and generations of human beings, even what little it said about the *Beginnings* contains many inspired additions and later modifications. Many details of Adam and Eve's life reflect Mesopotamian and Canaanite cultures of the days of Abraham and Moses; the blessing of Jacob in chapter 49 was retouched in the Davidic period. Why talk, then, about Genesis' taking the first step in the story of redemption?

Yet Genesis is first. We think at once of the name *Genesis,* a Greak word meaning *origins.* The title in Hebrew Bibles repeats the opening words of chapter one: *Bereshith,* which is translated: "In the beginning" or "At the first." Moreover, the subject matter of the book goes back to the first things, the beginning of the universe and the origin of the Israelite nation. These initial acts of God, by which He created the world and personally intervened in the lives of His creatures, are not told by eye-witnesses. Instead of any photographic account or play-by-play tape recording, the Scriptures contain a *religious interpretation* of these initial acts of God as understood by later, inspired authors.

Our problem, therefore, in studying Genesis is not the paleontologist's job of determining exactly what happened inch by inch in the formation of the earth's surface. The Bible reader wants to know, rather, *how* the inspired author *interpreted* the events, how he, a very religious man, viewed God's mighty acts "in the beginning."

To read Genesis as the story of redemption, we must be conscious of the various periods of Israelite history, reflected in this first book of the Bible.

It took centuries of editing and re-editing to produce the book of Genesis; its fifty chapters were certainly not written by a desperate author racing against a deadline of the year 1237 B.C. Genesis, in fact, is really a compilation from at least three different traditions, called the *Yahwist,* the *Elohist,* and the *Priestly.* Here we will attend only to the Yahwist and the Priestly. All three go back to a single origin in the days of Abraham and Moses and yet each also existed independently for many centuries afterwards. One of these traditions is called the *Yahwist* because from the very beginning it calls God by the sacred name *Yahweh* ("Lord" in English). From this Yahwist tradition comes the second to the fourth chapters of Genesis, the story of Adam and Eve. A look into the origin and development of the Yahwist tradition will enable us to recognize more than the history of our first parents. We will discover the story of every man's struggle with temptation.

The Yahwist, Master of Psychology

The Yahwist tradition originated around 1240 B.C. in the days of desert wandering, a period dominated by the gigantic personality of Moses. It grew steadily with the history of the chosen people. During the golden age of David and Solomon (1010-931 B.C.) the tradition solidified in the features by which it is recognized today.

We notice in the tradition a friendly familiarity between God and man. God is portrayed as though He were almost human. He works with His hands upon the clay of the earth . . . breathes into the nostrils of man to give him life . . . plants a garden . . . shares with man His inward thoughts in the soliloquy of verse eighteen. God's presence continually enfolds man. Even after the fall of Adam and Eve, the cool evening wind carries the voice of God to their ears. God is searching for Adam and Eve, that He may forgive them.

These and many other details show how the Yahwist tradition does not scan the surface but pierces deep into the heart of reality; it does not tell us about the biological aspect of man's body but speaks about man's religious origin and destiny as a beloved child of God. Chapters two and three of Genesis are masterpieces of depth psychology.

Stage Props and Costumes

The next feature of the Yahwist tradition may seem to reveal some inconsistency, but is not every human being a bundle of contradictions? The Yahwist openly opposed city life, not city life in the abstract, but city life as he observed it in the Canaanite culture of Palestine. Yet, he plundered this culture of its ideas and folklore to compose his own story!

If the cultured Canaanite ever looked at his reflection in

the mirror of the Yahwist mind, however, he would have shrieked. Instead of seeing a Dr. Jekyll, dressed respectably and acting politely as befitted an affluent gentleman, the Canaanite would have gasped at a Mr. Hyde, with a body soft and bloated, with eyes bleary from perverted pleasure, yet still burning with lust, with a mouth turned up in pride and cruelty. The Yahwist described the Canaanite as a descendant of Ham, the boy who boldly stared at his father's nakedness (9:18-25). The Yahwist also put the Canaanite in the ranks of Cain, the man who murdered his own brother and then "went out from the presence of the Lord" to become "the founder of a city, . . . the forerunner of all who play the harp and flute . . . [and of all who] forge vessels of bronze and iron" (4:7-22). The Yahwist had no use for Canaanite city life glutted in immorality.

The Yahwist, we said, seems inconsistent. In order to tell his story, he borrowed words and ideas from pagan mythology and culture. These elements, nonetheless, can be considered but stage props and costumes. The Yahwist washed them clean of sin before using them, for their moral worth will depend upon the nature of the play and the character of the actors.

The story of Adam and Eve begins in a way reminiscent of the Akkadian myth of creation, called from its first words *Enuma Elish;* it was a widely circulated tale, translated or adapted into many ancient languages. Such words of Genesis as *mist, side of man, Eden* and *Adam* have been found in Sumerian literature. The *tree of life* symbolized immortality in another Akkadian myth *Gilgamesh,* and various aspects of this divine plant show up in Canaanite sculpture. The motif of a sacred river which branches off into many streams to irrigate the world appears on a wall painting in the ancient city of Mari and on a sculptured scene in the fortress town of Megiddo. We naturally ask: why would the Yahwist have taken anything from the degenerate, sensual religion of his neighbors? This question may answer itself, if we touch another important feature of the Yahwist tradition, his penetrating insight into human nature.

Victory through Struggle

Borrowing from pagan mythology has left the Yahwist open to the charge that he was a writer of children's bedtime stories. Of course, children are fascinated by his pictures: animals parading before Adam; a snake talking to Eve. But if the modern reader sees nothing more than colorful fairy tales, he betrays a dull wit. The author most responsible for the Yahwist's characteristic features possessed a razor-edged mind. He was an expert psychologist. Under symbolic forms well-known to his audience he told the story of sin, sorrow and death in the life of Adam and Eve. He grappled with the deepest problems of the human heart. He sought to know why marriage, the most noble expression of human love, degraded itself? Why woman's most complete fulfillment, motherhood, caused her sorrow? Why everyone pretended to be what he dared not be? Why people tried to be gods in a way so ungodlike?

Coming to grips with the most basic problems of human life, the Yahwist laid bare the hidden self of every man and every woman. That is why he turned to the resources of pagan mythology for images, terminology and even ideas. He used a language which his audience could not fail to understand, words as much a part of their culture as bootlegging was to the 1920's, the quiz program to the 1950's and the telstar to the 1960's. As he told the story of Adam and Eve, he was forcing each man and each woman to admit the silent, devastating truth: "*I* am Adam!" "*I* am Eve!"

Gathering his details from foreign literature, the Yahwist admitted that he knew very little about the first human pair, not even their real name. In the Sumerian, "Adam" and "Eve" mean "my father" and "mother of life"; in the Hebrew, the same words signify "man" and "life." The names depend upon languages spoken in 3000 B.C. and 1200 B.C. In fact, the author is making a play on words here. Man is called *Adam* because he is taken for the Adamah (ground); woman is named *Hawah* (Eve) because she is the mother of all *hayah* (life).

What most interested the Yahwist were the religious truths received directly from God; he presented them in story form and in symbol. God was interested in the first man and woman and proceeded carefully in the formation of their bodies. Both man and woman were a curious mixture of earthly and divine elements. They did not make their own happiness. Rather, God surrounded them with delights and privileges far beyond their rightful claim. Their great pleasure came from God's companionship. But when pride drove them to try to devise their own happiness and thus become completely self-determining persons, they lost what God desired to give them. What they sought outside of God, the privilege of being God-like, was always waiting for them in God's hands. These are some of the religious-historical truths, presented in the thought-provoking form of symbols.

The Yahwist composed a sombre history of repeated infidelities. Adam and Eve rebel; Abel is murdered; Cain flees; the sons of God are corrupted by the daughters of men. The enmity between good and evil people, between the seed of the woman and the seed of the serpnt (3:15), continus in a struggle of world-wide dimensions. The head of evil is crushed, but only at the cost of sorrow, for the serpent strikes at the heel of his conquerors. Each fall, however, is an occasion for divine mercy. Man is driven back to God by sin's sad consequences.

The sorrows and trials occasioned by evil are symbolized for woman in the pain of childbirth and for man in the sweat of work. These difficulties are steps in the way of redemption. The flood waters do not destroy the world but cleanse the world of sin. Everyone who lives experiences in his flesh the struggle between good and evil. This is a dark truth to face, but faith pierces the darkness to discern stepping stones to salvation.

When the Yahwist wrote of the fall and the forgiveness of the first man and woman, he cast them in the role of contemporary people. Each person was seen to be ratifying the sin of Adam and Eve by his own sin. The sorrows of sin, nonetheless, were never meant to destroy but only to purify and redeem. Genesis, therefore, is the first step in the redemption not only of Adam and Eve but of every man and every woman.

Everyman is alive today. Here is the impact of chapters two and three of Genesis upon modern society. A twentieth century Christian is bewildred when he first learns that Genesis may contain very few details about Adam and Eve. When he is told further that there may be mythological elements in the Bible, he is stunned. While he is still numb and motionless, God strikes. The astonished person suddenly opens his eyes and finds Adam dressed like himself, acting the part of a high school teenager or of a father or a mother of a family. What the Yahwist of the time of David and Solomon did, can be done by anyone.

Adam and Eve are every one of us: proud and selfish, refusing to obey, grabbing for pleasure, letting sin destroy the most beautiful treasures of life, especially the loyal friendship of God. But to us as to Adam and Eve, comes the merciful voice of God: "Where are you?" We cannot hide from this "Hound of Heaven."

Whoever shares the Yahwist's faith and humility can say: Genesis symbolizes my first steps in redemption, leading me to the crucified arms of the Redeemer. There on the cross the most intense suffering is transformed into everlasting triumph.

Preface to Salvation

The story of creation in the *opening* chapter of the Bible existed very early in one form or another, but as we have it now, it is the product of the postexilic age, which dates it around 450 B.C.; roughly 800 years after Moses, 600 years after David, 100 years after the close of the Babylonian exile. The author was influenced by the book of Job, possibly by Psalm 103 (104), most probably by chapter forty to fifty-five of the book of Isaia.

The first chapter of the Bible belongs to what is called the *Priestly* tradition, which provided the basic framework of Genesis; into it were inserted other traditions like the Yahwist. The Priestly tradition receives its name from the clergy of the Jerusalem temple who were responsible for its preservation and transmission. It divided Genesis into a series of redemptive acts of God, each of which being introduced with the phrase: in Hebrew *'elleh toleoth; these are the generations,* in English. The formula occurs at the end of the creation story (2:4a), but in other cases we find it at the beginning: of Adam's and Sem's descendants (10:1; 11:10); of the stories of Abraham, Jacob and Joseph (11:27; 25:19; 37:2).

The Priestly author of Genesis used this phrase as a link to unite various ages of world history. Events like the creation of the world and the life of Abraham were parts of one, colossal world plan of redemption. Everything was preparing for *the* great redemptive act, the covenant of Mount Sinai. Creation, for instance, was so closely bound up with the law given to Moses on Sinai, that one part of the law, the Sabbath rest, was said to have been observed by the Creator Himself. The wisdom of the law and its power to save controlled the creation of the universe.

Genesis is thus a preface to the scriptural story of salvation. A preface should always be read first, because it acts like a master-of-ceremonies, introducing us to the principal actors and their various roles. A preface, however, is never fully understood, unless it is read again at the end, so much of the whole story does it condense into each of its sentences. Chapter one of Genesis, therefore, is most intelligently read only against the background of biblical history. No period of biblical history has left such a mark upon the creation story as the terrible ordeal of the Babylonian exile, 587-538 B.C.

Prophetic Influence

In July, 587 B.C. the Babylonian army broke through the walls of Jerusalem, to capture and sack the terrorized city. A month later, on the ninth day of Ab, word came from Nabuchodonosor to level the city to the ground. When Solomon's magnificent temple was burned, its marble walls came crashing down upon the smoldering ruins of a splendid past. The Israelites who had not been killed in battle or starved to death during the long siege, were marched off into exile. During the dismal, discouraging years which followed, God raised up not only the prophet Ezechiel but also another prophet whose name has been lost in the centuries. Scholars call him Deutero-Isaia, because sealed up in his heart were the teaching and the spirit of his namesake (Is 8:16). We find his beautiful, lyric poetry in chapters forty to fifty-five in the book of Isaia.

The people at that time felt that their world of happiness had exploded into chaos. The darkness which had surrounded the watery abyss before creation now swept down upon *their* world. Creation seemed to have been undone. Void and darkness again enveloped all things. At this desolate moment God commissioned Deutero-Isaia to:

> Comfort, O Comfort my people (40:1).

Deutero-Isaia strengthened the people with songs of exquisite beauty. Melody of sound matched magnificence of thought. Your God, he exclaimed, can re-create your world; He can put order and beauty where now there are chaos and darkness. Is He not God who created the world at the beginning? Listen to the prophet's own words:

> Thus says the Lord, your redeemer,
>   who formed you from the womb;
> I am the Lord who made all things,
>   who alone stretched out the heavens;
>   when I spread out the earth, who was with me? . . .
> I say to Jerusalem: Be inhabited;
>   and to the cities of Juda: Be rebuilt;
> It is I who said to the deep: Be dry (Is 44:24-27).

Deutero-Isaia, therefore, sang of first creation to sustain the people's faith in a future re-creation. God will redeem you, he promised, and will put happiness back into your life, just as "in the beginning" He spread out a world of happiness. God will make a new beginning.

The songs of Deutero-Isaia can be compared to the finale of a symphony. All the religious themes of the Bible join in full orchestration: the call of Abraham; the exodus through the Red Sea; Moses' striking the rock; God's sending food in the desert; the Covenant on Sinai; the promises to David. All of these great acts of God seem to happen all over again. In this glorious harmony of redemption, however, one theme constantly recurs. It is God's power to create. Creation in the beginning is the proof that God can redeem His people now.

God kept faith with His people. He re-created their Promised Land and led them back to it. The People continued to chant the songs of Deutero-Isaia, but now his prophecies looked beyond the return from exile to *distant* messianic glory. This messianic aura began to surround chapter one of Genesis, revised during the postexilic days as part of a larger collection of Priestly tradition. Although this tradition is often cold and dull, the creation hymn of Genesis echoes the majestic beats of temple bells, with the songs of Deutero-Isaia in the background.

Silver bells announce the divine plan. Before each new act we hear the words: *Wayy'omer 'elohim* ("And God said"); there is the soft mellowness of *wayyar' 'elohim ki-tob* ("And God saw that it was good") and the eternal, endless echo *wayehi-'ereb wayehi-boqer yom 'ehad ... yom sheni* ("And there was evening and there was morning, the first day, ...the second day"). It was the solemn recital and choral refrains of the songs of Deutero-Isaia, accompained by temple bells and trumpets, sounding within the soul of an artist which gave us this glorious hymn of creation, humanly as well as divinely inspired.

Creation Now

We now ask: how does this literary and historical background affect the interpretation of Genesis chapter one, as a story of redemption? The opening chapter of the Bible presents creation as an act of God which overcomes every obstacle and produces a place where man remains at peace with God. If sin separates man and God, earth returns to chaos. Chapter one of Genesis issues a solemn warning.

According to the ideas of his age, the author compared the earth to something like a pan-cake, floating upon a watery abyss. Although the earth has foundations sunk deep into the waters, it still endures a very perilous existence. These waters of the roaring depths can surge up and across the earth with destructive force. Above the earth, spans the firmament. The Hebrew word for firmament *raq'ia* means beaten-out piece of brass. It was thought to be a solid metallic substance, lifting an ocean of water into the sky. Here was more danger, because at any moment these waters could rain tons of fury upon the earth. These notions of watery abyss and of oceans lifted into the sky lie behind the description of the deluge: "The foundations of the great deep burst forth, and the flood gates of the heavens were opened" (Gen 7:11).

The nation's sins in the period before the exile provoked God to throw open the flood gates and to deluge the nation with sorrow. Surrounded by "waters" of death and destruction, the distressed people prayed to God in the words of Deutero-Isaia:

> Awake, awake, put on strength,
>   O arm of the Lord!
> Awake as in the days of old,
>   in ages long ago!
> Was it not you who crushed Rahab,
>   you who pierced the dragon?
> Was it not you who dried up the sea
>   the waters of the great deep? (Is 51:9-10).

Sorrow did its work well, washing the nation clean of its filth. The waters of exile subsided and a newly created

Israel appeared. God forgave His people and His act of forgiveness was considered an act of creation. In forgiving man's sins God re-created the world in a true sense. This redemptive feature of creation shines before our eyes once we put Genesis into the larger context of its historical development and prophetic influences. It sings of God's power to re-create postexilic Israel and the distant messianic kingdom.

This interpretation does not deny that God created the world in the beginning, no more than the previous explanation of Adam and Eve reduced them to legend. The emphasis, however, is placed upon creation as an *ever present* act. What happened in the beginning is repeated at each moment of time, but especially in periods of great crisis. To sing the creation hymn of Genesis is to revel in the glorious truth that the trees, the bushes and the flowers, the wind, the sun and the stars—all of these creatures which man touches or hears, sees or feels, were created, rather *are being* created *this moment,* in order that each man may live in happiness with God.

The created world shows God acting through its powers. Yahweh, however, is not immersed in material objects; He is far greater than they are. But He does wrap man round with His love in the beauty of the created world. Such an idea of creation thinks primarily of redemption, for it tells of God's wish to free man from sin and make him everlastingly happy in a new heaven and new earth.

To appreciate the book of Genesis, our thinking had to take on a friendly, neighborly attitude towards the Yahwist and the Priestly authors of the Bible's first books. There was need to breathe the atmosphere and to share the thoughts of their world. We had to become inhabitants of the ancient Near East.

Though they lived centuries before St. Paul, still they shared the universal sweep of sympathy of this Apostle of the Gentiles. The sacred authors of Genesis practised what St. Paul advised: ". . . whatever things are true, whatever of good repute, if there be any virtue, if anything worthy of praise, think upon these things" (Phil 4:8).

The sacred authors not only thought seriously about their neighboring world of culture and religion, but with the skill of an artist they introduced into their narrative the color and the costumes, the thoughts and the questions, the problems and the victories of this vast, surrounding world. Creation and the flood, Adam and Eve not only remained *real* events or persons, but they continued to have a real impact upon each succeeding age.

The past symbolized the present, and the present was pictured against a vista of future hopes. This symbolism never destroyed reality. Rather, it made the real of the past an actuality for each new age. The prophets were foremost among Israel's religious leaders, preventing worship from degenerating into a superstitious veneration of words and paper documents, keeping the ancient traditions what they really were, the *living word* of God, a gospel of redemption.